JS 331.793

725820

Resplendent Sites, Discordant Voices

Studies in Anthropology and History

Studies in Anthropology and History is a series that will develop new theoretical perspectives, and combine comparative and ethnographic studies with historical research.

Edited by Nicholas Thomas, The Australian National University, Canberra.

Malcolm Crick

Resplendent Sites, Discordant Voices

Sri Lankans and international tourism

Routledge
Taylor & Francis Group

LONDON AND NEW YORK

COPYRIGHT © 1994

Published by Routledge
2 Park Square, Milton Park, Abingdon, Oxon, OX14 4RN
270 Madison Ave, New York NY 10016

Transferred to Digital Printing 2008

LIBRARY OF CONGRESS CATALOGING-IN-PUBLICATION DATA

Crick, Malcolm
        Resplendent sites, discordant voices : Sri Lankans and
international tourism / Malcolm Crick.
        p.   cm. — (Studies in anthropology and history, ISSN
1055-2464 ; v. 16)
        Includes bibliographical references and index.
        ISBN 3-7186-5564-0
        1. Tourist trade—Sri Lanka—Social aspects.   I. Title.
II. Series.
G155.S65C75   1994
338.4'549304'3—dc20

                                        94-1708
                                        CIP

DESIGNED BY   Maureen Anne MacKenzie
                 Em Squared Main Street, Michelago, NSW 2620, Australia

TYPESET BY   P J & H Boes, Melbourne (Australia)

FRONT COVER   Seated Buddha at Polonnaruwa, Sri Lanka.
                 (Source: Tony Wheeler, Lonely Planet Publications, Melbourne.)

Publisher's Note
The publisher has gone to great lengths to ensure the quality of this
reprint but points out that some imperfections in the original
may be apparent

Contents

List of Illustrations

Acknowledgments

This book is largely the result of work carried out during one short vacation and two periods of study leave from Deakin University. I wish to thank Deakin for supporting my research proposals and for providing some financial assistance. I am also much in the debt of the university library for so efficiently meeting my numerous requests over many years for material in connection with the preparation of this book.

My first visit to Sri Lanka was of six weeks duration from December 1980 until the end of January 1981. A period of research leave was then spent there from April to October 1982, during which time I was a Research Fellow in the Department of Sociology at the University of Peradeniya. I would like to express my thanks here to the University of Peradeniya and to acknowledge assistance provided by the Department of Sociology and by the University Library. I am also indebted to the Ceylon Tourist Board, particularly to staff in its research section and library in Colombo who helped me with my inquiries. I am also grateful to staff in the library of the Central Bank in Colombo.

During my seven months of fieldwork in 1982, I lived in Kandy and made a number of friends to whom I wish to express thanks for information and companionship. Some of them are central to this book, but I have had to give them all pseudonyms, as indeed I have frequently had to omit details of or disguise events they related to me. International tourism in the Third World is frequently a controversial matter which can generate a good deal of resentment and antagonism, and my book, of necessity, has had to discuss this openly. I therefore owe various camouflages to my closest informants, lest they suffer because anyone takes exception to what I have written. I trust that enough time has passed since my fieldwork for the disguises to be effective.

For three years after my return from Sri Lanka, teaching responsibilities and other research interests intervened and I had no opportunity to do any systematic work with my field data. By 1986, when I was ready to look at my field material in a concerted fashion, the political situation in Sri Lanka had deteriorated so markedly that I decided not to make another visit but to write a book based on the material I already had. This book, therefore, is almost entirely based on information obtained in 1982, and was first drafted during five months research leave in 1986 when I was a Visiting Research Fellow in the Department of Anthropology at the University of Adelaide. I am grateful to colleagues and students for feedback provided both in casual conversations and in seminars during my time there.

I have much more recently acquired other debts in connection with the production of this volume, which has undergone a number of revisions since 1986. David Harrison carefully read the manuscript thoroughly and made a number of pertinent comments to which I have tried to respond. Michael Roberts kindly shared with me his extensive knowledge of Sri Lankan history and culture, resulting in significant revisions and additions to the text. Neither, of course, bears any responsibility for the shortcomings of the final product. I am also most grateful to Tony Wheeler of Lonely Planet Publications for allowing me to reproduce several of the maps which appear in the latest edition of his travel guide to Sri Lanka (Noble, Forsyth & Wheeler 1993) and for giving me permission to use some of his slides, some of which have not been previously published. Last but not least, I am grateful to Mary Werther for so efficiently handling the production of this book and to Nicholas Thomas for selecting my manuscript for inclusion in the *Studies in Anthropology and History* series.

Some of the material in this book has been previously published elsewhere. I wish here formally to thank: the editor of *Criticism Heresy and Interpretation*, for permission to reuse some material on hippies which first appeared in Volume 3 in 1989 under the title of 'The hippy in Sri Lanka. A symbolic analysis of the imagery of school children in Kandy'; and Belhaven Press, for permission to reuse material on street guides which first appeared in 1992 as a chapter in D. Harrison ed. *Tourism and the less developed countries* under the title of 'Life in the informal sector: street guides in Kandy, Sri Lanka'.

Finally, a brief explanatory note about the spelling of Sinhala terms. Different authors follow different conventions when rendering colloquial Sinhala words in an alphabetic script and in this book I have opted for both consistency (save in bibliographical entries where I have followed the author's own usage) and absolute simplicity. The latter inevitably introduces an element of inaccuracy, but I have chosen that rather than employ the large number of complex typographical signs required for a more faithful rendition.

Malcolm Crick

CHAPTER ONE

Anthropology and the Study of Tourism: Theoretical and Personal Reflections

The notion that tourism is the largest industry in the world seems to have acquired a wide currency over the past few years. Whether such claims are empirically correct or simply part of the industry's own propaganda, there are very good reasons for tourism to constitute a serious focus of attention for anthropologists. Yet anthropology, along with other social science disciplines, has been remarkably tardy in according tourism the importance it deserves. Indeed, during the late 1970s a number of social scientists with interests in tourism were relaying stories about how their research had been actively discouraged by others or even derided (Finney and Watson-Gegeo 1979:470; Leiper 1979:392; Mitchell 1979:236; Smith 1978:274). The reasons behind the neglect or discouragement may have differed from discipline to discipline, but in the case of anthropology the failure to come to terms with tourism is particularly curious given the self-evident fact that tourism, particularly international tourism, bears directly on a number of time-honoured themes in the discipline such as acculturation, socio-cultural change, inter-cultural relations, and so on (Nash and Smith 1991:13; Lett 1989:276).

Over a decade later, things have changed somewhat. There are now prestigious international journals devoted to the study of tourism, such as *Annals of Tourism Research*. In 1990 tourism was constituted for the first time as a 'Working Group' within the International Sociological Association. And within anthropology, tourism has become a respectable research topic in its own right, rather than being a spin-off or after-thought from projects with other main goals (Nash and Smith 1991:13). Over the past ten years a number of interesting analytical frameworks have been proposed by anthropologists and some fieldwork-based monographs have appeared (Jules-Rosette 1984; Moon 1989; Wagner 1982). To be sure, some very basic issues still require to be resolved. Is 'tourism' itself a field, or merely part of some broader field? What exactly should the relationships be between different social sciences such as anthropology, economics, geography, political science, psychology, and sociology in regard to the comprehension of such a complex industry, given that these disciplines have such different theoretical interests, as well as different methodologies? Clearly, with such a multi-faceted phenomenon no one discipline can claim any privileged insight (*pace* Pearce

1988:22). Another fundamental issue, and one on which opinion is clearly divided, concerns whether the more pressing need in tourism studies is for detailed case studies, or whether, quite the contrary, formulating a convincing and general theoretical framework is the highest priority.

It is clearly beyond the scope of an introductory chapter in a book devoted to the study of international tourism in Sri Lanka to tackle such basic and multidisciplinary issues.[1] Rather, this introduction has two aims: firstly, to set out some of the more important landmarks in the recent growth of anthropological interest in tourism with suggestions as to some key issues where anthropological interests and tourism coincide; secondly, to make explicit what issues are focussed on in the present study, the reasons for their choice, and the methods employed in the research on which the book rests.

AREAS OF CONVERGENCE

The father of touristic studies in anthropology is conventionally said to be Theron Nuñez, for his 1963 study of '*weekendismo*' in Mexico (1963). But while during the remainder of the 60s disciplines such as economics which climbed so confidently onto the bandwagon of 'development' and 'westernization' saw in tourism a rich vein to mine, there was no recognisable groundswell of interest within anthropology. The next major event as far as the discipline was concerned was the 1974 American Anthropological Association meeting from which resulted the significant collection edited by Valene Smith entitled *Hosts and Guests: The Anthropology of Tourism* (Smith 1978 ed.). Five years later there was an entire issue of *Annals of Tourism Research* devoted to anthropology (Graburn 1983 ed.) and at least three general surveys of the field 'the anthropology of tourism' had been written by the early 80s (Graburn 1983b; Nash 1981; Nuñez 1978). In the decade since there has been a steadily expanding number of anthropological articles on tourist topics based on field research, although the majority resulted from research which originally had little to do with tourism. In that sense, Nuñez's charge that the study of tourism by anthropologists has been "characterised largely by serendipity" (1978:207) continued to have the ring of truth, as did the perceptive suggestions made by Boissevain (1977:523–5) as to the weaknesses of anthropological writing on tourism and the reasons for those weaknesses. Full-length monographs on tourism by anthropologists are still very few, but in 1989 tourism acquired one symbolic benchmark of recognition within the discipline, namely the inclusion of a

---

[1] Crick (1989a), an extensive literature review of social scientific work on tourism, discusses some of these general problems.

chapter devoted to tourism in the *Annual Review of Anthropology* (Crick 1989a).

What is particularly interesting over such a short span of time is the sheer range of interests and approaches which anthropologists have brought to the topic. As Wilson has perceptively put it (1993:32–5), almost every passing fad — from 'development' to 'post-modernism' — has cropped up in the fairly limited volume of literature on the anthropology of tourism. In just twenty years we have seen the avoidance of tourism as a research topic, exaggerated and naive evaluations (both positive and negative) of tourism and its socio-cultural effects, efforts to devise taxonomies of tourism/tourist types (Smith 1978b), portrayals of tourism as neo-imperialism (Nash 1978), portrayals of tourism as play/ritual/sacred journey/pilgrimage (Graburn 1978), and finally the suggestion that in a reflexive age anthropologists should pay attention to tourism for the very reason that tourists and anthropologists are relatives of a kind (Crick 1985, 1989b, 1991).

At least two reactions are possible to the above catalogue. One is to suggest that the anthropology of tourism is chaotic and immature. But a second is to see in this diversity a very real richness and potential. I personally concur with the view expressed by Nash (1984:504) that there is much advantage to be gained by keeping open all theoretical options at this stage, and indeed by encouraging the different social sciences to deliberately follow their own particular approaches to the study of tourism (Crick 1989a:314) rather than aiming for standardisation or theoretical closure. My own view is that the most pressing need at the moment is for detailed ethnographic studies rather than for theoretical syntheses which might do little more than prematurely cast our relatively paltry data into ready-made, highly evaluative and patently lop-sided frameworks. A second reason for not wishing to press for an encompassing theory in the anthropology of tourism are the sheer number of general areas — from the global to the personal — where anthropology and tourism potentially intersect.

It is occasionally said that one of the most pressing issues facing anthropologists in the 90s is whether the discipline has a niche any more, given that the world in which anthropology was born and developed has ceased to be. Certainly the contemporary world, whether we call it modern, post-modern, post-industrial, post-colonial, or whatever, is a different world to that assumed in classical anthropological theory. But this is equally so for all of the social sciences. Anthropology is certainly influenced by the historical circumstances of its birth, but its future is no more determined by its past than is the case with any other discipline. The fabric of the modern world is a complex texture at one and the same time both compressed and fractured. It is a world in which global ideologies, the activities of multinationals, hordes of refugees and migrants, to say nothing of international tourists, substantially deterritorialise social identity (Appadurai 1991:191–2, 186). Such a system with its complex globalising forces, indeed, is often said to have dissolved clearly bounded cultural entities and therefore to have destroyed 'otherness' — widely regarded as anthropology's subject matter. This could clearly make somewhat problematic basic anthropological concepts like 'culture' and 'society'. But such difficulties are an opportunity for scrutinising our methods and theories, not for succumbing to the idea that anthropology has become an anachronism (see Abu-Lughod 1991; Appadurai 1991; Fox 1991 ed.).

In such a rethinking the phenomenon of international tourism possesses a strategic value in several ways. For a start, the social ramifications of tourism raise directly problems about such notions as 'culture', 'ethnicity', 'social change', 'authenticity', 'tradition', and so on (Hitchcock *et al.*, 1993:5). Secondly, being an industry which was from the outset encouraged by international agencies such as the United Nations and the International Monetary Fund and which is now dominated by multinational corporations, the contemporary processes of internationalisation bound up in tourism are very stark (Lanfant 1980). On a more philosophical level, the 'tourist', for MacCannell, simply is 'modern man', responding to the complexity of social experience in today's world by searching for authenticity in other cultures (1976:1–3). If such a view has any merit, there could be no more direct way of anthropology grappling with those features of contemporary life than a serious study of tourism. Dumont, reviewing MacCannell's important book, went even further: because the tourist is such a potent image for meta-inquiry, his work would prove frightening to anthropologists, a shock from which we could either recoil in dismay, or else make a sustained effort to reposition ourselves (1977:225).

Image, of course, is of the essence of the international tourism industry. There is a 'manufacturing of the exotic' (Rossel 1988 ed.), a 'commoditisation' of cultures (Greenwood 1978). The work of the image constructors makes Third World tourist destinations into veritable paradises where time-honoured themes in the depiction of the 'other' — primitivism, simplicity, sensuality, excess, harmony — some of which images have, of course, been well articulated within anthropology itself, are fervently recycled (Britton 1979; Selwyn 1993). In the process societies can come to be known by the international tourist in terms of cultural traits which are quite marginal or even embarrassing to many members of the society concerned; the brightly painted masks and devil dances of Sri Lanka are a good example (Simpson 1993:166–70). Nowhere in tourist advertising does an adequate story of the poverty, diseases, violence and malnutrition of the Third World get told since such elements are incompatible with the paradaisical imagery they are creating, but of course, in reality it is often a destination country's very underdevelopment which is, in fact, being sold. The fact that some holiday destinations are cheap is often a direct reflex of the poverty of their inhabitants.

Symbolic representation, of course, and particularly of late the whole issue of the representation of 'the other', are central anthropological interests, and since the writings of Foucault, Said and the like, the relationship between power and meaning creation has become a leitmotiv of the discipline. There can hardly be a more graphic illustration of this theme than the way in which tourism advertising, largely generated in the affluent industrial nations, merchandises the poor nations of the world. It is a 'spectacularisation' of the other, a deliberate play of signs in order to transform cultures into consumable products (van den Abbeele 1980:5). The economic and political power behind the images is immense. A Greek fishing village can be built in the West Indies, all the cultures of the Pacific can be assembled in one place, in a large enough tourist theme park one can create a simulacrum of the entire world (Britton 1978:202). Compared to the simulacra that tourism has to offer, social reality is a disappointing substitute indeed.

Besides providing anthropology with a rich field in which to explore the ways in which one type of society constructs others, international tourism also yields an opportunity for studying a whole host of inter-cultural processes with somewhat unusual characteristics. Host-guest relationships in international tourism are normally between pronounced unequals, and are of very short duration where one party is at work and another at play. There is much empirical work which needs to be done on the cultural rules which are developed to cope with relationships between strangers of this kind, and to trace the creation of new roles which emerge in response to tourism development (Nuñez 1978:209–11; van den Berghe 1980:378–9). International tourism, in fact, constitutes a fascinating field in which to develop further the significant anthropological interest in 'culture broker' roles.

There is another particular value to tourism as a field of study here, for if anthropology is normally concerned with people in culture, with international tourists one is dealing with people who are essentially 'out of' their normal cultural context; they are out of normal time and space, as Wagner (1977) put it. Of course, one might say that they are in a 'touristic culture' — surprisingly a concept which has not been well developed — but they are in a realm distinct from the normal workaday world. What is an especially attractive opportunity here is that much classical social theory has dwelt on rationality, work, production, structure, and the like, and with tourism, at least some suggest, we get the exact opposite — leisure, play, consumption, indulgence, and freedom from restraint. If it makes sense to use labels like post-modern, post-marxist, post-industrial, post-structural to describe a current style of theorising in the social sciences, if we now live in a world not according to Marx but according to Baudrillard and Eco — a world of hyperreality, sign saturation and spectacle — tourism would seem to a rich phenomenon to which these newer styles of analysis could pay attention. Tourism is certainly an area in which the still under-developed field of the anthropology of play could make some advances. Tourism, indeed, has been seen very much as a 'world of inversions' (Graburn 1983b:21) — again a time-honoured focus of anthropological attention, and it might well be that the considerable Turnerian legacy — 'anti-struc-ture', 'communitas', 'liminoid', and so on — will have a rich field of application here (see Lett 1983).

If tourism displays some of the ludic qualities which are sometimes said to characterise post-modernism in general, we need to caution ourselves before too readily accepting the imagery of 'sacred journeys', 'play' and the like. For a start, as Rojek has cogently argued (1985:73–5), much of the leisure organised by advanced capitalism clearly displays the same features of structure, routine and pressure as we find in our ordinary lives. Secondly, given the established links between tourism and activities such as prostitution and the drug trade, it is curious that some com-mentators can so readily see a sacred dimension in tourism and liken it so speedily to pilgrimage. Thirdly, if much international tourism is a gigantic potlatch, a case of conspicuous consumption by those from affluent industrial countries in front of the poor, then we squarely have to face the fact that the play and leisure have been made possible by the accumulation of assets in normal time (Schwimmer 1979: 223). In short, international tourism is only intelligible given certain very secular features of global political economy.

If it now makes sense to use phrases like 'global village' because expansion-ary industrial capitalism and modern communications technology have unified the world and set in train various processes of cultural homogenisation, nonetheless the continued reality of localism, of cultural and ethnic particularism, in the con-temporary world is also transparent. Certain well-established kinds of tourism — those normally labelled 'ethnic tourism' and 'cultural tourism' — in fact rely on the existence of difference. And even modern nation states with policies aimed at sup-pressing cultural difference within their borders have been quick to seize upon the chance to merchandise their ethnic minorities to earn tourism revenue (Crystal 1978:119–22). But not only is there still plenty of such 'otherness' left in the con-temporary world, the workings of the contemporary world clearly require that the various components that make it up be of very different natures. International tourism thus represents a potentially rich field for anthropology in which to explore the diverse way in which globalising forces are responded to in specific localities.

The various general analytical frameworks for understanding the meshing of these various components have all appeared in the history of tourism studies. In the 60s, for instance, the field of tourism studies was very much dominated by images of 'development' and by simple, unidirectional models of 'modernisation' and 'westernisation'. When the ethnocentric nature of that framework became widely recognised, a variety of 'dependency' and 'underdevelopment' theses then held sway. Such frameworks, however, whilst at the abstract level they may, depending perhaps on one's politics, appear to be either compelling or irredeemably ideologically scarred, are left wanting at the empirical level where they all appear to be incapable of capturing the complexity of what is going on in any particular instance (Harrison 1992a:9; Wood 1993). International tourism could well prove a fertile field in which to work towards an empirically more adequate framework for understanding international political economy, for to date the complexities of the tourism industry have not been convincingly captured by any of the available models.

In the 1960s tourist development was eagerly promoted as 'manna from Heaven', as a way in which the underdeveloped nations could acquire foreign exchange, diversify their export sector, and achieve faster rates of growth by tying themselves directly to the affluence of the western industrialised nations. The economic 'balance sheets' produced at the time looked very convincing. Thirty years later, however, they look far less positive; the multipliers far lower than projected, and foreign exchange leakages continue to be high, to say nothing of the unquantifiable but still very significant socio-cultural costs which the economists frequently omitted to mention. Far from being an industry with low start up costs because the 'raw materials' — sun, sand and welcoming smiles — already existed, tourism has, in fact, required heavy infrastructural outlays. Not only that, but the industry has been characterised by a high level of vertical integration; airlines own hotel chains which, in turn, control travel agencies, so often international tourists pay for virtually everything before even leaving their own country (Sinclair et al., 1992:50–5). And the foreign capital necessary for developing the industry, moreover, is often secured only by generous tax holidays provided by the governments in the developing nations.

There is inevitably a political dimension to all of this (Crick 1989a:314–26), for to the extent that many tourist destinations are ex-colonies trying to overcome the cultural and economic deformations produced by imperialism, tourism can so often seem like the return of their erstwhile rulers, only this time on vacation. Tourism, indeed, is referred to by some quite explicitly as 'leisure imperialism' and 'neo-colonialism' (Davis 1978:3–5; Nash 1978). So, on top of the stark realities that tourist destinations are tied up in what now has a reputation for being a fickle industry because of shifting consumer preferences and the obvious fact that the growth of the advanced industrial economies is inherently cyclical, is the experience, for some, of the re-creation of colonial race relations, of a largely unskilled workforce in servile relationships with foreigners, with areas of the country given over to the pleasure of outsiders (Karch and Dann 1981:250). Far from tourism being a vehicle for affluence and self-determination, for some, tourists simply complete the work of two earlier breeds of traveller from abroad — the conqueror and colonialist (Cohen 1972:82). Tourism and colonialism — and Bruner adds ethnography — are thus but variant expressions, at different points in time, of the expansive thrusts of the same western social formation (Bruner 1989b:439).

If this 'imperialistic' imagery be regarded as a gross exaggeration, perhaps it is worth remembering that the Vice-President of Edgar Rice Burrows Inc. once expressed his desire to take over the whole of The Gambia, to change its name, and to build a series of Tarzan 'vacation villages' there (Britton 1978:158–9). No doubt such an example is extreme. Some Third World tourist destinations no doubt do gain in certain economic ways from the advent of overseas visitors. But it is also clear that aspects of the relationships which grow up between hosts and guests can have colonial overtones. But, again, it is a far cry from acknowledging this to being able to assert convincingly that tourism is 'neo-colonialism'. The complexities of the tourism industry are such that such labels should be transparently inadequate — a point which, of course, applies equally to those such as 'a passport to development' which have also been bandied about. Detailed empirical studies will certainly be of value if they lead to the end of such sloganeering.

International tourism is also a very good topic with which anthropology can think through the whole matter of social change, for as the various social sciences began to take an interest in tourism in the 1970s and 1980s, the links between tourism and socio-cultural change very much fell to anthropologists to investigate (Crick 1989a:334–8). For some time it looked as if substantial progress was being made; there was an increasing number of rich ethnographic accounts of the socio-cultural repercussions of tourism development. Two problems soon emerged, however. The first was empirical. For every case where tourism could be shown to reinvigorate craft industries, there was another where crafts declined; for every case where tourist demand stimulated local agriculture, there was another where agriculture suffered; and so on with architectural conservation, ecological consequences, *et cetera*. In short, the patterns were very diverse; one had to know what sort of destination society one was talking about, how many tourists there were, what type of tourism was involved, what stage of tourism development had been reached. There were soon few general statements to be made in the wake of this realisation. Furthermore, it became clear that the links so confidently asserted by some between tourism and specific processes of change were little more than conjecture. As Boissevain pointed out, tourism is just one of a whole host of forces for change at work in the Third World — mass media, population increase, urbanisation, modern schooling, and so on — so one could scarcely convincingly attribute certain problems to tourism alone (1977:524). To the extent that this is true, tourists have often been no more than convenient scapegoats.

The second problem was conceptual. As Sahlins has so pointedly reminded us, anthropology is full of dichotomies — system/event, continuity/discontinuity, even anthropology/history — which are both analytically weak and phenomeno-logically dubious (1985:xvii). Such a realisation clearly makes the whole field of 'social change' much more complex than might otherwise be supposed. It seemed easy for Turner and Ash to declare that tourism was the enemy of authenticity (1975:197), but exactly what do we mean by 'authenticity'? What we commonly call 'tradition' is clearly not static, and nor is the contrast between 'tradition' and 'modernity' a simple polar opposition (Harrison 1992c:158, 162). In most Third World tourist destinations we are talking about societies that have been exposed for hundreds of years to western influences of various sorts. If we say that a tourist spectacle is a case of 'staged authenticity' (MacCannell 1973), what is abnormal about this? Culture is a process, it is in constant flux, it is constantly being created — that is staged — by someone for someone; why should tourism be regarded as so completely different? And if we can say that the very notion of what, for instance, Balinese culture is has been profoundly affected by tourism, where does one locate 'authenticity' and 'tradition', for Balinese culture in the late twentieth century is clearly the outcome of a complexity of forces — Dutch colonial policy, Jakarta's political imperatives, the writings of indigenous intellectuals, tourist images and the monographs of anthropologists, are only some of them (Picard 1993:73). It simply does not make sense to see tourism as an external force (Picard 1993:72) acting somehow on some pristine, traditional, authentic culture. Tourism always enters an already historically and culturally complex situation (Wood 1993:57–63), and in the case of Bali, tourism has been so important for so long that it is a part of Balinese culture, not an external agent; it has, in a very real sense, become a Balinese tradi-tion.

Some of the excesses of the earlier anthropological writings on tourism and social change are now beginning to be rectified. The early writing was often highly judgmental and its analytical naivety is now widely recognised. In her preface to the second edition of *Hosts and Guests*, Smith, in fact, candidly admits that ten years earlier anthropologists grossly exaggerated the power of tourism as a force for social change (1989:x). Even more recently, Wilson reports a number of anthro-pological 'restudies' which substantially undo the links between tourism and social change imputed by earlier authors. The problem, according to Wilson, is that those studies, being based on relatively short-term fieldwork, lacked adequate historical depth; the alleged causal connections were, in that sense, mirages produced by the anthropologists' methods (1993:36).[2] Hopefully, in future, anthropologists wres-

---

[2] It was largely because my fieldwork was confined to a seven month period that I decided not to focus on tourism and social change, difficult enough, in any case, in a city with a population of 100,000. Naturally, 'change' is a frequent theme in the voices of my many of my informants, but it did not constitute the focal point of my research.

tling with the complexities of social change in the tourism context will not only achieve a higher level of sophistication, but may also contribute towards a more adequate comprehension of the topic of change in general.

Having discussed several possible levels and areas of convergence between contemporary anthropology and the phenomenon of tourism, I want to end this section by exploring the pertinence of a study of international tourism to anthropology at the personal level. One of the things which we can say about anthropology in the 1990s is that it is a period of anxious reflexivity in which our own identities are under scrutiny as we attempt to define the discipline for the contemporary world. It is suggested here that the tourist may be a good image for anthropological self-examination in that anthropologists and tourists are partially overlapping identities. Tourism, in other words, can act like a cracked mirror in which we can glimpse something about the nature of our discipline and our professional practices (Crick 1985, 1989b, 1991).

Van den Berghe has posed the question whether an anthropologist is "an in-depth tourist or an entirely different breed of sensation seeker?" (1980:376). The overlap of identities intimated here has, in fact, been commented on by a number of anthropologists over the years (see Crick 1985:76–83), but the topic is never dwelt on for very long; some colleagues, indeed, find it somewhat distasteful (Errington and Gewertz 1989:51–2). But clearly anthropologists and tourists are both metonyms of the western world (Dumont 1978:44). Both go to other cultures as temporary strangers, with interests derived very largely from their home culture rather than the one they visit. Both occupy marginal roles, endeavouring from an intrinsically liminal position and with inadequate means of cultural communication to make sense of 'the other'. Both utilise their resources to develop relationships with the sort of culture brokers they require in order to access what it is they wish to obtain from the other culture, the one using a guide and the other an interpreter or research assistant. Tourists leave their 'pleasure periphery' (Turner and Ash 1975) after a period of conspicuous consumption with souvenirs and photos to remind them of their experiences, which are then told and retold to enhance status back home. Anthropologists leave their 'ethnographic periphery' after a period of conspicuous consumption of data, to be written up elsewhere to craft an academic career. The tourist is at play, of course, while the ethnographer is engaged in work — fieldwork — but both are equally out of normal space and time, which for the anthropologist is not 'the field' but routine teaching and academic administration. Even etymology robs anthropologists of a difference on which they might like to insist, namely the serious theoretical intent of their professional presence as compared to the frivolity and spectacularisation of tourism; the term 'theory' itself derives from the Greek for 'sightseer' and 'spectacle' (van den Abbeele 1980:13). And if anthropologists require 'thick' descriptions whilst tourists are satisfied with 'thin' (Bruner 1989a:112), that, after all, is only a difference in degree.

The sketch above omits the obvious fact that anthropologists do very different types of research. It also omits that fact that there are very different types of tourism and tourist. But if there is any merit in the suggestion of overlapping identities, it makes the comparatively late start in the anthropology of tourism all the more intriguing. Almost anywhere an anthropologist goes in the modern world to do research there will be tourists, yet, in monograph after monograph during the 1960s, 1970s and 1980s it was as if tourists were non-existent (Nuñez 1978:207, 212; Pi-Sunyer 1981:272). Perhaps the very sensing of an overlap itself explains why tourism was a neglected topic; it constituted a reminder about the nature of anthropology that was unwelcome. Anthropologists denying that they have anything in common with tourism is perhaps something like the denial in an earlier age of links with the colonial administrator and the missionary, despite the fact that it was the same discrepancy of power between different races and societies which allowed all three to be present, irrespective of the divergence of individual intentions. Moreover, denying that one is a tourist is very much a part of tourist culture itself; one is a 'traveller', it is always the other person who is the 'tourist'.

Whatever the validity of this line of speculation, what one is in the field is only partially a matter of one's own self-definition in any case, for what one is and what roles are available is very much a matter of what 'they' will let you be. In Sri Lanka, a small island in the throes of a tourism explosion in the early 1980s, my immediate identity as a foreigner in their midst was that I was a tourist. I quite expect that many of my informants, despite my best efforts to explain to them my purpose, still regarded an anthropologist as a kind of tourist. And, to the extent that in the personal encounters that make up fieldwork there are no privileged positions, there is no way in which I can deny the legitimacy of their construction of the situation. I can say — and it is important that I do so in this introduction — that the identity of 'tourist' was difficult for me in that I felt no closer to the tourists I met in Sri Lanka — even those from the U.K. and Australia — than to the locals. I do not have positive associations with journeys, holidays or leisure and was, in fact, far less widely travelled than most of the tourists I met. In that sense, my choosing international tourism as a field in which to do research is clearly over-determined in ways I probably cannot fully unpack. It corresponds, perhaps, to that irony in Lévi-Strauss' career, that it was *Tristes Tropiques*, an account of his travels in South America, which brought him professional fame, and yet he chose to open the work with the words: 'I hate travelling' (1984:17). The irony is the more gripping for anthropologists since we are, in a fairly obvious sense, the beneficiaries of those travellers who, in previous ages, amassed stories about other cultures (Fabian 1983:82), and it is those self-same travellers whose modern-day descendants are none other than tourists.

RESEARCH FOCI AND METHODS

Having set out a range of general issues in contemporary anthropology to which a study of international tourism can be pertinent, the rest of this introductory chapter deals exclusively with the present work itself. It will make clear what the book does and does not attempt, explain the reasons for the focus adopted in the research, outline some of the methods employed in the research, set out the content of the text chapter by chapter, and finally raise some ethical issues about my own research and tourism research in general.

As said earlier in this chapter, tourism research at the present time is faced with what some have seen as a stark choice, namely that between crafting a convincing general theory of tourism or piling up largely empirical case studies guided only partially, if at all, by some loose analytical framework. The choice need not be that stark, of course, and in any case one can hardly contend that theory and ethnography are unrelated. Nonetheless, in this book, there has been a deliberate opting for a presentation that remains close to actual events and particular relationships, rather than attempting something more abstract or theoretical. There are two main reasons for this. Firstly, it is clearly the case that many of the frameworks so far developed within the anthropology of tourism, whilst highly suggestive, are transparently lop-sided. Be it tourism as a 'sacred journey' or tourism as 'neo-imperialism', such frameworks strike one as more a case of using tourism as a convenient hook upon which to hang a set of values than of an attempt to create an adequate account of what is a phenomenally complex industry.

My second reason for remaining largely at the relatively descriptive level is to be found in the less than satisfactory circumstances of my fieldwork (see Crick 1989b, 1992). This book is not the result of afterthoughts or a spin off from research with a different focus. My fieldwork was about tourism from the word go. On the other hand, having to fit the project into a period of research leave lasting for only seven months — indeed having been conducted quite literally during a 'stopover' on my way back to Australia after an anthropology conference in the U.K. — much that I would like to have attempted in more protracted fieldwork was out of the question. This is particularly so since teaching and writing commitments immediately prior to my research leave, neither of which had anything to do with tourism, so interrupted what was to have been a solid period of field preparation and language learning that I had to proceed to Sri Lanka with almost no preparation. Given my limited time in the field and given the fact that English was the language in which most host-foreigner relations in Sri Lanka were conducted, I quickly realised that by the end of my brief stay my Sinhala would still be so inferior to the English of most of my hosts that I conducted almost the entirety of my research work in English. I could have spend my seven months acquiring a fair level of proficiency in colloquial Sinhala, but I would then have to wait some three years for my next period of research leave before getting on with the tourism research; this did not seem like the best use of my time, though it obviously restricted the range of voices accessible to me.

Given the short period of time in the field, certain other restrictions were placed on the research which mean that this book is in no way a complete account of the international tourism industry in Sri Lanka. Firstly, I worked almost exclusively in Kandy. I did not work in a village; I did not work in a coastal resort. More than that, I scarcely worked in the 'formal' tourism sector (that sector approved by and regulated by the Ceylon Tourist Board, the world of the graded hotels and 'package tours') but very much in the 'informal' sector (the realm of the unlicensed guesthouses and the street guides). One reason for this was simply lack of funds to be able to afford to stay in accommodation in the formal sector for any length of time. A second reason, which may not be at all well founded, was an instinct that working outside the approved sector would be anthropologically richer. This world of the beggars, the cheap cafes, the semi-literate culture brokers, and those normally referred to as 'touts', is one that does not appear in the glossy brochures of the travel industry, but it is assuredly a very real part of tourism in most Third World destinations, and one, besides, for the study of which anthropologists are better equipped than their colleagues in other social sciences. One last qualification needs to be made as to what this book does not cover. The study concerns Sri Lankan views about tourists and tourism; it does not concern itself with tourists' perceptions of Sri Lanka. Clearly, the latter topic is a legitimate one, but during my fieldwork I decided to concentrate on just one side of the whole, that in which Sri Lankans speak and the tourists are spoken about.

The reason I chose to concentrate on the 'native voice' — that is an exploration of the views of Sri Lankans about tourism — had less to do with any fashion current in the early 1980s for 'dialogical' anthropology and the need to create a text in which one's informants were not silenced, than a very salient fact about the social science literature on tourism, namely that hosts in the tourism industry are largely "shadowy figures" about whose viewpoint we know relatively little (Dann *et al.*, 1988:22). An anthropologist reading the literature on international tourism in the Third World by geographers, economists, psychologists, and so on, will immediately be struck by the almost complete absence of attention to the voices of the human beings caught up in tourist developments. Whether such local voices are silenced in these disciplines because of their level of abstraction, their methodologies, or simply because of a lack of interest in the first place (Simpson 1993:179), they normally do not ask questions about how people on the receiving end perceive international tourism, what they understand by the behaviour of foreign visitors, what sense they make of the changes going on. It is important for each social science discipline to pursue unabashedly its own particular interests in tourism employing its own particular methodologies, and this means that one discipline can strategically focus upon what it sees as the glaring omissions in the purview of others. Concentrating on the 'native voice', especially when obtaining much of my information by the time-honoured anthropological method of participant observation, seemed a focus by means of which anthropology could make a distinctive contribution to the study of international tourism. International tourism inevitably brings into play a whole host of cultural meanings about foreigners, and reflecting on 'the other' in this way inevitably activates cultural themes about the values of one's society, tradition, cultural change, commerce, jealousy, and the like; it is a potentially rich field for anthropological investigation.

In using such expressions as 'native voice' or 'local voice', I must make it clear immediately that Sri Lanka does not have one voice on international tourism, any more than it has only one voice on any other important public issue. Not only are many of the individual expressions decidedly ambivalent, there are also many conflicting viewpoints within Sri Lanka, and several sections of this book concentrate on the ways in which Sri Lankans in different niches perceive and evaluate tourism differently. The voices are sometimes those of bystanders, but for the most part they are those of people involved in tourism in one way or another. Inevitably the different kinds of voices were heard in different circumstances and were made audible by a variety of research methods. Those of small-scale tourist entrepreneurs were heard as a result of participant observation in guesthouses. Senior management of local hotels was accessed through formal interviewing. The views of municipal officials were expressed in a seminar which I organised in the Kandy Town Hall. The voices of those at school in Kandy were accessed by organising a writing exercise in several local schools (Crick 1993). Newspapers were the vehicle for yet other voices. Written documents available in the Ceylon Tourist Board's library and in the Central Bank in Colombo gave expression to the voices of the policy-making elite and the pro-tourism lobby. Simply being observant in the local shops, market, and cheap cafes on a regular basis brought a different kind of information. Waiting and listening in the streets of Kandy allowed many of the poorer sectors of society, but particularly the street guides, to tell their story. One street corner near the famous lake in Kandy, frequented by guides, prostitutes, beggars and street vendors, became an important research 'base', the place where I worked extensively with Ali, one of the pavement vendors who also occasionally did tourist guiding, who became my main informant. This spot gave me a good view of several shops, banks frequented by tourists, and a leading hotel; it was also on the route tourists travelled on leaving the rail and bus stations in their initial search for accommodation (Crick 1992).

Throughout this book, not only do different sectors of society have their say, I attempt to contextualise their remarks so that the voices are not 'disembodied' but located in terms of sets of cultural values and patterns of social relationships, unlike the methodologically prim and statistically immaculate, but otherwise culturally meaningless, examples of tourism 'survey research' so frequently found in the literature. Having said this, I should make it clear that I entertain no romantic notion that anthropology can ever give direct expression to any 'native voice' (see Hastrup 1993:176–7). Most of those who speak in this book spoke because of my interests and because of my presence. Many were literally speaking to me, responding to my queries. One of the ever-present voices throughout this text is obviously my own, with all the values and presumptions which I brought to my research. Besides, as said, I, a stranger in Sri Lanka, of necessity would have been regarded by many of those to whom I spoke as a kind of tourist myself. That needs to be taken into consideration when evaluating what I was told and what I present in this book.

There is a second slightly different sense of 'contextualise' which must also be clarified here. Whilst I have been concerned to 'locate' the particular voices heard in the text, I have also attempted throughout the book to locate the overall development of the tourism industry in Sri Lanka within a historical, political, economic and cultural framework. It might seem superfluous to dwell on such an obvious matter, but in fact it is not redundant to make the point explicit, for literature on tourism in Sri Lanka and contemporary literature on other aspects of Sri Lankan life form two almost totally separate bibliographies. Apart from that type of literature which very much stresses the 'cultural pollution' said to follow in the wake of tourism (for instance, Mendis 1981), the vast bulk of tourism writing in Sri Lanka is technical, statistical, and concerned exclusively with the industry; the wider social and political economy framework is largely absent. On the other side, in the extensive social scientific literature about contemporary Sri Lanka — whether it be about kinship and land tenure, ethnicity, Buddhism, politics, social change, development, civil violence, and so on, there is almost no mention of tourism, other than the occasional dismissive or derogatory aside by serious academics making clear their own contempt for the trivialities of tourist behaviour.[3] This omission is somewhat curious in that the growth of the tourism industry is so clearly bound up with quite explicit economic policies, has a range of socio-cultural concomitants; and civil strife clearly affects the health of the industry directly.

As Britton has so correctly remarked (1982), accounts of tourism in the absence of such historical, political and economic frameworking are woefully inad-

---

[3] Daniel (1990) is an exception here. An ex-patriate Sri Lankan anthropologist, he writes insightfully as an anthropologist/tourist/pilgrim revisiting the sacred sites of the land of his birth amidst the contemporary scene of turmoil and carnage.

equate because they inevitably present the tourism industry in an ahistorical vacuum which renders it unintelligible. Despite the obviousness of such a point, the tourism literature consistently omits the larger social framework, just as the social science literature on Sri Lanka largely omits serious reference to tourism, which had by 1982 become one of its top foreign exchange earners. Given that situation, the construction of this book has as one of its foci to provide a cultural and historical context, so that the broader circumstances in which the industry has developed are made clear. At both the national and local levels, a sketch is provided of demographic, historical, political, economic and cultural factors. Such contextualisation unfortunately still falls short of the ideal, namely placing tourism squarely in a convincing and agreed upon overall picture of the evolving social structure of contemporary Sri Lanka, but I have supplied such context as my field data and subsequent reading have allowed. Unfortunately, perhaps because of a rural bias in research in Sri Lanka, little has been written about contemporary Kandy where I did my field research, and despite the ready availability of large quantities of national statistics and a large literature about politics, communalism, religion, and so on, no usable, overall empirical picture of the 'social structure' of contemporary Sri Lanka presents itself, quite apart from the issue of theoretical disagreements over the adequacy in the Sri Lankan context of concepts such as 'feudalism', 'caste' and 'class'. Clearly, given the shortness of my research time, undertaking the fundamental research required to generate an overall picture was quite out of the question; hopefully others will, in time, fill this vital gap in the literature.

THE STRUCTURE OF THE BOOK

Having discussed some of the methods used in the field and made clear some of the themes stressed in my research, I now wish to outline in concrete fashion the structure of the book, chapter by chapter. It has often been said that anthropologists typically study social phenomena at 'ground level', and in writing a book which deliberately stays close to concrete events and relationships, I have no doubt worked at ground level in the most obvious sense of that expression. But 'ground' is a spatial metaphor which can be deceptively simple when talking about social phenomena. What is 'ground' obviously varies with perspective and with something as complex as international tourism, it is important to view the phenomenon on a number of different levels.

This book has been arranged explicitly so that different levels are highlighted. Each chapter looks at similar material, but as if through a microscope where the level of magnification used is altered from one chapter to the next. This introductory chapter addresses tourism from a theoretical, comparative and personal viewpoint. Chapter 2 focuses on the development of the modern tourism industry in Sri Lanka at the national level, paying particular attention to the economic and political forces behind that development and then examining some of the cultural 'costs'. Chapter 3 concerns the growth of tourism in the city of Kandy, thus yielding a regional version of a national story. Chapter 4 investigates images of tourism and tourists in Kandy by analysing the topic from three different viewpoints — officials in the Town Hall, senior students at school, and those on the streets. Chapter 5 looks at the so-called 'informal' tourism sector in Kandy, that is to say the operations of the guesthouses which are not licensed by the Ceylon Tourist Board and the activities of the street guides who similarly are not licensed by any authority; in particular it analyses the activities of guides in relationship to shopkeepers in the city and the unlicensed guesthouses. Individual guesthouses are examined, just as the lives of particular street guides are described. From Chapter 1 to Chapter 5, then, we move from the comparative level to the national level, through the regional level down to the sectoral level, and finally to the level of the individual, acquiring en route multiple glimpses of the reality of international tourism in Sri Lanka. As one alters the focus on the microscope, certain phenomena fade from sight, and others come into view; some appear on a number of levels. The final chapter, Chapter 6, is a brief account, largely based on statistical information, which surveys what has occurred in the tourist industry in Sri Lanka in the decade since my fieldwork in 1982, ten years of almost unremitting civil turmoil and ethnic violence.

AN ETHICAL NOTE

I cannot end this introduction without raising a number of ethical concerns, both about aspects of my own research and about the relationship between anthropology and the tourism industry generally. Boissevain (1977:525) once alleged that there was frequently so much bias evident in the social science literature on tourism that it was sometimes difficult to tell whether an author was engaging in serious analysis or merely indulging in outbursts of emotional hostility. Embarking on tourism research acutely aware of this problem is, of course, no safeguard against its appearance in one's own work, the more so when in the field one hears such a discordant set of voices that one scarcely knows how to secure a starting point for one's investigation, or indeed whom to trust. There is no doubt that my own less than optimistic views about international tourism in the Third World — to say nothing about my personal attitudes towards leisure activities in general — have both affected the information I acquired and coloured the way in which I have chosen to present it. S.J. Tambiah, one of Sri Lanka's most distinguished anthropologists, has written of his profound unease and ambivalence while contemplating the topic of 'development' (1985:341, 347); I find inescapable a similarly equivocal sense when confronted by the phenomenon of international tourism in the Third World.

Personal ambivalence about international tourism apart, I have a number of obligations to my informants and hosts which fit less than comfortably with standard professional responsibilities. From the outset of my stay in Kandy, street guides would ask me whether my investigations would harm them, and I am bound to say that, to the extent that much of what goes on in the informal tourism arena is dependent upon tourists not fully comprehending what is going on, any account does have the potential to disadvantage those who gave me information. It is little comfort that my work will be read by a specialised group of academic colleagues rather than by an army of tourists. Another difficult issue concerns my responsibilities towards the Ceylon Tourist Board, which was, in one sense, my ultimate host. On my last day in Colombo in October 1982, I was the guest of the then Chairman of the Tourist Board, who was presiding over a farewell dinner in a Colombo hotel for a group of visiting Australian travel agents. I had had an interview with the Chairman earlier that day, as I had had seven months earlier at the outset of my research. The Chairman, a man of advanced years, had not come to the tourism field from an entrepreneurial background, but from the national library system in Sri Lanka. His view was the same as that of the then Minister of State (whose portfolio included tourism), that international tourism was a vital force for peace and inter-cultural understanding, and that without this dimension, tourism was just a "shoddy little show". His main concern, he put it to me, was not with foreign exchange and profitability, but with the various forms of cultural 'pollution' attendant upon international tourism.

When interviewing him, he made the point that what we were doing together — talking about the differences between cultures — that was tourism in the best sense of the term. I told him that evening that my book would have to make a number of critical points about the tourist industry in Sri Lanka, and he replied that criticism was both needed and welcome. That assurance notwithstanding, some of my comments in this book will likely not please the Sri Lankan tourism authorities. It in no way impugns the professionalism of Tourist Board officials to point out that the basic role of the Board is to promote tourism, not to criticise it, and it may be, therefore, that even so obvious an observation as the fact that tourism is a highly controversial industry and that many Sri Lankans are bitterly opposed to it, may not be welcome. To discuss dimensions of international tourism not contained within the official rhetoric of the industry of necessity casts doubt on the image of tourism and, indeed, to a degree, the image of Sri Lanka itself, which the authorities are attempting to disseminate. I can see no way of solving this dilemma. The role of advocate and social scientist are normally very different, and as other tourism researchers have felt obliged to point out (Pearce 1988:217–18), it is vital in the establishment of an insightful social science literature on tourism that we distance ourselves from the tourism industry itself and its particular interests.

Anthropologists have in the past acquired something of a reputation for being ideological enemies of tourism (Smith 1980:29), so it is important that we now strive to give this complex industry a fair hearing. As Nuñez stated: "the anthropological community [should] resist the temptation to condemn tourism as unnecessarily intrusive, as exploitative, as deculturative". But he went on to say that: "we would not be acting ethically, however, if we did not expose the cultural fakes and human zoos for what they are" (1978:214–5). These twin obligations pose a very real quandary for any social scientist who might be called upon by governments, tourism authorities, developers and the like, to give professional advice concerning the tourism industry. Valene Smith has argued that academic researchers and the tourist industry have common goals of which we should be more aware, and that the proven power of the anthropological profession to communicate with the public at large on vital issues could be turned to the service of tourism; anthropologists, for instance, could help to ameliorate the difficulties which permeate relationships between hosts and guests by providing tourists with better information about another culture (1980:15, 29).

This is not the place to open up an extended discussion on the nature of applied anthropology, but consultancy work by anthropologists in regard to tourism will clearly involve a number of very basic difficulties. To start with, the areas of misunderstanding are not only between hosts and guests. International tourism can bring to the surface fundamental conflicts between different classes in a society, between a government and its people, between national authorities and local communities, and even between nation states. It would be miraculous if an academic researcher could produce a view of tourism equally acceptable to all who have a stake in it and all who are affected by it. The other point to remember is that the anthropological study of tourism is still in its infancy, and that being the case, the highest priority really must be to establish a substantial body of high quality work. It will likely be somewhat hazardous for an anthropologist to pose at any time as an 'expert' in this field, given the often widely diverging goals of policy makers, developers and various community groups, but this is bound to be the more so when the field cannot yet display, at either an empirical or theoretical level, solid and secure academic foundations.

CHAPTER TWO

The Development of International Tourism in Sri Lanka: An Economic, Social and Political Portrait

S ri Lanka, the Resplendent Isle, the small tear-drop shaped nation off the south-eastern tip of India, has excited the imagination of those looking for a paradise on earth for centuries (Garcia 1988:94–100). Officially abandoning her British colonial name of Ceylon in 1972 for her present one, she was known in much earlier eras as Taprobane and Serendip, but has also commonly been referred to as 'The Pearl of the Orient'. As Goonetileke put it: "Ceylon has long been the dream island of nearly every traveller from the intrepid voyagers of ancient Greece and Rome, Arabia and fabled China to the peristaltic globe-trotters of the present charter flight era" (1976 ed.:xv). Even Marco Polo felt obliged to declare that for its size Ceylon was one of the finest islands in the world. During the early years of British missionary zeal, Bishop Heber's infamously derogatory hymn about Ceylon, could still manage a begrudging admission of the attractiveness of the place itself, even if not of its people — "Where every prospect pleases, And only man is vile" (cited in Goonetileke 1976 ed.:xxi). An island nation of some 25,000 square miles and in 1982 just over 15 million people, Sri Lanka is certainly a land of contrasts — from beautiful tropical beaches to spectacular mountain scenery, from massive modern hydro-electric schemes to ancient temples. Diversity also characterises her social and cultural life, for apart from the numerically preponderant Sinhalese, there is a sizeable Tamil population; apart from Buddhism, there are significant Hindu, Christian and Muslim minorities. With such cultural richness in addition to its legendary beauty, it is no wonder that when the tourism industry began to expand throughout the Third World after the Second World War, Sri Lanka should seek to become a significant tourist destination.

When Sri Lanka achieved independence in 1948 after more than four centuries of European domination (first by Portugal, then by Holland and finally by Great Britain), she did so in a condition and by a path which was the envy of many other nations. Indeed, at independence, her position looked positively rosy compared to that of many of her Asian neighbours (Peebles 1982:10). She had almost entirely avoided the bloodshed of a protracted anti-colonial struggle, she had a well-developed transport infrastructure, a profitable export sector, an efficient bureaucracy, a sizeable indigenous bourgeoisie, and a record in the spheres of edu-

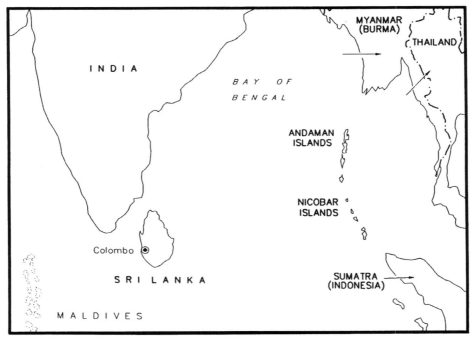

Map 1   Sri Lanka and her neighbours.

cation and public health which far surpassed the standards found in nations with comparable per capita income levels (Gunatilleke 1978:38, 54, 84–7; Higgins 1982:15). Unfortunately, with a population which roughly doubled between independence and 1982, but with an economy which failed to grow significantly over the same period, the maintenance of such impressive welfare achievements became an increasing burden (Gibson 1982), achievable, in fact, only by a massive increase in public debt which exceeded 75% of the GNP by 1977 (Peebles 1982:13). Sri Lanka's second tragedy is that her very ethnic and religious diversity has proven to be incompatible with the unity and homogeneity many apparently require in a modern nation state (Wriggins 1960:4, 20, 211, 218), hence the violence which has characterised the last decade of her history. Whatever advantages she enjoyed in 1948, she emerged at independence very much as a collectivity of highly self-conscious religious, ethnic and linguistic communities rather than as one nation, and events since have made things considerably worse. The bloodbath which has ensued and which at the present time seems insoluble has, of course, done nothing to help Sri Lanka solve her economic woes. It has also significantly set back, but perhaps only temporarily, her growing tourism industry. This chapter examines closely the growth of that industry after the Second World War, particularly from 1966 until 1983, when the upsurge in violence reversed what to that point had been a story of almost uninterrupted expansion.

A POLITICAL AND ECONOMIC FRAMEWORK

Depending on whom one asks, and what one is thought to mean by the term 'tourist', the question 'When did tourism begin in Sri Lanka?' can yield three very different answers. One answer can be that Sri Lanka for well over a thousand years has had pilgrims and other travellers visiting its shores. A second answer can be: the second half of the nineteenth century, when Colombo became an important staging post for those travelling between Europe and the Orient, so that Sri Lanka experienced a constant flow of "boat tourists" spending one or two days in the island (Seneviratne and Peiris 1991:47). For those who feel that neither of those kinds of travellers has very much in common with modern mass tourism, the answer is most likely to be 1966 because this was the year in which J.R. Jayewardene, then Minister of State, established the legislative and planning foundations for the industry.

Despite the impetus which might have been given to the growth in the visitor industry immediately after the Second World War, no substantial developments occurred in Sri Lanka for another twenty years, despite the considerable growth in international tourism during this period experienced by other Asian countries (Attanayake *et al.,* 1983:243–4). In fact, for some of those years, the number of foreigners arriving in Sri Lanka actually declined (Gamage 1978:17; Kovach 1965:9). There was after 1945 a small number of travellers and a fairly constant, if small, flow of 'excursionists' in Sri Lanka for a day or so as ships called in at Colombo, but there was no concerted, and certainly no successful, attempt to increase the number of tourists. There was virtually no travel research being conducted and, in fact, no clear tourist policy at all. Well could it be said that in 1946 not only most of the people, but also the Government itself, treated tourism as a "big joke" (Ediriweera 1969:23). After 1966, by contrast, international tourists became a very serious matter for governments, entrepreneurs and subsequently for many others in Sri Lanka.

The idea that 1966 was an *annus mirabilis* is, however, to some extent, but a part of a politically charged version of Sri Lanka's recent history in which the origins of the modern tourism industry constitute an element in a set of representations celebrating the United National Party's coming to power. As an article entitled "Five years that changed a nation" (*Sun,* 22 July 1982) makes clear, the development of mass tourism and the commitment to maximise foreign exchange are quite explicitly listed as achievements of the Jayewardene years and of the U.N.P. The ousting of the Sri Lanka Freedom Party was represented as the transition from nepotism to democracy, rationing to choice, bureaucracy to freedom. To

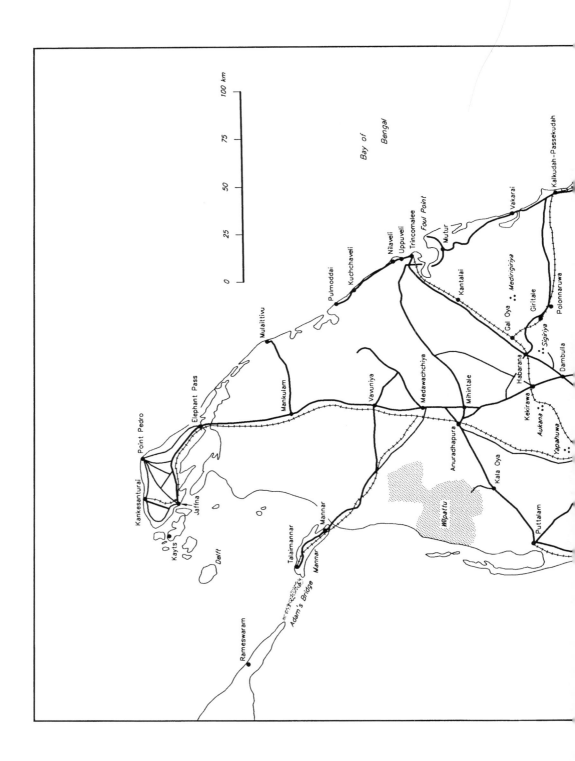

25

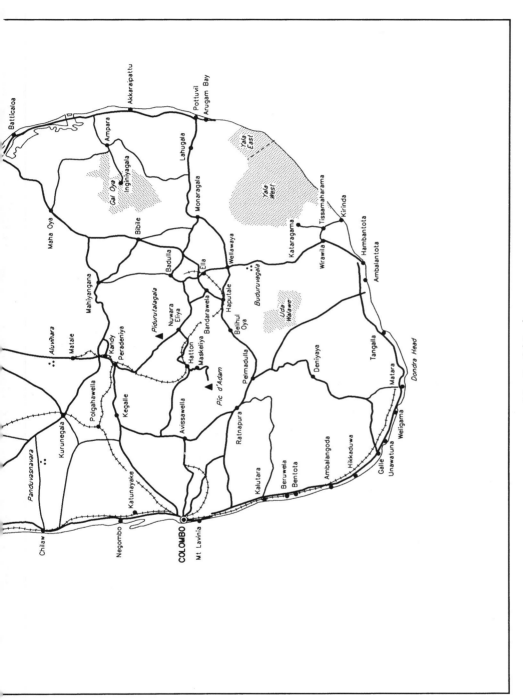

Map 2 Sri Lanka.

the extent that the story of international tourism in Sri Lanka is often portrayed as part of that set of collective representations, when we read appraisals of the tourist record we have to bear in mind this wider and, of course, not undisputed framework.

In the late 1950s and early 1960s there were, in reality, a number of moves afoot to put some momentum into the tourist industry, but very little changed and the record of arrivals continued to be unimpressive. In fact, a total tourism revenue for 1950 of 6.4 million rupees had only risen to 6.5 million rupees by 1965. 1966, however, saw the Ceylon Tourist Board Act (No. 16 of 1966), which established a statutory authority, appointed by the Government, and under the wing of the Ministry of State. This body replaced the Ceylon Tourist Bureau, which, even with a 'Six Year Plan' in 1954, had failed to produce noticeable growth (Due 1980:48). The overall brief of the new Board was to encourage the growth of the tourism industry. 1966 also saw the Ceylon Hotels Corporation Act (No.14 of 1966), which empowered this new body to acquire land to establish tourist developments, and to establish other needed facilities such as a fleet of tourist cars. The Corporation was a body in which both the government itself and a number of entrepreneurs invested heavily. Two years later came the Tourist Development Act (No.14 of 1968) enabling the Tourist Board to regulate the provision of tourist services. In this period, too, was established the Ceylon Hotels School, a body originally created with overseas help, to train the managerial and specialist personnel required for the new industry.

Although it is often difficult to get reliable information on the precise pressures behind policy formation (Richter 1993:179), in the case of Sri Lanka it looks as if the political elite rather more than highly influential domestic pressure groups were behind the thrust towards massive tourism development (Richter 1993:193). Indeed, tourism development can be a relatively easy policy area for a government because, tourism being a new industry, there are no well-entrenched powerful groups opposed to it, at least not to begin with (Richter 1982:108). The government has certainly always been of central importance in the tourist industry in Sri Lanka. As Anandatissa de Alwis, Minister of State in 1982 (whose portfolio included tourism) said: "the responsibility for stating objectives and value judgments in growing industries like Tourism, rests firmly with the Government" (1982a).

When one examines the parlous situation prior to 1966, the need for that central direction was clearly vital. In his 1965 report, Kovach claimed that tourism in Ceylon was the "Cinderella of her economic development projects", and that "with her natural tourist attractions and location it should have been her Croesus" (1965:9). He pointed out that more market research was required, statistical data needed to be collected, border formalities needed simplification, the guide system had to be reorganised, and specific plans should be implemented geared to the needs of international rather than domestic tourists. He also stated (1965:10) that a total reorientation of thinking was required and a replacement of the system where, as under the Tourist Bureau, tourism was at the mercy of a succession of short-term civil service appointments. In 1968 the International Bank for Reconstruction and Development pointed to the need to arrange investment incentives and to acquire capital from abroad. It also set out some alarming statistics: about 70% of Ceylon's foreign exchange gains were lost through 'black market' operations (1968:6). S.N. Chib, previously Director-General of the Department of Tourism in India and in 1967 U.N. adviser to the Government of Ceylon on tourism, painted a very grim picture of tourism in that country (1967). In 1963 tourist numbers were not only miniscule, their average stay was only 4 days. The airport was grossly inadequate; a building programme for new hotels was vital. Indeed, at that time some of the hotels were converted nineteenth century barracks or the 'rest houses' constructed during the nineteenth century for the leisure of planters, civil servants and merchants (Sievers 1983:17). Above all, according to Chib, the private sector and government would need to co-operate closely (1967:11).

During the 1960s, besides government enthusiasm, there was a small but vocal private sector eager to be part of a modern tourism industry. In fact, a recognisable pro-tourism lobby group had formed. In 1969, V.E.H. de Mel, Chairman of the Association for the Promotion of Tourism in Ceylon, had this to say at a seminar held in the Hotel Taprobane, Colombo: "We are conscious of the fact that Tourism has not been accepted as a good thing by everyone, and it is our endeavour to propagate and do all we can to promote Tourism because we ourselves, those connected with the business and those interested in the health and wealth of the country, do feel very strongly that tourism can bring a lot of good" (1969:iii). In the following year, the same organisation held a seminar on tourism for 'Local Bodies' at the Chamber of Commerce in Colombo.

Apart from setting up a range of organising bodies, the government of the day took the same course as many other Third World nations in commissioning a 'tourism plan'. The Ceylon Tourism Plan was drawn up by Harris, Kerr, Forster & Co., a firm of hotel and travel consultants based in Hawaii. This plan, a '10 Year' blueprint, was part of a package of assistance given by the United States to Ceylon through the Agency for International Development. This utilisation of foreign 'experts' to plan the development of Third World countries was standard at the time, in tourism as in other industries (Goonatilake 1975: 4). It is only recently that we have recognised how inexpert such assistance often was and how frequently consultancy reports enshrined values at variance with declared national goals (Goonatilake 1975:4–5). Many a Third World nation unhesitatingly followed the advice of the World Bank and other prestigious international organisations, but such organisations are seldom neutral; their function is often to foster the development of tourism and other activities, not to raise fundamental questions about whether such developments might be beneficial for a particular country or not. In the case of Sri Lanka, the small Harris, Kerr, Forster & Co. team visited the island for only three months during 1967, and despite the obvious limitations of understanding this entailed, many critical commentators argue that their resulting plan guided tourism development, not just for the first decade, but well into the 1980s and that its fundamental assumptions have never been challenged or revised (ibid:2). Richter has noted pertinently that: "what is good for the travel industry is almost never the only criterion a developing nation should consider, though it is often the only consulting perspective the nation may get" (1989:32). To the extent that the Ceylon Tourism Plan was very much an overseas travel industry view, some would argue strenuously that there was considerable cause for concern when in 1978, more than a decade after its publication, the Chairman of the Ceylon Tourist Board could state baldly: "I see no reason for a new plan" (de Zoysa 1978:12).

The Ceylon Tourism Plan spoke of tourism in Ceylon as "an export industry of enormous proportions, offering unlimited prospects as a growth resource" (1967: 27). It spoke of the foreign exchange which could be earned, thus solving Sri Lanka's acute balance of payments problem, and of the need to attract foreign capital. It spoke of the income derived from tourism flowing "quickly and directly with a wide distribution into the local economy providing a rapid, cumulative and circulating flow of income" (ibid:239). Tourism was an "inexpensive instrument for creating good will, development of other industry and the circulation of desirable public and political relations with neighbouring nations and the world community" (ibid:239). Predictions were for 300,000 tourists by 1976, with North America supplying almost as many as western Europe (ibid:54–5). The greatest need was suitable quality accommodation, virtually no new plant having been constructed in the previous thirty years (ibid:60). The government itself would have to be heavily involved in investment in the initial stages. In its optimism about growth potential, foreign exchange earnings and so on, the Tourism Plan was not alone. Kovach felt bold enough to declare that "under proper direction, tourism should be her permanent fourth industry" (1965:23).

In 1980, tourism did, in fact, attain fourth place as a foreign exchange earner, although it subsequently slipped. But many of the other expectations of the Ceylon Tourism Plan were nowhere near realisation by 1982. As Mendis shows (1981:2–3), by 1976 Sri Lanka was earning only half the foreign exchange predicted, and tourist arrivals were only a little over a third of those projected. Visitors from North America were only 7% of those the Plan had led the authorities to expect. Nor is the foreign exchange 'leakage' anywhere near the low 20% forecast (ibid:246). One of the things that has become clear from the fortunes of the tourist industry in several Third World countries is that links between the tourist sector and the rest of the economy are not strong, and therefore the predicted employment and income multipliers have not been achieved. The multiplier of between 3 and 4 which the Plan had envisaged for Sri Lanka (1967:240) has proven to be a complete fantasy.

Apart from specific predictive errors, the Ceylon Tourism Plan was grossly defective in a very basic way. As Gamage, Director of Research at the Ceylon Tourist Board in 1982, put it: "the report had been adopted in its entirety by the authorities without discussion of the wider implications of the tourism development" (1978:19). Thus, not only were a number of economic issues not considered, but the socio-cultural consequences of tourism development were ignored. There was no consideration of the difference between the acquisition of foreign exchange, economic growth and the broader topic of socio-economic development. Nor was there any consideration of how tourism growth might form part of much wider economic and social planning in Ceylon. In short, vital present day considerations in the field of development such as the social distribution of benefits and the interlinking of economic growth with other social objectives, were absent. But establishing a tourism industry in the Third World, in fact, normally involves heavy governmental outlays on infrastructure and the soliciting of international capital by the provision of tax holidays and other incentive schemes, all of which have an inevitable 'opportunity cost', namely the results achievable by directing such expenditure and revenue to other needy areas. Indeed, the rapid growth of the tourism industry has been claimed by some to have been very much an artefact of the tax-privileged conditions of its early years which made the industry so attractive to invest in (Karunatilake 1987:87, 90). This was even more the case in the early 70s under the left wing S.L.F.P. government when nationalisation of plantations and other major land reforms meant that ownership of property was no longer a favoured method of capital accumulation; many a wealthy Sri Lankan immediately turned to investment in tourism as the way out of this dilemma (Gunatilleke 1978:67, 78).

Collaborating with international capital is also clearly not without political costs for the Third World. The control exercisable from overseas in respect of industries requiring foreign investment is considerable. Moreover, narrow economic goals may obscure other national programmes and even be incompatible with them. Of India, Berindranath (1980:5–6) comments acerbically on the strategy of 'Indian socialism' which has opted for capital-intensive tourism of the graded hotel kind from which local people and local resources are largely excluded, and also on the utilisation of public money which could be put to other uses, so subsidising the holidays of rich foreigners in luxury accommodation when millions of Indians are malnourished and without shelter. The same irony in connection with international tourism in Sri Lanka under the 'democratic socialism' of the U.N.P. has been commented on by observers.

Looking back from the 1990s with more understanding of the operations of the international tourism system and with considerably more scepticism about the whole issue of development in the Third World, one still needs to ask the question why, during the 1960s, international tourism appeared to the Director-General of the Ceylon Tourist Board to be such "an easy and relatively quick" (Silva 1978:11) way of solving several basic economic problems, indeed to be a "passport to development", in de Kadt's well chosen phrase (1979 ed.). Much of the answer lies in the particular economic pressures facing Sri Lanka in the immediate post-war years, pressures similar to those confronting other Third World nations who also eagerly embraced tourism.

Sri Lanka's economy in 1966 was still largely a legacy of the demands of the colonial system for primary produce exports; it had, for several centuries, very much been structured around the needs of Europe. Specialised production enclaves had been created during that time and trade links organised along political lines. So in the decade or so after the end of the Second World War, those countries gaining independence from colonial rulers found themselves to be extremely vulnerable economically. Economic diversification was underdeveloped and inter-sectoral linkages were weak. They were hazardously dependent upon the export of raw materials and agricultural products — in Sri Lanka's case very much tea, rubber and coconuts — and during the 1960s severe balance of payments problems were occurring given the need of such countries to import manufactured goods with revenue earned from the sale of primary commodities whose value was declining.

In this situation, tourism as an industry seemed to have much to recommend it. Gamage rightly points out (1978:4) that Sri Lanka, like many lesser developed countries beset with such problems, and particularly by a lack of diversification, could see tourism as such a different type of venture that it could be referred to as "manna from heaven" (1978:4; cf. Balakrishnan 1979:101,119). Many of the essential 'raw materials' for a tourist industry — scenery, climate, good transport facilities, 'friendly people' — were already there. Given the increasing affluence of the industrialised world and the substantial growth in leisure time in those countries, tourism seemed to have a rosy future assured. It is also necessary to add that in Sri Lanka's case, as in the case of many other Third World countries, there were no obvious alternative activities where the necessary raw materials and trained manpower were available in abundance. Tourism particularly, as a service sector undertaking, was thought to bring economic rewards without the heavy infrastructure costs associated with setting up manufacturing enterprises. As it has turned out, however — and Sri Lanka had to learn this lesson the same way as other countries which leapt onto the international tourism band wagon — establishing a tourism industry is not without substantial infrastructure costs. Nor, given the periodic recessions in the industrialised world, does tourism offer the Third World an untroubled road to affluence. The optimism of the 1960s was also short-sighted in another way. International tourism in the Third World is, precisely, an industry gearing, once again, sectors of the economy of countries like Sri Lanka to the needs and desires of those in Europe and the rest of the affluent, industrialised west. Consequently, if Sri Lanka's economic troubles in the 1960s were a result of deformations produced by imperial political economy, of being the 'periphery' to a metropolitan centre, developing international tourism was a strategy which, of necessity, created similar structural arrangements.

The 'political' nature of tourism was also evident in the domestic context of Sri Lanka. Nimalasiri Silva, Director of the Ceylon Tourist Board in 1970, stated that one would have to teach hospitality to the people by a "systematic propaganda campaign" (1970:44). The people would need to be educated about the benefits of tourism; the subject would be introduced into the school curriculum. By films and radio, children would be made aware; essay competitions would be run by teachers to inculcate the proper attitudes (Silva 1970:42–4). Posters of 'do's and don'ts' would be displayed. Slogans were adopted to the effect that foreigners should be greeted with a smile and not by outstretched arms begging for money. A magazine entitled *Sancharika* would be distributed to teachers to instruct them on how to teach the topic of tourism. Besides this, Colombo would be cleaned up and beggars would be removed from the streets. The original Tourism Plan itself, in fact, had made a number of suggestions along these lines: social policy was required to free areas of beggars and other undesirables who stood and stared (1967:149). "The aims and objectives of the Ceylon Tourism Plan must be understood and supported by all segments of the country ..." (ibid:235). There were very few voices pointing out the fact that the socio-cultural repercussions of affluent tourists in the Third World would make such actions or simplistic propaganda unrealistic. A.T. Ariyaratne, the influential social reformer, was one who made his views clear at the 1970 seminar: "How can you expect a discontented people who don't have even their basic necessities to greet a tourist with a smile?" (1970:51). Ariyaratne envisaged that the international tourism industry being developed would not benefit the mass of the people and felt that a form of tourism should be developed which involved the people at large, and, moreover, which could be developed specifically to aid their social and spiritual welfare. "The foreign-exchange mania is morally degrading to all of us as a nation. If we are in the economic plight today as a nation as a result of the west exploiting us in the past thus reducing us to be international beggars we should not adopt the identical philosophy of exploiting the tourist to earn foreign exchange ... even from a practical point of view this philosophy is wrong because the West is better equipped than we are for exploitation of the Third World" (ibid:50).

In 1970, particularly in the company of enthusiastic Colombo entrepreneurs intent upon success in a new commercial venture, Ariyaratne's idealism and con-

cern would have been distinctly out of place. But it is also important in surveying
the modern history of international tourism in Sri Lanka to grasp the fact that idealism about tourism was also there at an official level at the origin of the government's involvement in the venture. 1967, the year of the Ceylon Tourism Plan, was
'International Tourism Year' and had as its theme: "Tourism — Passport to Peace".
In that year J.R. Jayewardene as Minister of State had asserted: "The economic benefits of such a venture are obvious and abundant. But the primary object ... is to
encourage understanding, tolerance and goodwill amongst peoples. ITY could
therefore partly be described as a crusade against ignorance and prejudice, and also
a friendship campaign" (Jayewardene 1982). Over a decade later in 1978, the World
Tourism Organisation's theme was "Tourism for International Understanding,
Peace and Co-operation", and during that year President Jayewardene opened a
Pacific Asia Travel Association Conference with the theme of tourism's contribution to enhancing the brotherhood of man. Thus, when Anandatissa de Alwis,
made his Vice-Presidential speech at the World Tourism Organisation Conference
in Manila in 1980 entitled "Tourism. The Greatest Movement for Peace and Understanding" (1980), the rhetoric was not really new. What was new was the Buddhist
framework in which the message was clothed. Quoting the Buddha's words in Pali,
that the consequences of human actions are bound up with the motivations behind
them, he urged that tourism must be given a new direction; it could not simply be a
materialistic quest for foreign exchange, because actions rooted in greed are des-
tined for self-destruction. Tourism should be a matter of people meeting each other
and learning to understand each other (1980). This ideological dimension is not, in
fact, surprising, given the 'image creation' role in the Jayewardene government of
de Alwis, previously head of the Thompson advertising agency in Colombo. As
Kemper puts it, his job was to sell to Sri Lankans the image of the U.N.P. as creator
of *dharmista samajaya* — a righteous Buddhist society — and to sell to foreigners
the image of Sri Lanka as an attractive tourist destination (1991:10, 168).

   The sizeable gap between social reality and the rhetoric used by the controlling interests in international tourism has been widely remarked on in the context
of Third World tourism. If in previous centuries a great deal of travel may have
been very much concerned with education in the broad sense (Adler 1989:16), it is
doubtful whether this connection is strong in twentieth century mass tourism,
although, of course, some learning inevitably accompanies the experience of cultural difference. I asked many people in Sri Lanka how they felt about the official
'peace and understanding' view of international tourism and received a range of
responses. Some said that it was simply a cynical case of an elite adopting a camou-
flaging ideology to disguise the links between themselves and international capitalism. Ali, my pavement hawker informant in Kandy, was more charitable. It was not
that the Minister was dishonest, he claimed; he truly believed what he said, but he

had little appreciation of the nature of tourism on the streets. One wealthy guest-house owner in Kandy simply asked: "Who is going to invest their money in peace and understanding?" I raised the issue of a possible tension between the emphasis on profit-making and gaining foreign exchange, and the lofty moral claims as to the nature and consequences of international tourism with senior employees at the Tourist Board itself and at the Ministry of State. The Director of Development at the Board, after all, was on record as stating that the objective of tourism planning was to maximise economic benefits (P. Seneviratne 1982:96). A direct question about whether tourism was a force for international peace and understanding drew two replies: "You must ask the Minister that", and "A very dangerous question to answer".

Some evidence regarding the relationship between international tourism in Sri Lanka and lofty motives on, at least, the visitors' side, is available in the Ceylon Tourist Board's own published data. In 1982 (1982c:25), 88.7% of arrivals claimed that their prime reason for visiting was pleasure; 6.7% visited for business; and only 2.9% for religious, cultural, and similar reasons. 1982 was in no way atypical. Since 1969 the percentage arriving 'for pleasure' has always been in excess of 75%, and frequently around 90%. If such 'airport statistics' are any real indication of tourist motivations for travel, 'cultural understanding' would seem to be fairly insignificant, although it has to be admitted that 'having fun' and 'learning' are not mutually exclusive. Whatever the official rhetoric of the policy makers about peace and understanding, from the customers point of view, quite clearly tourism in Sri Lanka is about the sun, sand, sea — and as Sri Lanka has also learned — the sex that foreigners can purchase in the Third World. This must be additionally disappointing to the degree that Sri Lanka has stressed its rich cultural heritage as a tourist attraction to distinguish itself from nearby destinations such as the Maldive islands which it regards as able to offer beach resorts and no more.

Although one might expect a somewhat chequered political history for the tourism industry in a country like Sri Lanka given the ideological differences between her two main political parties which have vied for power since 1966, this does not really appear to have been the case to any great extent. Perhaps during the years the Sri Lanka Freedom Party was in power (1970–7) there were differences in emphasis. The government was prominent in organising a State-run tourist program of rail and coach tours, which by 1982 were a thing of the past. There was also a greater emphasis on domestic tourism than subsequently. Perhaps, too, the 'nationalistic' thrust of S.L.F.P. policy meant that tourism was smaller in scale and less in the hands of international capital than under the U.N.P. (Due 1980:126–7). But whatever the founding myth of 1966, the facts show clearly that the S.L.F.P. also was constantly pro-tourist, and during its years in office growth in the industry was substantial. It was during those years — some being periods of severe domestic hardship and rationing — that foreign tourists were exempt from many of the restrictions placed on nationals. Far from being a bleak period in the growth story, some U.N.P. supporters who spoke to me on the subject paid the opposition a back-handed compliment, stating that it was during those S.L.F.P. years that the tourism industry first started to get "out of control" because of too rapid a growth rate, and so started to display a worrying range of adverse socio-cultural side-effects.

Whilst it is important to recognise the pro-tourism attitude of the S.L.F.P., it is equally important to acknowledge the tourist explosion which occurred immediately after the U.N.P. regained power in 1977 with a massive electoral mandate for widespread economic reform. Welfarism, it was widely believed, could no longer sustain the basic needs of or employment of a rapidly growing population (Higgins 1982:19), so there had to be a fundamental change from economic nationalism with its controls, rationing, subsidies, and policy of import substitution to one which liberated the Sri Lankan economy. The so-called 'open economy' involved freer international trade, the attraction of foreign capital and encouragement of the export sector (Gunasinghe 1984:128). The encouragement of tourism was a central expression of this new outlook (Simpson 1993:166), which could indeed be symbolised equally well either by the accelerated construction of the massive Mahaweli hydro-electric dam near Kandy or by the rapid construction of massive tourist hotels on the seafront of Colombo (Spencer 1990:4). 1977–82 were the years when tourist arrivals increased by leaps and bounds each year and when, in response to the criticism of the International Federation of Airline Pilots, Jayewardene himself directed that there should be a massive upgrading of the facilities at Katunayake airport outside Colombo (Economist Intelligence Unit 1979:12). These were years of substantial economic deregulation when Prime Minister Premadasa could state that there were no class distinctions in Sri Lanka any more and that anyone with talent could make money (*The Island*, 5 May 1982). Foreign capital was financing an increasing amount of the hotel construction in this period under conditions of generous tax incentives.

It is vital that this overarching U.N.P. philosophy be kept firmly in mind, for when the tourist industry came under attack during the early 1980s, it was very often as an exemplar of the 'open economy' in general. Whatever the need for a redirection in economic policy in the late 1970s, many have been critical of the new order. Not only did it create rapid inflation and a steadily mounting external debt, by dismantling some of the long-established subsidies in food prices and generous support to public education and health it greatly increased the insecurity of life for many; it also, for some, substantially increased the levels of social inequality (Karunatilake 1987:190, 190n1, 213–5, 466–7; Isenman 1980; Ivan 1989:48–9; Nissan 1987:16) and greatly exacerbated ethnic tensions (Gunasinghe 1984:198). For some

Photo 1   Beach at Unawatuna.

left wing political critics the very idea of a 'democratic socialist' republic under Jayewardene was a misnomer.

For members of the traditionalistic cultural elite, such as the distinguished author Sarachandra, the 'open economy' of which tourism was such a fundamental part, was undermining the very *dharmista samajaya* (righteous society), that Jaye-wardene was meant to be creating. For him, tourism was part of an insidious west-ernisation process which stripped Sri Lanka of its cultural integrity, introducing western films, nudism, consumerism, hedonism, and a whole host of things which would, over time, do serious damage to the moral and cultural fabric of Sri Lanka (Manor 1984:16–17). For him, basic Buddhist values combined with modernisation would produce moral schizophrenia (Sarachandra 1965:119, 125). Many felt that the whole rhetoric of development was deeply divisive raising, as it did, the issue of whether Sri Lankan society was based upon spiritual (*adyatmika*) or materialistic (*laukika*) values (Tennekoon 1988:301). Some Sri Lankans saw the fervent official adherence to the ideas of development and growth, of which tourism promotion was a part, as being intrinsically deaf to deeper questions of value and as uncaring about the victims created along the way. It is perhaps no exaggeration to suggest that *samvardhana* (development) acquired at that time the status of a quasi-sacred discourse, which was dislodged only when 'national security' took over centre stage (Tennekoon 1988:295).

Given the polarisation of political and economic outlooks in the early 1980s, and the relatively straightforward way in which attitudes towards the tourism industry could express the differences, I had expected tourism to emerge as one of the themes around which the two main political parties might crystallise their rivalry in the Presidential election campaign in 1982. Politics in Sri Lanka, it has been well said, is something of a festival of disunity (Spencer 1990); some have even seen the regular and sizeable swings in electoral fortunes in Sri Lanka in the decades after independence as symbolic substitutes for massive eruptions of violence (Ilan-gakoon 1978:32). Sri Lanka is certainly a nation with a finely developed social cos-mology, being acutely conscious of its external geographical boundaries and internal social divisions (Kapferer 1988). Sri Lanka is, after all, *dhammadipa*, the tiny island citadel of Theravada Buddhism, but a stone's throw away from the mighty sub-continent of India where the Buddha was born but where Buddhism was expunged. India is also the homeland of the Tamils, whence have come con-querors in centuries long past and plantations labourers during the British period, and who today are widely seen as such a potent internal force for the dissolution of the state (Manor 1984:8).

Tourism could very easily have been used as a symbolic weapon in a political contest over images of the 'national good', for international tourists, too, are clearly 'foreign bodies' within, and bodies, moreover, strongly connected in popular thought to such social ills as drug abuse, venereal disease, as well as 'cultural pollution' of a more diffuse kind. A drawing of international tourism into the political arena never occurred, however, because, I was told, tourism was so vital an industry that no party could seriously be seen to oppose it. An official at the Ministry of State was quite candid: "Unless any political party is bent on suicide, it will not give up tourism". Informants who were more cynical pointed out that the S.L.F.P. and the U.N.P. were two interrelated parts of the one elite whose economic interests were really very similar; the difference between them was largely rhetorical, and so one would not expect there to be any substantial differences of outlook. Given the ongoing 'feud' between sections of the one elite, the election was not really about inequality, justice, poverty, and the like, so a good many issues, including tourism, which might easily generate such themes, never got on the political agenda at all.

A STORY OF GROWTH: 1966–82

Comments about a political dimension to tourism development in Sri Lanka or its rhetorical packaging should not blind us to the simple fact that from 1966 until 1982 the industry in Sri Lanka experienced not only spectacular but also uninterrupted growth (see Table 1), with the exception of 1971 when the insurrection against the S.L.F.P. government of Mrs Bandaranaike kept foreign tourists away in droves. In 1966 Sri Lanka had only 18,969 tourists and earned only $U.S. 1.3 million from them. Those figures had climbed to 118,971 tourists and $U.S. 28.2 million by 1976 and to 370,742 tourists and $U.S. 132.4 million by 1981. From 1975 to 1982 foreign arrivals virtually quadrupled. Over the entire 1966–1979 period arrivals grew at an average rate of 21.9% per annum, making tourism Sri Lanka's fastest growing economic sector (Attanayake *et al.*, 1983:267, 330). Such a growth rate far outstripped the world growth rate in international tourism and also by far surpassed the growth rates of other South Asian countries.[1] The Tourist Board's *Report on the Performance of the Tourism Industry* in 1981 reported on an industry bringing in 10% of the nation's foreign exchange, with a leakage of only 30%;

---

[1] In making such a statement we must remember what a low point Sri Lanka was starting from. Also, to put things into a comparative perspective, the vast bulk of international tourism still takes place within and between the affluent countries of North America and Western Europe. According to World Tourism Organisation statistics (C.T.B. 1983b:1–2, 6), in 1982 the whole South Asian region received only 2.1 million of the 279.9 million international tourists; Sri Lanka's share of that was only 407,000. In terms of receipts, South Asia received approximately 1% of total expenditure, a percentage which has been fairly stable for a number of years. Total world receipts for 1982 were $U.S.99,925 million; South Asia's share $U.S.1000 million; Sri Lanka's share $U.S.147 million.

much of the revenue, it claimed, went into government coffers for "broad-based public expenditure and resulting public benefits" (1981c:1). So impressive a record was it that in 1979 tourism was even granted a chapter to itself in the annual review of the economy by the Central Bank in Colombo.

In 1982 as in 1981, tourism was Sri Lanka's fifth largest earner of foreign exchange after tea, personal remittances (largely from contract labourers working in the Middle East), textiles and petroleum products. A number of travel magazines were publicly proclaiming tourism in Sri Lanka as one of Asia's success stories. Indeed, 1982 was actually a year in which globally there was a contraction in the number of international tourists, but Sri Lanka still experienced a 9.8% increase on the previous year to 407,230. Receipts increased over the same period from $U.S. 132.4 million to $U.S. 146.6 million. The number of rooms in graded accommodation increased from 6,891 to 7,539 and direct employment rose from 23,023 to

Table 1 Tourism Trends in Sri Lanka 1966–82.

Year	Arrs	Excurs	Rev.	Dur.	P.D.	Rms	D.E.	I.E.
1966	18969	7909	1.3	-	-	-	-	-
1967	23666	59052	1.2	11.0	4.52	770	-	-
1968	28272	41407	1.8	10.3	5.98	903	-	-
1969	40204	68054	2.9	10.0	7.05	989	-	-
1970	46247	68529	3.6	10.5	7.39	1408	5138	6940
1971	39654	58292	3.4	10.5	8.63	1767	6397	8640
1972	56047	48310	7.3	10.9	11.87	1891	7040	9500
1973	77888	27920	12.8	10.3	15.93	2468	7134	10780
1974	85011	23434	16.4	10.2	18.71	2905	8551	11550
1975	103204	25490	22.4	9.8	22.02	3632	10148	13700
1976	118971	14499	28.2	10.0	23.75	4581	11752	15900
1977	153665	7672	40.0	10.7	24.29	4851	13716	18520
1978	192592	8494	55.8	10.8	27.07	5347	15404	20795
1979	250164	5563	77.7	11.1	27.97	5599	18472	24937
1980	321780	8636	110.7	11.0	31.20	6042	19878	28022
1981	370742	7737	132.4	10.5	33.88	6891	23023	32232
1982	407230	6632	146.6	10.0	36.21	7539	26776	37486

(Source: Ceylon Tourist Board, Annual Statistical Report 1982:42). Explanation of abbreviations used: Arrs= tourist arrivals; Excurs= excursionist arrivals; Rev.= revenue in $U.S. millions; Dur.= average duration of stay (in nights); P.D.= average per diem receipts per tourist in $U.S.; Rms= no. of rooms available in graded accommodation; D.E.= direct employment; I.E.= indirect employment (estimate).

26,776, indirect employment rising from 32,232 to 37,486. We can compare these 1982 figures with the situation in 1970: 407,230 arrivals instead of 46,247; $U.S. 146.6 million instead of $U.S. 3.6 million in receipts and an industry employing overall 64,000 instead of 12,000. There were however three potentially troubling signs evident in the 1982 figures. Firstly, although arrivals were still increasing, the rate of increase was slowing down significantly; 1982 saw an increase of less than 10% over the 1981 figures, compared with an increase over the previous decade of over 20% per annum. Secondly, whilst tourists were spending slightly more *per diem* than before, the average length of stay in Sri Lanka fell slightly to 10 nights, lower than for most of the years during the 1970s. Thirdly, the occupancy rate in graded accommodation fell back to the level achieved in 1977. The first two statistics were not particularly significant, but the third, in part a sign of the increasing flow of tourists away from the approved sector and into unlicensed accommodation, certainly was. The People's Bank felt fit to express alarm about the state of tourism in the country, selecting for particular mention the rapid rise in prices and the flow away from approved accommodation. It urged a serious look at some of the contemporary trends before the tourist drive actually became counter-productive (People's Bank 1982a:22). A sizeable flow of tourists into the informal sector, for instance, not only gave the tourism authorities less control over standards and so, inevitably, less influence over the image of Sri Lanka being taken away by foreigners, it also permitted a large leakage of potential government revenue through tax evasion (Yacoumis 1980:96).

Although the period 1966–1982 was one of rapid growth, and although even in 1982 the statistical indicators were still looking good in the main, it would not be accurate to describe those years as completely untroubled. A number of difficulties which came to the surface in 1982 had been in evidence several years earlier. Many people were increasingly concerned that tourism brought adverse socio-cultural consequences and, indeed, despite continual references to foreign exchange, employment opportunities, regional diversification and the like, the Central Bank very noticeably refused to make an overall cost-benefit assessment because such cultural aspects could not be quantified (1979:163). It was also increasingly apparent that different sectors of the tourism industry had divergent interests, so that some very real tensions underlay the overall record of growth. The stories of Air Lanka, the 'Duty Free' Shopping Complex in Colombo, and the Tourist Board's guide training programs are richly illustrative in this regard.

All Third World countries involving themselves in international tourism have a fundamental choice to make: to remain substantially at the mercy of the airlines of other countries, or to establish, at considerable cost, a prestigious national airline which might never achieve financial viability, given the entrenched position on the main air routes of overseas carriers. Air Lanka was born in 1979 to overcome the very poor carrying record of Air Ceylon, which for many years had created sizeable losses and achieved little success in bringing an increasing proportion of tourists to Sri Lanka. Air Lanka was heavily subsidised by the government, and for several years was party to a training scheme in alliance with Singapore Airlines, inevitably one of its own main competitors. For many years of its operation losses have been substantial, for instance in 1979–80 it lost $U.S. 12 million (*South Asia Travel Review*, April 1982), and over the period 1978–86 the estimate is a loss of 5.6 billion rupees — not an unsubstantial drain on government revenue (Karunatilake 1987:159n1). There have also been rumours in the Sri Lankan press of scandal, demands that the airline be opened up for public scrutiny, complaints at enormous untaxed salaries being paid to expatriate advisers and experts, and suggestions that some involved in tourism planning and development were making fortunes through secret commissions (*Sun*, 8 August 1982). As for carrying success, in 1982 Air Lanka was still bringing only 122,729 out of 407,230 tourists; 51,274 still arrived by sea, either in Colombo or by ferry from South India, and charter flights still carried 65,792, approximately 16% of the total (C.T.B. 1982c:22).

The story of the Duty Free Shopping Complex in Colombo is similar in several respects. The 'duty free' shops at Katunayake airport had throughout the 1970s been a severe disappointment to tourists, and so a large complex was constructed in the centre of Colombo. During 1982, the area around the complex daily became a congested scene of long lines of impatient tourists, Indian 'day trippers', Sri Lankan contract labourers returned from the Middle East, fleets of taxis, several clusters of police, and small groupings of individuals lurking on the pavement nearby and generally believed to be engaged in one kind of illegal activity or another. Entry to the shopping area required a passport and foreign currency. There was also an entry charge which generated revenue for the government, but which was deliberately introduced to discourage the entry of local people up to no good.

Despite these various precautions on entry and also a system of checks at the exit, soon after its opening the complex was enmeshed in controversy. Accusations of fraud on a wide scale were rampant. There were stories about the selling there of stolen goods, about forgery of passports and currency, the over-pricing of goods and a system of immediate sale of items on the pavement outside to people not entitled to enter the complex themselves. One commentator in the press referred to the shopping complex as the "biggest legalised smuggling racket this country has ever had" (*Daily News*, 22 January 1982). Apart from illegality, the complex was caught up in another form of unfavourable news coverage for the Tourist Board. By far the most numerous users of the complex were Indians who had crossed by ferry from South India to the Jaffna peninsula for one day of shopping in Colombo, to return to India with goods not available in that country, many of them easily sellable at very high prices. Thousands of such people, not 'tourists' in the normal sense of the term, were being included in the statistics collected by the Tourist Board, inflating the 'success' story at a time when, without such shoppers, overall 1982 foreign arrivals would have declined substantially. An angry letter in the press accused the Board of deliberately lying about its record by classifying these Indian shoppers as tourists (*Island*, 9 July 1982).

It was partly because of a desire to avoid the proliferation of unedifying images of Sri Lanka that the Ceylon Tourist Board had been making strenuous efforts to train a large number of guide/lecturers who could present the country in a professionally competent and favourable light. Ironically, the official tourist guides in Colombo operating prior to 1966 were frequently rehabilitated criminals (Kovach 1965:75), whose job essentially was to show visitors around the city. The newly formed Tourist Board quickly put an end to that system and has since run training programmes in Colombo in order to prevent so-called 'touts' from cornering the market. The Board is well aware that for many tourists, the guide has a critical role in creating the image of Sri Lanka that will linger in the memory of the visitor. By its educational programmes and codes of conduct, it hoped to stamp out the bad impressions which quickly grow when tourism is controlled by 'fast buck' merchants, who scarcely create a good impression, particularly with their frequently broken English.

The four month training course being run by the Board in 1982 required attendance at a series of lectures, essay work and examinations in English on a broad range of topics concerned with Sri Lankan geography, society and history. Clearly (C.T.B. 1981d), given the enrolment fee charged and the language requirements, most of those people undergoing training would have been to the better Colombo schools, and in many cases had already received a tertiary education; some even spoke other foreign languages besides English. Such guide/lecturers on completion of the course were to work under conditions strictly set down by the Board. These included a fee of 125 rupees (approximately $U.S. 6) *per diem*[2] and there was a prohibition on receiving any commissions from the tourists. The stated aim in 1982 was to have 500 trained guide/lecturers to accompany groups of tourists. Not only would this lessen the impact of the touts, it would also effectively dispense with the foreign guides accompanying 'package tour' groups who were a significant source of foreign exchange leakage. There were also some plans in 1982 to set up, on a reduced scale, other training courses for those who wished to be 'regional' rather than 'national' guides. Such courses would involve a system of municipal licences, granted only with the approval of the local police, and hence, again, would be a method of keeping 'undesirables' away from foreigners.

---

[2] During the period of my field research in 1982, the exchange rate was fluctuating around $U.S. = 20 Sri Lankan rupees.

The three cases discussed above — Air Lanka, the Duty Free Shopping Complex and guide training schemes — are all indicative of the extent to which in Sri Lanka, as elsewhere in the Third World, the national tourism organisation needs to contend with the power of overseas interests, local corruption and the mushrooming of fringe activities beyond its control, such as the conduct of untrained guides and the opening of unlicensed guesthouses. For the Ceylon Tourist Board the growth in the so-called 'informal' accommodation sector was becoming a real worry. Between 1976 and 1980 the proportion of tourists staying in unlicensed premises outside the approved accommodation sector had increased significantly from 22.4% to 38.8% (C.T.B. 1980b:9), thus jeopardising the profitability of capital invested in the formal sector. The Ceylon Hoteliers Association was urging the Tourist Board to stifle its development (Economist Intelligence Unit 1981:14) and municipal authorities were also being called on to stamp out the 'grass roots' entrepreneurs who were alleged to be ruining Sri Lanka's image by lowering standards (*Island*, 7 October 1982; *Daily News*, 26 January and 6 October 1982). In Sri Lanka as in many other Third World countries, such widespread grassroots developments had not been officially encouraged, so it fell to the Tourist Board to find an effective means of controlling them. Some, however, saw the situation in a very different light. R. Perera, for instance, argued that with the downturn in 1983 and the half empty hotels this was producing, Sri Lanka would have done well in the early days to have conscientiously explored the possibility of so-called 'alternative tourism' rather than to concentrate so much on a capital-intensive hotel-based version (1985:3–4). It is also the case that grassroots tourism can very significantly reduce that inflow of foreign capital which so often hands over the control of the new industry to overseas interests which, for many, would be a desirable goal in itself.

By 1982 there was also much protest directed towards the Tourist Board by hoteliers about the level of taxation being imposed by the government on the tourist industry. Given the tax privileged status of the industry in the late 1960s for both domestic and foreign investors, Business Turnover Tax had subsequently risen as high as 25%. The Chairman of the Tourist Hoteliers Association of Sri Lanka complained that the industry was being crippled and that, if not careful, the government would "kill the goose that lays the golden egg" (*Daily News*, 2 July 1982). A prominent hotel owner in Kandy listed the various financial impositions being suffered during 1982 and advocated that the Board impose a two year freeze in order to "create a climate of hope for the future" (*Daily News*, 13 August 1982). The Hoteliers Association was also pointing out the inadequacy of the Board's Hotels School to train sufficient personnel to meet the needs of the industry. In 1982 the Hotel School could offer only 125 places to the 2000 or more people who were eager to begin careers in the industry, so the Association was pressing for the creation of a second, but privately run, establishment. If in 1970 tourism had locally been perceived as a somewhat dubious occupation in which to plan a career, by 1982 it was no longer necessarily frowned upon by people from respectable backgrounds. For a start, top hotel managers could command very high salaries in the region of 7000 rupees per month plus perks. Indeed, the rewards to all levels of staff, even those performing menial tasks, were fairly high compared to other sectors, a fact which created considerable ill feeling among those employed in other occupations (Manor 1984:16). The Minister of State even portrayed the tourism industry as one in which profits were shared out with all its employees via the distribution of service charges (*Sunday Times*, 4 July 1982).

In the midst of an escalating antagonism between the private sector and the national statutory authority, and between the approved and informal sectors, earlier statements by the Minister of State about an industry of "grace, spirit and service" (de Alwis 1978:35) began to take on a less than convincing air. "There is peace within the industry and excellent relations between the government and industry at all levels. In fact there is no 'them' and 'us' attitude of mistrust. There is a 'we' attitude of seeking common objectives along agreed lines of policy" (*Island*, 27 September 1982). The Minister's official message may have been of an industry happily and harmoniously going about it business, but in reality considerable friction between various interest groups in tourism were clearly evident. For instance, in 1982 when the Board drew up and published information concerning the scale of operations of travel agents in Sri Lanka as part of its efforts to establish a Travel Agents Code, the Travel Agents Association, fearing that publishing such information would harm some of its members, threatened the Board with legal action. Loud also were the denunciations of the Board's efforts during 1982 to complete a star classification of hotels in Sri Lanka so that tourists might have a better idea of what type of facilities to expect. Many alleged that this was a bureaucratic waste of time in a period when the industry was facing very basic problems, although in another light it was but one of the areas of professional research, monitoring and control which the Board had been carrying out for over a decade.

Not unnaturally, with such sectional interests in collision, it was not long before policy options would be discussed and implemented where categories of tourists themselves, as well as locals, would feel themselves unfairly treated. Bound together with the issue of the mushrooming informal accommodation sector, for instance, arose the issue of which types of tourists Sri Lanka wanted to encourage and whether certain types should be forbidden entry altogether. All countries developing a tourism industry have a series of basic policy options to resolve: direction by government or free enterprise; emphasis on international or domestic tourism; integrated tourism or a virtual 'enclave' system; high spenders only or an 'open door' policy. Actually, from relatively early on in Sri Lanka's modern tourism history the last question about the kind of tourist desired had been raised

(Nanayakkara 1971:60), and Due (1980:169) even suggests that in the 5 year period 1977–82 there was already a distinct emphasis on exchange maximisation by attracting the more affluent type of tourist. However marked this emphasis was, in 1982 the policy dilemma came to the fore in quite explicit terms: should Sri Lanka cater to an increasing number of budget tourists and so-called hippies or should she limit overall numbers and concentrate on high spending foreigners by specifically imposing a minimum *per diem* expenditure requirement.

At some time or other most Third World countries involved in international tourism have confronted this issue and solutions have varied widely: from a total insistence upon high *per diem* spenders who are ferried around on highly circumscribed routes, thereby creating few cultural repercussions but also making few cultural links of any kinds, to the opposite approach of encouraging anyone to come (People's Bank 1982b:14–15). The economic consequences are equally diverse. For instance, in 1979 when Sri Lanka was deriving an average of $U.S. 310 per visitor, Bhutan was deriving $U.S. 1000 (Ahmed 1985:640), over three times as much. Sri Lanka's Minister of Finance and Planning (*Daily News*, 15 July 1982) was certain that going for the low density high spending variety was the means by which Sri Lanka could maximise economic benefits and such a choice became embodied in a Specified Tourist Services Code. Being drafted during 1982, it was finally enacted as a regulation in 1984 under the 1968 Tourist Development Act.

The intended effect of the new Code was to enforce minimum standards of accommodation, to force providers of any tourist service to register with the Board and to pay a licence fee, thus becoming liable, among other things, for taxes, or to face punishment and the closure of the establishment. If minimum standards were not met, a licence would not be granted, nor would a licence be granted to anyone with a recent conviction relating to currency offences or moral turpitude. Operators of all services were to maintain registers of their clients, services provided, currencies paid for services, and employees, whilst Tourist Board officials could enter business premises without notice to ensure that the regulations were being complied with. These various requirements imposed on providers would automatically require tourists to spend more money because, over a period of time, the cheaper forms of accommodation, operating without approval, would be closed down or would voluntarily go out of business for fear of incurring fines. Such provisions would not confine accommodation exclusively to the hotel sector, but as is clear from Tourist Board pamphlets such as 'Rooms in Homes', the standards being insisted on in private homes were such as would require the taking out of bank loans for the installation of facilities such as fans, refrigerators, etc., a level of investment beyond the resources of those of modest means.

I was told by a senior Tourist Board official in Colombo that driving less wealthy Sri Lankans out of tourism was not the aim of the new policy, although that would inevitably be a consequence. My informant added, however, that the legislation was not likely to be strictly policed, and so was not as draconian as it seemed. Nonetheless, I was told that "not everyone in Sri Lanka can be an entrepreneur", a view which perhaps contradicts the Prime Minister's that in 1982 anyone in Sri Lanka could become rich. Whatever the intentions as regards the illegal guesthouse owners, there were certainly moves afoot to crack down on other sections of the population to rectify the perceived problems arising from tourism. For instance, the Board's *Performance Report* for the period 1st January to 30th September 1982 set out plans by the Tourist Police in Colombo and the Social Services Department to round up beggars and put them into rehabilitation camps such as that at Gangodawila (1982g:5). This policy was to be extended from Colombo into the Ancient Cities region including Kandy. The Report also states that the Colombo Tourist Police will be liaising with other police authorities "to curb harassment of tourists by touts and beggars" (1982g:5).

On the tourist end of things, during 1982 the Board was stepping up its campaign against those tourists it considered undesirable, either because they spent little money in Sri Lanka or because they blatantly disregarded local culture. Spending $U.S. 20 per day (or $U.S. 15 for those entering Sri Lanka by ferry from South India) were established as minimum requirements and visa renewals during 1982 were tightened up considerably, now requiring the production of records of amounts of foreign exchange converted into rupees to establish that an acceptable amount *per diem* was being spent. Cautionary articles began appearing in the press about the standards of behaviour expected of foreigners. The *Sunday Observer* (18 April 1982), for instance, carried a headline: "Warning to tourists. Behave well or no visas". While such warnings would no doubt have been aimed at a fairly broad category of tourists, hippies were singled out for special treatment. Discriminated against in many Asian countries and denied entry altogether by some, they were subject to a public campaign of vilification and harassment. They were declared to be of no economic value to Sri Lanka, living for such protracted periods of time on virtually no money. They, in fact, were beginning to symbolise all that was evil in the cultural repercussions produced by tourism. They, it was claimed, were the ones who were encouraging youths to drop out of school and to emulate a western life of idleness. They were the drug traffickers. They were the ones who strolled nude on the beaches in total disregard of local standards of decency. Hippies were regarded as the worst offenders for avoiding the visa renewal process in Colombo.

The Tourist Board estimated that in mid 1982 there were something in the order of 6000 to 7000 foreigners staying in Sri Lanka with expired visas. "Operation Overstay" (*Sunday Observer*, 11 June 1982; *Daily News*, 15 May 1982) was thus announced in which the Tourist Board, Department of Internal Security and police would combine forces to launch raids in areas of the country such as

Hikkaduwa, Arugam Bay and Passekudah especially frequented by hippies. Hippies without visas were to be fined and deported and the locals harbouring them were to be prosecuted. The use of a detention camp in Colombo previously reserved for illegal Indian immigrants was proposed as a place to house these undesirables. Despite the uncertainty of knowing exactly what a 'hippy' is and so of correctly spotting who is one — a problem admitted by some Board officials to whom I spoke — a number of police swoops occurred, a number of drug prosecutions were successfully pursued, and a number of deportations carried out.

What is striking about both the Specified Services Code and the anti-hippy campaign was the parallel way in which they act against the less affluent. The wealthier tourist operators would control more of the market as the informal sector contracted, just as the wealthier tourists would form a more sizeable fraction of the arrivals as the lower spending tourists were denied access or were removed by the non-renewal of visas. Two comments might be made about this. Firstly, however little foreign exchange budget tourists bring with them, what they spend stays in the local economy; it goes to private home owners, to arts and crafts workers, to owners of small cafes and shops. By contrast, many of the higher spenders, whether on package tours or not, spend most of their money on accommodation or meals before setting foot in Sri Lanka or in establishments where there is the maximum leakage of foreign exchange in the form of profits back to overseas investors. The economic arguments about high *per diem* spenders, then, are not entirely clear cut. Secondly, the 'cultural pollution' arguments which are frequently marshalled against budget travellers and especially hippies are less than compelling.

Arthur C. Clark, the famous Australian science fiction writer, who was a permanent resident of Sri Lanka, had observed the peculiarity of the campaign against the hippy. He remarks (*Daily Mirror*, 31 October 1978) how the people so often classified as hippies are simply the young, determined to experience the world, who do not possess as much money as most other tourists. The menace posed by such people, he went on, "is being grossly exaggerated. In fact in many ways culturally they are much more akin to the natives of this island and its people than more affluent tourists". Whilst it is no doubt easy to romanticise the extent to which various types of budget traveller mix with locals, they do, in fact, enjoy a fairly positive image with some Sri Lankans (Samarasuriya 1982:82), precisely because they are easy-going, relaxed and often have the time to talk to local people. By contrast, there are many negative characterisations of those more affluent tourists who travel from hotel to hotel in air-conditioned luxury never stopping to speak to anyone. Moreover, as many people were observing in 1982, it was simply not convincing to lay at the feet of hippies the various forms of cultural and moral pollution which Sri Lanka was suffering in the way of drugs, prostitution, and so on, and the authorities were therefore misdirecting their efforts if they thought they could eliminate these problems by cracking down on them and the unlicensed premises they stayed in. For a start, the authorities risked alienating a very wide category of young, relatively well-educated budget travellers, who would certainly not define themselves as hippies (Riley 1988). Secondly, quite clearly affluent tourists staying in expensive hotels were also involved in prostitution and drugs. Lastly, the newspapers were full of cynical letters during 1982 about how the police were allowing the 'big fish' to go free in the drug trade while arresting and punishing the 'small fry'. The cynicism was even more pronounced because of the widespread belief that the 'big fish' operated with the protection of the senior people in the very organisations who were making things so difficult for the hippies.

As if to emphasise the emerging troubles of the tourist industry in Sri Lanka in 1982, on the very day in June of that year that the South Asian Chapter of the World Tourism Organisation opened its conference in Kandy, the newspapers carried ominous headlines. The *Island* ran a story headed "Death knell for Sri Lankan Tourism" (29 June 1982). The day before, Maureen Seneviratne, a distinguished Sri Lankan journalist, examined the continuing planning and building of luxury hotels in Colombo against the background of falling occupancy rates, and posed the question whether Sri Lanka would be the 'graveyard' of the Five Star hotel (*Island*, 28 June 1982). After a less than good 1981–2 peak season because of the European recession, there was gloom about the coming 1982–3 season. A substantial drop in the profits of the Ceylon Hotels Corporation was also announced, amidst charges of gross corruption and the call that its affairs should be handed over to private industry (*Daily News*, 14 July; *Island*, 1 July). The increasingly popular tourism industry in the nearby Maldives, shrugged off as insignificant only two or three years earlier, was beginning to be taken seriously by those who felt that Sri Lanka might become a mere 'stopping off' point for those on their way to these islands.[3] The Minister of State was warning the tourist industry that if the price increases of 1981 and 1982 were not curbed, Sri Lanka would price itself out of the market (*Sunday Times*, 4 July 1982). The one clearly positive note from Sri Lanka's perspective during the Kandy conference was its proud announcement that it would be hosting the 1984 Pacific Area Travel Association Conference. Given the abysmal showing of the tourist industry in Sri Lanka only fifteen years earlier, such a choice of location was certainly a mark of recognition of Sri Lanka's remarkable achievements as a tourist destination.

Nonetheless, in 1982 there was a feeling for some that perhaps a turning

---

[3] Since 1982 tourism has boomed in the Maldives. With substantial airport improvements, her industry is no longer reliant on Colombo as a 'stop over'. Also, having opted for segregated, 'resort' tourism, she has attracted foreigners without the same level of social and cultural disruption experienced by Sri Lanka (Sathiendrakumar and Tisdell 1989:259).

point had already been reached, not only in terms of numbers of tourists, but also in the sense that it was now time to start seriously looking at the structure of the industry and its attendant difficulties. On numbers alone, Tourist Board officials and the press became very concerned that there was a decline in the numbers of arrivals from western Europe, traditionally Sri Lanka's main source of tourists. This was partly because of European economic problems, but it did introduce a significant new element, namely that Sri Lanka's chief source of arrivals was now India. And as the Board's *Performance Report* for 1st January to 30th September 1982 made clear, the substantial leap in Indian tourists from 48,520 in 1981 to 92,940 in 1982 was really caused by the availability of 'duty free' shopping in Colombo (1982g). From 1981–2 the foreign exchange gained from duty free shopping saw a 200% increase (C.T.B. 1982c:8, 40), but, as already said, many hostile to the tourism industry argued that it was quite inappropriate to count these 'day shoppers' as tourists.

It was in his address to the Tourism Marketing Conference in Colombo on 15 June, 1982, that the Minister of State made his memorable remark that Sri Lanka was "not the only girl on the beach" (1982b:2); she was not, in other words, in a position to rest on her laurels by virtue of having a captive market since there were so many other tourist destinations offering very similar attractions. He added to that message another which he urged his colleagues to take seriously: international tourism could not be relied on for ever to be the fastest growing industry in the world (ibid:3). Actually, earlier that year, the *South Asian Travel Review* which had previously commented so glowingly on the success of Sri Lanka as a tourist destination, carried a 'survival of the fittest' theme; the days of early growth were over, there now had to be sophisticated marketing and the industry would need a good 'shake out' (April 1982:9). Advice was already coming in that because of the increasing number of tourist destinations in Asia, Sri Lanka really did need to examine herself and make some changes in order to maintain market share (Ahmed 1984:282, 88). For Maureen Seneviratne (*Island*, 27 June), Sri Lankan tourism was "at the crossroads". Wijeratne (1982) gave further voice to the growing sense of uneasiness that some very basic imbalances had now come to the surface — the extent of informal accommodation, over-pricing, over-capitalisation, the Maldives — and was suggesting that it was not adequate for different sections of the tourist industry simply to blame each other. P.C.S. Fernando (1982) spoke of "tourism in turbulent times", and of the need for the industry to prepare itself for a rough stretch ahead.

THE ECONOMIC BALANCE SHEET

Given the politics and ideological discourse surrounding international tourism in Sri Lanka, it is not surprising that balanced appraisals are hard to come by. The Ceylon Tourist Board, generator of most of the available statistical information on the industry, is, of course, part of the industry itself, rather than an unbiased commentator on it. Commentary in the press and elsewhere stems more often than not from those with interests to defend, or from those implacably opposed to tourism, or at least from those who wish to focus only on its negative side. The Director of the Marga Institute in Colombo, a leading centre of socio-economic research in Sri Lanka, therefore quite pertinently commented that discussions about tourism were often acrimonious, sometimes simply an indulgence in interminable controversy, and occasionally degenerated to "juvenile debate" (Gunatilleke 1981:2). There had earlier been calls for the tourism industry to "subject itself to a thorough scientific examination" (Goonatilake 1978:25) given the fixed positions already taken by prominent commentators, but certainly by 1982 the Marga Institute had not itself devoted any detailed attention to the tourism industry.

When one looks back to the state of Sri Lanka's economy and its poor showing in the international travel industry in 1966, the achievements attained by 1982 are noteworthy. According to the Ceylon Tourism Plan, tourism would: earn extensive foreign exchange; stimulate the local economy through income and employment multipliers; increase economic diversification; create direct and indirect employment; promote regional development; raise standards of living; and through government revenue produce infrastructural improvements for the community in general. Using certain yardsticks, Sri Lanka had achieved much by 1982, but as a United Nations publication states: "On paper prospects may look pretty rosy for a lively romance between developing countries and the international tourist industry. In practice, this area can be as tricky as an Irish bog, complete with will o' the wisps" (quoted in Hills and Lundgren 1977:255). In the case of Sri Lanka we might particularly remember this cautionary note in the light of the depressing predictions of one of the first international appraisals of the industry in that country. Working with data to 1972, Radke commented: "the actual beneficiaries of the present development of tourism in Sri Lanka are the countries of tourist origin, i.e. the industrialised states. Sri Lanka has no prospects in the near future of altering this distribution in its favour" (1975:19). Sri Lanka was, in Radke's view, already maximising the gain it could derive — a retention rate of only 23% of foreign exchange (1975:19–20).

Subsequent studies have painted a considerably more positive picture. Compared to some economic sectors, most notably agriculture, tourism certainly has been a local success story bringing considerable benefits to several sectors of Sri

Lankan society. Gamage, for instance, estimates that between 1967 and 1980 tourism revenue rose from 0.07% to 2.9% of Gross National Product (1981:1). Tourism was Sri Lanka's fastest growing economic sector. According to *Tourism on Track* (C.T.B. 1982e), in 1981 employment generated by tourism was 52,000 and the government derived 250 million rupees (approx. $U.S. 13.5 millions) by way of Business Turnover Tax, embarkation tax, entrance fees and the like, which was then available for public expenditure. The net retention of foreign exchange was put at 70%. The foreign exchange obtained was 10% of the gross earnings by Sri Lanka and had more than quadrupled in only five years. According to the Director-General of the Tourist Board (*Daily News*, 1 September 1982), average monthly earnings in the tourism industry were 900 rupees (approx. $U.S. 45) in 1982 as compared to the overall average in Sri Lanka of 500 rupees (approximately $U.S. 25). The Board's *Market Intelligence News Release* was claiming tourism to be a labour-intensive industry and painted a picture of an industry where employees benefit from free meals and service charges, on top of getting higher wages than those in other sectors (March/April 1984:2, 4). In addition, for every rupee spent by the government, 1.67 rupees were returned in taxes and charges, which could contribute towards its general public expenditures.

Sceptical comment has taken the gloss from much of the statistical information published about tourism, whether it be about employment levels, multipliers, diversification, and so on. Firstly, it is necessary to remember that international tourism is precisely that — part of an international system where the odds are heavily stacked against the small players (Gamage 1978:35–6). When the Economist Intelligence Unit produced its 1972 study of tourism in Sri Lanka it felt it necessary to qualify the foreign exchange earnings picture by pointing out the heavy infrastructure expenditures, the leakages and the operations of the black market which such gains entailed (1972:14). Nearly a decade later it was still making the same points, and stating that because of these factors, profit repatriation and the importation of food specifically for tourist consumption, it was extremely difficult to be certain what the net benefit to Sri Lanka of tourism really was (1979:11). The Central Bank too remained non-committal on the whole issue, citing absence of data and methodological problems as reasons why it could not be more forthcoming (1980:198).

When a Third World country acquires a tourism industry, it does so as part of the overall international division of labour, where economic and political power are already very unequally distributed. The image may well be of a well-paid industry, but the fact is, as the Board's own statistics reveal (1982c:41), that whilst the industry directly employed 26,776 people, only 2,176 were at managerial or professional levels. The overwhelming proportion of tourism jobs are menial. Sri Lanka's record here is in no way atypical. Gunatilleke (1981:6) may well be right in claiming that those who have been critical of the employment-creating capacity of tourism have tended to underestimate the employment multiplier of the industry, and we should certainly bear in mind the large informal sector surrounding tourism where much indirect employment not recorded in the official records is generated — batik making, metal, wood and leather crafts, folk dancing, jewellery manufacture, and so on (Karunatilake 1987:257). On the other hand, a sizeable proportion of the direct employment created is lost after the initial construction phase of tourist developments is over. A high percentage of the service jobs also tend to be seasonal. There has long been a debate over whether tourism is labour-intensive or capital-intensive (de Kadt 1979:381), but Due's conclusion for Sri Lanka (1980:82, 97) is that tourism is an inefficient means of creating employment, especially within the hotel sector. Contrary to representations of the tourism industry being labour-intensive, there is much evidence to show that the creation of just one job in the hotel sector requires a very large outlay of capital (Mendis 1981:9–10). One estimate (Attanayake *et al.*, 1983:304, 308) is that it takes 59,000 rupees to create one job; Gamage (1981:23) puts the figure as high as 65,000 rupees. This is certainly not capital-intensive when compared with some industrial sectors in the Sri Lankan economy, but it is, on the other hand, very capital-intensive when compared with a good many others; in ceramics, for instance, one job is created for less than one third of this level of capital expenditure. At 124,000 rupees for the creation of one job in a Colombo hotel (Gamage 1981:23), luxury tourism is capital-intensive by any standards.

When considering the statistical record it is also important to remember that investment in the tourism industry, as in any sector, has an opportunity cost. Public money spent on hotel construction could have been spent on education, roads, health facilities, and so on, for the benefit of the community as a whole. However much some infrastructural projects may benefit the community in general, their chief beneficiaries are clearly the tourists. Moreover tourism, because constituting an increased demand for certain foodstuffs, inevitably has some inflationary effect (Gunatilleke 1981:15–6), further disadvantaging the many who do not gain from tourism, although it is difficult to know how much price rises are due to tourism as opposed, say, to the increasing export of foodstuffs. It is also somewhat doubtful in Sri Lanka's case, as in the cases of other Third World tourism destinations, just how much the new activity has stimulated regional economic growth (Mendis 1981:13). Radke, early on, doubted whether rural communities would be greatly benefited because of the inevitable advent of the parasitic 'middle man' (1975:16–9). His suspicions are confirmed in a study of Hikkaduwa (L. Perera 1978:53–4). Beach-front land was sold to wealthy Colombo developers who reaped windfall gains; craft people in cottage industries have not done well because the profits are siphoned off by the middle men; and even in employment, the record has not always been good because hotels have often not offered jobs to the local unemployed but have brought in labour from elsewhere. Sri Lanka's economy lacks many of the linkages which produce the beneficial high multipliers frequently claimed for the tourism industry and which do frequently obtain in more developed industrial economies. With a 1.59 multiplier (Attanayake *et al.*, 1983:290–1), all one can say is that Sri Lanka's achievement is considerably better than many other developing countries (for instance, the Bahamas at 0.78), but also worse than those achieved by the industrialised countries, and certainly far below the predictions contained in the original Ceylon Tourism Plan. Gamage concluded that there was little evidence of tourism stimulating other sectors of the economy (1978:78).

During the late 1970s, Sri Lanka was putting greatest emphasis on the construction of graded hotels, a policy trenchantly criticised by many (Gunatilleke 1981:10,13). Not only is there a considerable tourist population which cannot afford or which does not want this expensive sort of facility, research also suggests that the commercial profitability and employment-generation capacity of less luxurious institutions are higher (Gamage 1981:28). Luxury hotels also tend to increase levels of foreign ownership. Surveying the 1967–76 period, Gamage estimated that the foreign portion of overall investment in tourism plant and ancillary services (such as tourist vehicles) was 31% (1981:25). For the hotel sector alone, an estimate of 15% has been given (Attanayake *et al.*, 1983:275–7). This is certainly less than was expected in the original tourism plan and very low compared with many Third World countries, although one should be cognisant here of a trend by which tourist destination countries have increasingly been allowed to shoulder the direct risks of investing in tourism plant, while multinationals have merely endeavoured to gain control of the running of such facilities by means of various management contracts (Sinclair *et al.*, 1992:47). From the outset, however, Sri Lanka had strict rules governing the extent of foreign participation in tourism. The 1982 *A Guide to Investors in Hotel Projects* issued by the Board sets out the rules for foreign investment in tourism. There had to be a Sri Lankan partner where control must ultimately lie, and the Sri Lankan equity must exceed 50%. Such stipulations could be relaxed in extreme circumstances, however (1982d:5). There were generous tax holidays, other financial incentives, and relief from tax on capital gains (ibid:7–9), a pattern common in the establishment of the tourism industry in the Third World.

If Sri Lanka has managed to steer clear of the situation into which some Third World nations have fallen where their tourist facilities are substantially owned by foreigners, nonetheless the opting for luxury hotels has still had significant effects. Tourists coming on 'package tours' and staying in such establishments will have spent nearly everything they will spend, before leaving home. Those eating in graded hotels are also likely to be eating a higher percentage of imported foods for which Sri Lanka must expend foreign exchange. The loss of foreign exchange through import content in Sri Lanka is estimated at 25%, compared to a tourist economy such as Hawaii where it is 45% (Gamage 1981:25); such estimates, in fact, put Sri Lanka in a far better situation than most developing countries (Attanayake *et al.*, 1983:333). The overall leakage for Sri Lanka (the difference between gross and net foreign exchange receipts) has often been estimated to be 25–35% (Central Bank 1981), but it was suggested to me in 1982 by a researcher in the Central Bank that this figure might be somewhat on the low side given the operation of the Free Trade Zone and the Duty Free Shopping Complex. It was also suggested that the announcement during 1982 that foreign equity in new hotel plant could go as high as 70% would mean that the overall leakage rate might increase to around 40%.

Leakage calculations have always been somewhat hazardous. Geshekter has claimed that trying to arrive at an estimate of net receipts is like "trying to nail jelly to a wall" (quoted in Smith 1977:131). Every year, for instance, the Central Bank in Colombo and the Ceylon Tourist Board differ, sometimes quite appreciably, in their estimates of foreign exchange receipts (Mendis 1981:8). There is thus some justification for the hesitation expressed in the Central Bank's 1981 *Review of the Economy*: "in the absence of adequate and accurate data firm conclusions cannot be arrived at with regard to the net contribution of tourism to the government budget or to the national economy" (1981:180). Such caution needs to be remembered when reading about a 'success story'. After all, some look at the same statistical picture and are very critical of the industry. Due claims that tourism's widely alleged economic benefits have been swallowed wholesale by a small Sri Lankan elite, an elite which perhaps does personally benefit. He comments: "neither the government nor the foreign 'tourist experts' have deemed it necessary to analyse tourism's viability and appropriateness in the development context or examine the social and economic costs to the local people" (1980:11–12). His overall view is that capital-intensive tourism development does not contribute positively to development in Sri Lanka; it has high employment costs, diverts scarce resources from local utilisation, causes socio-cultural dislocation, creates over-dependence on foreign capital, thus undoing the goal of self-sustained economic growth; it does not cater to the economic needs of the local people, nor does it lead to greater internal integration (1980:iii-iv).

We need, as suggested above, to remember that the tourist industry is part of a complex international system, in which the different players have very unequal allocations of power. Indeed, in many senses, Third World destination countries are very often simply on the receiving end of decision-making which has, to all intents and purposes, taken place elsewhere. Sri Lanka, for instance, cannot control the number of foreigners who come to her shores, nor can she control prices. There are countless factors, such as the economic health of the tourist-generating countries and shifts in perceptions about desirable tourist destinations, which are outside her control. However Sri Lanka likes to advertise herself internationally, she cannot control shifts in consumer preferences in the affluent tourist-generating countries; she cannot control airline routing decisions; she cannot control the price of aviation fuel which is so critical a factor in the attractiveness of long-haul destinations; she cannot control international exchange rates. And, as Third World nations have realised, it is a somewhat rocky road tying themselves to the affluence of the industrialised west for it is in the nature of such capitalist economies to experience considerable cyclical shifts from boom to bust and back again. For Sri Lanka to invest in an industry such as tourism, therefore, is necessarily to create considerable vulnerability to overseas forces. Sri Lanka and other South Asian nations were exploring the possibilities of regional co-operation during 1982, to make themselves less dependent on tourist flows from Europe and also to increase their collective bargaining power in the international tourism system, but as Gamage has observed, such efforts carry a risk that overseas travel agents will simply redirect their clients elsewhere where increasing demands are not being made of them (1978:77). To that possibility we have to add the competitiveness between destinations in the one region which makes such co-operative ventures hard to get off the ground. Regional co-operation in 1982 was hence still very much an "unwanted child" (N. Silva 1982).

It is quite clear, surveying international tourism in the Third World, that if very stringent safeguards are not created, a tourist industry will work to the benefit of the affluent, tourist-generating countries. But we should also remember a point expressed clearly by de Kadt: "Even with planning it is difficult enough to ensure that the poor share in the benefits of development ... local capacity to control tourism development appears to be generally weak, especially where such development is rapid and massive. This is partly owing to the lack of trained personnel and effective organisation at the local level, but mostly to the sheer strength of outside interests that move in" (1979:9). He goes on to state that:

> Governments do not deliberately set out to assess the overall effects of alternative types of tourism in order to promote those that appear to promise the greatest net social benefits ... [they] ... inevitably represent the interests of certain groups more than others ... To the extent that policies in any sector, such as tourism, reflect the existing socio-economic situation, the development of the sector is likely to reinforce the position of the more powerful classes, confirming existing social patterns ... It is a nation's overall political economy that will, in effect, largely determine eventual social outcomes ... 'Planning' can do little to alter this fundamental fact (1979:21, 32–3).

If this is the reality within any nation state and the international inequities which produce international tourism are also taken into account, we might well ponder again on the message of Anandatissa de Alwis that tourism should not be seen as an essentially economic enterprise but as a much more noble concern. If the deck is already stacked against the underdeveloped countries, what may the effects be of statements such as: "Hard currency and hard hearts go together. Soft currencies often go with a kindly compassionate people worth knowing"? Or the following: "In our country we are not commercialising this industry. We are not making it part of the economic plans of the development of Sri Lanka, to make it a number one exchange earner. No. The policy of this Government is to bring tourists into this country as part of a world-wide exercise of human understanding ..." (1982a:3, 5). The hard-hearted in the international tourism industry might well hear such a message with glee, believing that such a declared non-commercial orientation will make it even easier for the affluent west to turn international tourism to its own advantage. If such a reaction were possible then there might be many in Sri Lanka who would be relieved that the statements are perhaps made essentially for rhetorical effect, or at least do not, as some put it to me, in any substantial way direct the daily activities of the Tourist Board.

CULTURAL 'POLLUTION'

The troubles of the tourist industry which seemed to be almost daily news during 1982 were not only of an economic kind. Increasingly people were speaking out about the adverse social and moral consequences of rapid tourism development, what is frequently referred to in tourism literature as cultural 'pollution'. The Ceylon Tourism Plan of 1967 had omitted consideration of these wider cultural issues, but tourism is an industry unlike most other forms of development in that it is one where the consumer comes personally to collect the goods (Gamage 1978:92–3). It is therefore obvious today, as it perhaps was not in 1967, that any serious evaluation of tourism development must pay close attention to its socio-cultural ramifications (Cater 1987; Dogan 1989; Harrison 1992b). Narrowly defined cost-benefit analyses will inevitably be seriously inadequate, not only because many of the 'costs' are social, but also because they are also largely unquantifiable. Although therefore difficult to incorporate into any precise model, it is often the case that when properly considered they can substantially affect the answers to basic questions about the desirability or otherwise of actively pursuing tourism growth. Belatedly recognising this home truth has seen many Third World national tourism organisations endeavouring to shut the stable door after the horse had bolted.

It is not my intention here systematically to discuss all the social problems perceived to be consequences of tourist development in Sri Lanka. For a start, such problems and their extent are, in many instances, less a direct consequence of tourism itself than of a complex host of more diffuse forces for social change operating in the Third World. And as Wriggins rightly pointed out in 1960, it is hard to imagine any society east of Suez more open to European influences for such a long time as Sri Lanka (1960:13). In the present day and age, Haas, for instance, comments that returning migrant workers from the Middle East are a far more potent contemporary force for change in Sri Lanka than tourism. He also adds that it is supremely arrogant of westerners to see themselves as the cause of cultural change, as if the inhabitants of Sri Lanka were just passive victims of European influence (1984:3–4). In fact, during the 1970 Colombo tourism seminar, V.E.H. de Mel, Chairman of the Association for the Promotion of Tourism in Ceylon, stated: "Our culture is far too old and too deep to be corrupted by merely the visit of tourists or by our catering to their legitimate demands. Tourists are not all seekers after the flesh pots and we have no need to think only in terms of satisfying the baser demands of the tourist" (1970:2).

This view that Sri Lanka was culturally resilient was still being voiced in 1982. Ali, my chief informant, frequently told me that the mere presence of tourists did not require anyone to abandon their beliefs and values, and that no-one was obliged to live like a foreigner. For him, Sri Lanka gained from tourism; there were obvious employment gains, local culture was better known to the wider world and Sri Lankans also learned about countries which they would never visit. He admitted that tourism had made worse problems such as drugs and prostitution, but he did not blame the tourists for this because, in his view, no one could make a Sri Lankan imitate a foreigner. The owner of a private guesthouse who had previously been involved in running a large hotel on the outskirts of Kandy took a similar line: "If one is a good Christian or a good Buddhist, tourism will not affect one's values".

Most commentators, however, had a somewhat different view. They automatically connected international tourism with very serious social problems, and saw Sri Lanka as very vulnerable indeed. Consequently, 'pollution' was one of the dominant representations of international tourism in the island. Pollution, of course, as anthropologists have amply demonstrated, can only be understood against a background of much larger systems of cultural meaning, and to the extent that this is true tourism merely 'triggers' well-entrenched cultural themes. In that light we can see much of the modern outpourings about the negative consequences of tourism in Sri Lanka as but restatements of the same message uttered by a variety of indigenous voices over the centuries about the pernicious effects of the west.

Sri Lanka has a highly developed historical consciousness (Kemper 1991; Spencer 1990 ed.), even if elements of that present-day consciousness were in fact moulded during the nineteenth century by European philological, ethnological and religious scholarship (Obeyesekere 1976:238). Because the Sinhalese widely regard themselves as a "chosen people" (K.M. de Silva 1979:135), chosen in fact by the

Photo 2   Seated Buddha at Polonnaruwa.

Buddha himself for the historic mission of preserving his teachings, a marked sense of being a two thousand five hundred year old Aryan civilization was predictably a central element of the cultural revitalisation movements associated with figures such as Anagarika Dharmapala (Obeyesekere 1979: 279–82, 287) and Piyadasa Sirisena (Amunugama 1979) in the late decades of the nineteenth century and early decades of the twentieth. Part of the same broad tradition in this century is Vijaya-vardhana's 1953 Sinhala nationalist tract denouncing the west as barbaric and pol-luting, as the source of those ruinous Christian missionaries who damaged Buddhism and those violent, greedy vandals who so systematically robbed Sri Lanka of her wealth during the colonial period (1953:53, 75, 79, 93, 512–3). When Sarachandra rails against the evil influence on Sinhala Buddhist values of western films, nudism, materialism and the like, it is thus part of a centuries-old tradition in Sri Lanka of associating the west with corruption and decay.

International tourists, in this cosmology, are sometimes clearly seen as just another source of social ill, as are Tamils and anything else alien. When tourists are portrayed as low, vile, dirty, materialistic, depraved and hedonistic they are thus joining a long line of other foreigners who have been stereotyped in intensely derogatory ways by Sri Lankans for hundreds of years (Roberts *et al.*, 1979:2–21), ways which contrast so strikingly with the moderation and soberness which is often portrayed as the essence of Sinhala Buddhism. It matters very little that the opposition 'tradition'/'modernity' is vexed at best from an analytical perspective. It may also be the case that the somewhat protestantised version of Buddhism and its highly moralising outlook is very much a modern, as well as lower middle class, ideology (Obeyesekere 1979:302–8; Warrell 1990b:72). That having been said, how-ever, one should not underestimate the political power of this cosmology. Sinhala fundamentalism, after all, was largely responsible in the 1956 election for ousting the political elite that had governed Sri Lanka since independence on the grounds that that elite was westernised, out of touch with the masses and culturally alien-ated. Given that political elites in Third World nations are invariably hopelessly separated by education and class from the electorate at large, there is much mileage in using cultural themes as political weapons. This needs to be appreciated in the Sri Lankan context, for it not only explains why tourists can so easily emerge as scape-goats for social ills, it also explains why, very often, the enemy is frequently depicted as lurking within.

On 19 September 1982, for instance, the Sri Lankan newspaper *Weekend* carried an article originally published in the September 1982 issue of *Asian Business* entitled "Sri Lanka's Image Blasted". Sri Lanka, the article claimed, had become a jungle of "beggars, greedy hoteliers, dishonest shopkeepers, touts, rip-off artists, pimps and prostitutes". And, as for Sri Lankan 'hospitality' and 'friendliness': "In Colombo where the head offices of these hotels are situated, financial wizards with the shrewdness of Jews ... and ruthlessness of concentration camp commanders control the 'comforts' and amenities of their clients in close collaboration with foreign agencies who have brought them here with their vast and colourful propaganda". A Sri Lankan living abroad wrote (*Weekend*, 18 January 1982): "There are so many slimey snakes crawling around now in what used to be the brightest jewel of the British crown". For another writer (*Sun*, 22 July 1982): "Our religion, society and cultural atmosphere has been polluted by the foul air of tourism". For another commentator, all the foreign exchange earned would not compensate for the "irreparable damage that threatens us" (*Island*, 9 September 1982). Sri Lanka had become a society of human parasites fleecing people (*Island*, 29 August 1982); people had become so greedy that they would destroy themselves (*Daily News*, 26 June 1982). Clearly, given a culture where hospitality and consideration are highly valued and where certain forms of commerce are looked down upon and associated with specific minority ethnic groups, tourism, with all its associations of money-making through a pretence at friendship was profoundly worrying to some.

For other bitter critics, tourism was the vehicle by which to rail against the super-wealthy who were in league with the overseas capitalists. Not only that, some alleged that tourism was often but a camouflage for illegal activities used by those with political connections, that the elite found investment in tourism an easy way of hiding the fortunes they were making out of secret commissions and from dealings in the drug trade. Commenting on the evils to which the young are exposed in the tourist travel business, Maureen Seneviratne detailed the plight of those young boys who drop out of school to work as fare collectors on the private buses, living by their wits, learning dishonesty, to say nothing of the crowds of begging children running after such buses. Politicians are responsible for the fate of these youths, she argued: "They cannot dare plead ignorance. Would they expose their own children to these horrors?" (*Weekend*, 1 August 1982). For one critic in 1978 the real culprits were the wealthy Sri Lankans investors in the tourism industry, "denationalized people without much feeling towards this country" (Endagama 1978:61). If the above letters and comments are more than the outpourings of a very small hyper-critical minority, then Ahmed's comment that "by taking a planned, gradualist approach to tourism development ... the Sri Lankan government has avoided the severe negative impact that tourism can have on a country's social-cultural fabric" (1987:51) is clearly somewhat amiss.

The list of cultural ills alleged to stem from tourism in Sri Lanka[4] is the same

---

[4] They have been documented for Sri Lanka by Mendis (1981:19–25), L. Perera (1978) and Samarasuriya (1982), among others, and even appear in the foreign press. *Le Monde*, in 1980, for instance, carried an article detailing the 'corrosive effects' of the tourist shock in Sri Lanka, even labelling tourists '*les nouveaux conquistadores*' (de Beer 1980).

as one finds in most other Third World countries where international tourism has become significant. The problems most widely mentioned are: increasing dishonesty; heterosexual prostitution; homosexual prostitution of young boys; drug abuse, particularly among the young; irresponsible behaviour among the young through emulating western ways. Increased begging was also a concern to many, especially by the young whose insistent cries of "school pen, one rupee, bonbons" (Karasek 1980:236) cause humiliation to elders, particularly when many such children are not needy but drop out of school just to earn money. There was also evidence of the use of tourist visas to engage in gem smuggling. There was also the illegal selling of Sri Lankan babies to foreigners, a business from which it is said lawyers were making vast sums while the mothers received a mere pittance (*Daily News*, 20 July 1982). Indeed, Sri Lanka had the reputation of being "one of the main world centres for the sale of babies", some travel agencies even running "baby excursions" (Garcia 1988:119–10). There have also been several cases of religious antiques being stolen from temples and smuggled out of the country (Mendis 1981:24); in some cases, it seems, monks themselves have been the culprits. Commentators have also pointed out that some monks have been very quick to seize commercial opportunities by charging tourists sizeable sums of money to enter temples, and that many younger monks are eager to fraternise with tourists to get their addresses hoping, like other Sri Lankans, that this may lead to the opportunity to leave Sri Lanka altogether.

Child prostitution was a very real concern in 1982. German 'gay' magazines were quite openly speaking of the cheapness and allure of small Sri Lankan boys (Seneviratne and Peiris 1991:48–9). A survey ranked Sri Lanka second to the Philippines in 1981 for the prostitution of young boys, estimating that 2000 boys aged between 8 and 17 years old were in the trade (Ecumenical Coalition on Third World Tourism 1983:31–3). Very few paedophiles had been fined and deported from Sri Lanka by 1982, and a move to adopt harsh measures to deal with the problem was stopped by the Minister of State himself in 1983 when he withdrew draft legislation because the tourism downturn caused by mounting civil unrest seemed to solve much of the difficulty (Seneviratne and Peiris:50–1). By 1982, Sri Lanka had also come to be regarded as an important staging post in large international drug rings, and local police were working with the police forces of the United Kingdom and Australia to try to break the racket. While tougher anti-drug legislation was in process of being drafted during 1982, however, the suspicion consistently being expressed in letters to the press was that while renewed efforts would be made to prosecute, deport and fine hippies and small 'pushers', the 'big fish' (both locals and foreigners) would continue to escape detection. Indeed, there was the frequent allegation that these "Mr. Bigs" carried on their work with the protection of the police because of their political connections (*Sun*, 14 July 1982).

The Ceylon Tourist Board, like national tourism organisations in other countries, has produced a number of brochures informing visitors what standards of conduct they expect from foreigners while in Sri Lanka, in order to minimise undesirable cultural influences. *'Come share our way of life'* was one such brochure in circulation during 1982, which graphically set out a list of 'do's and don'ts' in regard to drugs, nudity, the taking of photographs, antiques, and so on. As with comparable literature in other countries, it is an effort to have a form of international tourism which respects one's culture. In his address to the Tourism Marketing Conference in Colombo in 1982, de Alwis labelled it "tourism with care" (1982b). Sri Lanka's aims in this regard, of having tourism on her own terms, are shared by most tourism destinations, and the rhetoric of safeguarding a way of life is almost universal in official tourism pronouncements. Whether such policies have any significant effect upon the industry and its local repercussions is a moot point, however. Some critics of tourism and, indeed, some hard-headed people engaged in tourism suggested to me that the statement was so much 'hot air'. One private hotel owner in Kandy put it to me candidly: tourism was about making money from foreigners, and given that, one should be consistent; all the talk about preserving one's culture was so much nonsense — "one cannot serve two gods".

Others took a different view, recognising the contradictions or at least the ironies of the situation, and the double standards to which it was giving rise. One might imagine a profound incompatibility between modern international tourism with its emphasis on hedonism and extremes in general, and a culture based upon Buddhism, with its emphasis on balance and moderation. But some commentators have queried the invocation of Buddhist values in this modern context. They claim that much of the prudish denunciation of tourism stems very much from a nineteenth century anglicised Buddhism. Furthermore, they allege that for many who condemn tourism as decadent and against the Buddha's teachings, Buddhism is personally of no consequence at all, simply a convenient image to express middle class disapproval, or perhaps jealousy because they are not personally profiting from the industry. Some point to the contradiction between the authorities decrying nudism on Sri Lanka's beaches but charging 75 rupees to see the ancient murals of half-naked'women at Sigiriya. They are also quick to point out that prostitution (and indeed homosexuality) has always existed in Sri Lanka, that tourism only alters the scale and the prices; the presence of the foreigners is not the cause. Some Low Country Sinhalese I spoke to in Kandy even informed me that many a Kandyan aristocrat had held onto, or enhanced, his power during the nineteenth century precisely by making his wife available to the British.

Allegations about moral decay invariably feed off idealised images of the past. One very senior member of the Tourist Board suggested to me that tourism was just one of several modern malaises afflicting and confusing the people. He placed it alongside democratic elections, newspapers and television as sources of cultural chaos, painting a rosy picture of an orderly, harmonious Sri Lankan way of life before those contemporary ills appeared. Clearly he was not so much criticising tourism as expressing his disaffection with the modern world in general. But what exactly is meant by the expression 'Ceylonese culture' in the twentieth century? Lalith Athulathmudali, Minister of Trade and Shipping in 1982, responded to criticisms that the U.N.P.'s policy of the 'open economy' was destroying Sri Lankan culture by arguing that culture did not mean 'the past' (*Sun*, 8 July 1982). An academic I spoke to concerning the question of tourism and cultural change in Kandy replied: "What culture?" For him, Kandy was just a modern city. The derogatory term "convenience culture" was also used to describe the ceremonial opening of a tourism conference in Kandy. Oil lamps were lit and a choir of school children dressed in white sang greetings in Sinhala to the overseas delegations. The person who used the expression "convenience culture" was a professional man, and pointed to the wearing of white cloth by leading politicians as being an example of the same kind: it implied no genuine attachment to traditional culture, Buddhism, or anything else. I had expected a somewhat different view from Buddhist clergy on the relations between tourism and cultural values, and was therefore surprised by the response I received from a young monk studying French at the nearby University of Peradeniya. He told me that there would always be differences between generations and between cultures and that tourism was a good way of learning about different ways of life. As for the changes caused by the presence of tourists, instead of moralistic judgment, he simply quoted to me a basic tenet of Buddhist teaching that all things were in a constant process of change.

A common version of the connection between international tourism and moral decay attributes most of the problems to the lower orders in both societies: the beggars, the touts, the hippies. It is convenient to believe that the budget tourists staying in the cheapest accommodation are those mainly involved with drugs and prostitution, but in Kandy it was quite obviously the wealthier tourists in air-conditioned cars who were being whisked away by their drivers after their rapid tour of the Temple of the Tooth to liaisons with prostitutes in expensive accommodation in, or just outside, the city. By no means were the several guesthouses in Kandy with reputations for prostitution those which catered to 'bottom of the market' visitors. Coach loads of tourists would arrive in Kandy for a one or two day stay in one of the best known hotels, and it took only a few hand signals from the coach driver to a woman on the pavement to indicate how many of these guests wanted *ganja* that night. All these links between hire car drivers, taxi drivers, hotel waiters, prostitutes, and so on, are well established in the licensed tourism arena, so the notion that these problems would go away by the authorities cracking down on hippies and unlicensed guesthouses was just wishful thinking.

For double standards one could not do better than the stories I was told by the owners of a large guesthouse/hotel complex just outside Kandy. At the same time that the husband was telling me of his outrage that drivers delivering guests would demand from him a woman for the night, his wife was explaining to me that it was necessary in the provision of tourist services to "cater to human nature". Her establishment had *the* reputation in Kandy for supplying young, local girls and even its own servants to tourists; some of my informants even told me that the owner herself was not averse to offering herself in the same way.

Anandatissa de Alwis who, as Minister in charge of tourism in 1980, had made the famous Manila speech about tourism, peace and understanding, had, a decade earlier and before his political career had begun, written a number of short stories. One of these was entitled "Star Sapphire" and revolved around tourism. It concerns the relationship which grows up between Prema, a Sinhalese waiter, and Mrs Fawn, a rich American tourist crippled with polio. The tourist hotels are described in that story as "prisons of glass and aluminium ... coldly clinical and the cold had nothing to do with the air conditioning" (1970:10–11). Here the people in the tourist industry are portrayed as "tetron suited receptionists with narrow ties and tooth-paste grins, exuding copy book gentility" (1970:11). The irony about social morality is well stated: "It was a peculiar twist of the law that it pounces on a poor man who went to bed with a woman and called it vice but smiled indulgently at a rich man who took a woman to his estate bungalow and called him a playboy. No vice squads raided him" (1970:37). "Everywhere there were double standards" (1970:36). The story ends with Prema going to the United States, leaving his wife and children behind, but making sure that they were well provided for. de Alwis clearly depicts the double-edged nature of international tourism. As a relative says to Prema's wife: "After all the fellow has done something, hasn't he? Seela, don't look so glum. If Prema worked for another twenty years he couldn't have done as much for you and the children as he has done now" (1970:45).

NEO-COLONIALISM

Any adequate 'balance sheet' on tourism must pay due attention to social costs and moral dilemmas as well as straightforward economic factors, but there is also an inherently political calculation involved in the overall assessment of international tourism too. John Bright, over a century ago, likened British imperialism to a great outdoor recreational system for the well off (quoted in Palmer and Palmer 1976:26). Some have reversed this proposition and suggested that international tourism has a clearly colonial dimension to it (Britton 1982; Nash 1978); indeed Krippendorf has argued that tourism has a colonial dimension "everywhere and without exception" (1987:56). During the 1970 Colombo tourism seminar only A.T. Ariyaratne saw the matter in these terms, but since then many contributors to the tourism debate have highlighted the 'neo-colonial' aspect of international tourism. If before the formal establishment of empire, trade patterns made for imperial (albeit 'informal') relations, so, after decolonisation, economic ties can perpetuate essentially 'colonial' links, albeit without the political responsibilities. A letter to the *Daily News* (22 January 1977) is pertinent here:

> If the object is to turn this country into another rest and recreation camp for the jaded foreigner, then of course we cannot complain ... we are on the right track. But to a land struggling to find its identity after 400 years of colonialism, to a State pledged to seek a more equitable distribution of power, wealth and resources, surely this is a mockery ... it is tragic to think that a bare 30 years after political independence we are on the verge of ... an era of neo-colonialism.

It may be significant that in 1982, a decade after Ceylon changed its name to Sri Lanka, the Tourist Board was still known as the Ceylon Tourist Board, perpetuating, as some other public institutions do, a colonial name familiar to Europeans.

The neo-colonial dimension of tourism appears in various guises. One is the diversion of resources from local people for the benefit of foreigners. There have been occasions when hotels providing swimming pools for tourists were exempt from water restrictions imposed on the rest of the community. In some coastal areas, hotels have taken the best beach locations and displaced local fishermen, some of whom have ended up selling trinkets to tourists on those same beaches instead of fishing. Also domestic tourism in Sri Lanka has fared badly as compared with tourism geared towards overseas visitors, despite the emphasis in the original Ceylon Tourism Plan (1967:95) that the recreational interests of the host population should not be ignored. Many were the complaints from lower middle class Ceylonese in 1982 that they could no longer afford a holiday in their own country because the prices were so high. Letters to newspapers (*Weekend*, 2 May 1982; *Sun*, 16 June 1982) have even spoken of *apartheid*, of the way Sri Lankans are treated as second class citizens in their own country and how security guards employed by hotels endeavour to keep local people out of such establishments.

Goonatilake entitles a section of his insightful 1978 analysis into tourism in Sri Lanka: "Tourist Encounters — Class and Colonial Dimensions". He draws parallels — perhaps somewhat stretched, and certainly not very accurate as regards the activities of the thousands of budget tourists who visit Sri Lanka — between the tourist industry and the nineteenth century enclave system. In both, areas of the country are effectively set aside for the use of foreigners. Europeans are walled in to protect fort-like spaces away from the locals, just as with the planters' clubs of yesteryear, those leading symbols of British aloofness and arrogance. Indeed, in some cases in Sri Lanka, it is those self-same buildings which have been converted to hotels. In such enclaves, relationships are not based on 'friendship', 'understanding', and the like, which tourist literature likes to pretend exists, but on commercial transactions; 'service' is simply a marketable commodity. Not only that, but the foreigners who already possess well-entrenched stereotypes of the Third World, partly derived from their knowledge of the colonial past, arrive to find waiters barefoot and wearing sarongs, even if they are from good homes and have been well educated. All this creates an overwhelming atmosphere of subservience and privilege (1978:7–9).

For Mendis, this attitude of servility threatens to make Sri Lanka into a "nation of butlers" (1981:24). What is exchanged culturally are not noble thoughts of peace and understanding but "often the worst aspects of culture on both sides" (1981:21). He provides a description utilising the same neo-colonial representations as Goonatilake and then goes on to state:

> In a sense, we are compelled to create these tourist enclaves since we are obliged to fulfil the expectations of our visitors who come here to sample a taste of paradise. We must make it possible for them to enjoy the sun and the sea and relax in peaceful, tranquil surroundings, oblivious of the poverty around them. If we do not insulate them from the stark miseries of our country, they may perhaps be nauseated or conscience-stricken, and not visit us again. Hence the strenuous efforts at window-dressing, camouflaging the hell-holes of squalor that blot the landscape, and sweeping the dirt under the carpet, take the form of rounding up beggars, keeping the cities clean, and planting colourful flowers on our roundabouts. We cover up the festering sores with bright raiment and present to our visitors a cheerful, smiling Lanka who in reality is nothing but a sick and anaemic lady with a painted face (1981:22–3).

There is another political dimension to the tourist industry which Goonatilake has particularly commented on. This is the possibility that the attractive pictures of the Resplendent Isle created by the international tourism industry may prevent the Sri Lankan political elite from having a realistic assessment of the severe domestic problems which confront them, and indeed may simply entrench in them even more deeply the alien attitudes and values of the affluent overseas countries that send their citizens on holiday to Sri Lanka, thus making it even harder for them to empathise with their own people (Goonatilake 1978:10). In this respect tourism is a classic confirmation of the views of those theorists of imperialism who have stressed the role of indigenous collaborative elites (Harrison 1992b:24; Truong 1990:123, 158–9). Due is extremely caustic: tourism accentuates the inequalities and class divisions in Sri Lankan society; it channels benefits mainly to the local political elite who in so many ways identify their interests with those of international capitalists; under the pro-western, 'open economy' U.N.P. version of tourism this is particularly the case (1980:101, 114, 124). Instead of the 'peace and understanding' of the official rhetoric, what we actually have is a situation where the local elite profits while most local people are subject to a number of dislocations and are little more than mere spectators of the cash flow. As we will see when we examine the situation in Kandy, the feeling one most associates with tourism is not friendship but rather *irisiawa*, a deep-felt resentment and social jealousy. Bugnicourt's striking depiction is apt here:

> One wonders whether the effort of a few individuals to open doors and to seek international understanding makes up for the damage caused by or aggravated by tourism as it encroaches upon the Third World ... There is no doubt whatever that a change in the overall economic and social relations between industrialised and Third World countries and a consequent evolution of behaviour will be needed before there can be any real prospect of a tourism which no longer leaves itself open to the charge of colonialism (*Sun*, 12 October 1977).

It is important not to leave the impression in this discussion of the social, economic and political history of international tourism in Sri Lanka that there is anything unique about this one industry, for much of what has been set out above also applies to other industries. Tourism is not atypical, for, as Ponnambalam puts it, the entire Sri Lankan economy since 1948 has been "dependent capitalism in crisis" (1981). For him, the economic problems of Sri Lanka since independence are quite separate from the issue of which particular party has been in power, because no government has endeavoured to tackle the structural deformities of the colonial economy. This is because the upper middle class benefited from colonialism and so is now the ally of neo-imperialism; to attempt structural transformation would be to undermine their own power and wealth (1981:13, 15, 29, 173–4). 'Socialism' in Sri Lanka, according to Ponnambalam is simply 'State Capitalism' (1981:39). Over the years the increasing reliance on foreign aid and international borrowing has perpetuated not only economic dependence but also political control from overseas (1981:57; see also Karunatilake 1987). The I.M.F. and the World Bank are Sri Lanka's new masters and Article 157 of Sri Lanka's constitution even guarantees co-operation with international capital (Ponnambalam 1981:147, 164–5). The establishment of the Duty Free Shopping Complex and the provision of tax privileges for overseas investors involved in establishing hotel plant is thus just part of a broader picture, and is not really greatly different to other features of the 'open economy' policy set in motion in 1977. The Free Trade Zone established near Katunayake airport in 1978 is a region in Sri Lanka where some of the laws of the land are suspended to enable capitalism to pursue its goals in an unfettered environment

(Ponnambalam 1981:156, 160–1); wage rates are low, working conditions inferior, and it is surrounded by secrecy and has been widely associated with systematic smuggling (Karunatilake 1987:424, 430–1). For some, it is simply re-colonisation, just another enclave system separate from the rest of the economy, like those of yesteryear. For some left wing critics even that characterisation would be regarded as over-generous for the simple reason that for them Sri Lanka has not yet attained any real form of independence: neither separation from Britain in 1948, nor the 1956 election, nor the political changes in 1972, add up to real freedom since who-ever has been in power the fundamental imperialistic economic ties have never been effectively dismantled (Ivan 1989:xi, 1, 4, 20–1).

The international tourism industry is not, then, unique. When Ponnam-balam comments on the U.N.P.'s "whole-hearted commitment to right-wing eco-nomic policies for the benefit of a tiny body of Sri Lankan ultra-rich capitalists at home and the giant Western multinationals abroad" (ibid:167), it becomes very clear that tourism is only part of a larger picture of development and dependence. It is vital to make such a point forcefully lest features of the international tourism industry erroneously be thought to belong to that industry *per se* rather than to the overall structural context of political and economic ties in the Third World which, as one of the particular manifestations of these broader circumstances, has been made into a "pleasure periphery" (Turner and Ash 1975) for the affluent, industrial nations.

CHAPTER THREE

Tourism in Kandy: A Historical and Contemporary Portrait

THE CITY AND ITS ENVIRONS — PAST AND PRESENT

The city generally known to foreigners today as Kandy and to many locals also as Maha Nuwara (literally 'Great City') was founded in the fourteenth century with the name Senkandesala Sirivaddhana according to the *Mahavamsa*, the 'Great Chronicle' of Sri Lanka which stretches back over a thousand years of her history (Nanayakkara 1977:1). The present name of Kandy derives in all probability from a Portuguese corruption of the Sinhala word *'kanda'* in the expression *'kanda uda rata'* meaning 'hilly up country'. For three centuries after the Portuguese and subsequently the Dutch established control over the coastal regions of Sri Lanka, Kandy, flanked on three sides by the largest river in the island and nestling in a thickly wooded valley amidst the central hill ranges, proved impossible to capture, largely because of the difficulty of the terrain (Karunaratna 1984:3). Sri Lanka has had her capitals in numerous locales over the centuries, with shifts often being made for strategic considerations. At the end of the sixteenth century, Sri Lanka consisted of three semi-independent kingdoms centred on Kotte, Jaffna and Kandy, but when the European presence was secured along the littoral, and when the resistance of the Sitavaka Kingdom came to an end (K.M. de Silva 1979:130–1), Sinhala resistance decisively shifted inland to Kandy (Gunasinghe 1990:19; Roberts *et al.,* 1989:5, 32). Burned and looted on several occasions by both the Portuguese and Dutch, Kandy was always able to repel the invader, but existed nonetheless for well over two hundred years in a more or less permanent state of readiness for war. Finally, in 1815, amidst a welter of intrigue by members of the Kandyan aristocracy against their ruler (Dharmadasa 1979:102–4, 118–21), Kandy, the royal heart of a kingdom which extended over much of the inland areas of the island, finally fell to the British, the first colonial power to secure control of the entire island.

These historical events lend the city of Kandy considerable national importance, for many see the Kandyan region as embodying the very essence of Sinhala Buddhist civilization. Seneviratna has recently even referred to Kandy as the "cultural capital" of Sri Lanka (1983:7). Kandy certainly radiates a strong historical, even sacred, aura. As Goonetileke observes, even amidst the hustle and bustle of

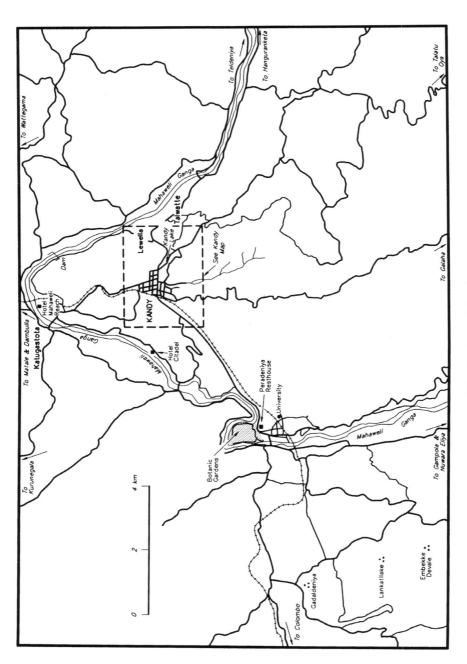

Map 3   Around Kandy.

Photo 3   View of Kandy across the Lake.

modern life there is still the "compelling patina of its ornate and many-splendoured past" (1976 ed:214–5). Indeed, not only is Sinhalese history physically present in Kandy, the very architectural design of the town enshrines, as do other South Asian royal capitals, far more basic religious, mythological and cosmological themes (Duncan 1990:22, 48, 59). Kandy is thus a key site in the UNESCO 'cultural triangle' archaeological project in Sri Lanka which also embraces other ancient capitals such as Anuradhapura and Polonnaruwa. Indeed, it was in the Audience Hall in Kandy in 1980 that President Jayewardene, who has contributed large sums of money to this project, spoke of these archaeological treasures as revealing the ancient glories of the Sinhala race, a decidedly political comment both repudiating a colonial past and also disavowing the Tamil contribution to Sri Lanka's history. (Ministry of Cultural Affairs 1980; Nissan 1989:74; Kemper 1991:135, 148, 174).[1]

Kandy is certainly supremely important because of its connection with Buddhism, a religion intimately bound up with Sri Lanka's sense of herself as a civilization of great historical depth. There is even a foundation myth which links the city

---

[1] To the extent that many of these archaeological sites are tourist spectacles as well as pilgrimage centres, tourists inevitably move in politically contentious spaces, though doubtless few are aware of the fact. It is partly the hefty entrance fees paid by foreigners at such places which allow much of this archeological work to continue and thus assists the rewriting of the past by contemporary ethnic and political interests.

with stories about the Buddha's own clan (Duncan 1990:91). Also in Kandy is the *Dalada Maligawa*, the Temple of the Tooth Relic, the repository of one of the most important religious treasures in the Buddhist world. This Temple is a centre of pilgrimage for Buddhists from beyond the shores of Sri Lanka and has been visited by devout Buddhists for centuries. The *Asala perahera*, the spectacular procession which takes place through the streets of Kandy over a ten day period at the end of July and the beginning of August, is possibly the largest pageant in the Buddhist world. Kandy is also the home of the Asgiriya and Malwatte monasteries, whose chief monks are the two most powerful Buddhist monks in the island. Kandy's continued importance is also transparent in the national political arena. Kandy, as Daniel puts it "has provided legitimation to every Sinhala party and politician since Independence ... who, on being elected to office, visit the temple to receive the blessings of the Triple Gem" (1990:236).

Moore is possibly correct in saying that Kandy is the only city in Sri Lanka apart from Colombo with any national significance (1985:132), but Kandy is not a 'capital' in this day and age in any sense, cultural or otherwise. Very early during the nineteenth century she was eclipsed in both political and economic importance by Colombo. With a population estimated at a mere 3000 in 1817, what was the royal centre of a regional, pre-capitalist feudal structure assumed another role under British rule (Roberts *et al.*, 1989:86–7, 98–100). Kandy became the hub of the inland transportation network which focused on Colombo which, as the principal port, tied Sri Lanka into a structure of global political economy (Moore 1985:131). As for culture, it was Colombo and the southwestern littoral more generally which saw the Sinhala renaissance in the late nineteenth century and the pressures for independence in the twentieth. The Kandyan region had almost no input into these events. Nowadays, the political, economic and cultural hegemony of Colombo cannot be disputed. Colombo with its suburbs is a city of over 1,000,000 people whereas Kandy in 1982 had a population just a little over 100,000; its importance today is largely symbolic (Roberts *et al.*, 1989: v, 2, 4, 27, 100, 178).

Basic changes in Kandy took place within a few years of the British conquest of 1815. A Colombo-Kandy road was started in 1820 and finished in 1830 (Jennings 1958) with a rail link started in 1857 and completed a decade later. Such developments were partly to open up the interior for economic exploitation, but the former was also very much for military reasons. Kandy after defeat, in fact, became a garrison town; part of the Temple of the Tooth became a prison, part of the Malwatte monastery became a military hospital, and the Queen's chambers in the Palace complex became a gunpowder store (Karunaratna 1984:6). A rebellion was brutally suppressed in 1817, with much loss of life and a massive destruction of crops and housing, as also occurred in 1848 (K.M. de Silva 1979:136–43; Karunaratna 1984:6). Whilst coastal areas had been involved in European affairs for centuries, the British regarded Kandyans with deep suspicion, and throughout the nineteenth century few were thus in a position to take advantage of new opportunities. Thus, a few decades after 1815 the populational structure of Kandy was substantially altered. Because of the presence of the royal court, there had been both Muslims and Tamils in Kandy prior to conquest, but after conquest there was a sizeable movement of different kinds of people into Kandy from the low country. Many Burghers (those of mixed Sinhalese-European descent), because familiar with European ways, took up clerical, administrative and other professional positions. Carting, tavern keeping, peddling, and other commercial jobs attracted Muslims and considerable numbers of low country Sinhalese. (Gunasinghe 1990:48; Moore 1985:128–9; Roberts *et al.*, 1989:56). By 1911 census data reveal that there were actually more low country Sinhalese in Kandy than there were Kandyans. Given that the export of up country plantation crops was so fundamental to the colonial economy of Sri Lanka, some have argued that the Kandyan region bore the brunt of British exploitation. In addition to that, for many Kandyans of strong regional loyalties, the hill country was exploited and local people dispossessed, not only by the British but also by low country Sinhalese and a variety minority ethnic groups, as this erstwhile royal capital and its environs changed physically and socially with the substantial influx of newcomers (Roberts 1979:44).

Kandy, at the hub of a very quickly established network of roads which linked up country towns, villages and plantations (Gunasinghe 1990:46) around the export needs of the colonial economy, very much grew throughout the nineteenth century as 'a planter's town', and thus attracted a sizeable working British population. But Kandy also became very much a town for recreation for the planter community throughout the hill country in general, and indeed for the well-to-do throughout the island, in particular those from the Colombo area wishing to escape the stifling heat and humidity of the capital for the more temperate climate of the Kandyan region. In that sense, even in the nineteenth century Kandy was something of a tourist site. Indeed, Burrows, a member of the Ceylon Civil Service, in one of the earliest local travel books commenting on the increasing popularity of the island as a pleasure resort sought fit to claim that Kandy had become a household word with the travelling public at the end of the nineteenth century (Burrows 1899:preface). Situated only six degrees north of the equator but at approximately five hundred metres above sea level, for many Europeans the local climate was like an eternal spring. Hurst, an American theologian visiting in 1891, commented that the beauty and serenity of the place was reminiscent of the English Lake District (cited in Goonetileke 1976 ed:229), and when Auden and Isherwood visited the region between the wars they likened it to the Thames Valley (Goonetileke 1984 ed:59).

Few who have visited the hill country of Sri Lanka around Kandy fail to be impressed by its striking beauty. A British officer in 1803 stated that the area deserved the title 'Paradise' (cited in Nanayakkara 1977:6), a little later Davy described it as "beautiful and romantic" (1821:365), and at the end of the century an American visitor spoke of "scenes as beautiful as the hand of God ever created" (cited in Goonetileke 1976 ed:229). Comments about the town of Kandy itself as distinct from its environs, however, have been rather more mixed, reflecting perhaps the very admixture of east and west, old and new, that is so evident there, and recognising the substantial changes that the city has undergone in the past one hundred and fifty years. Burrows in 1899 informed visitors that because of the periodic burning and sacking of Kandy by Europeans that there were no really ancient buildings left (1899:2). Percival, early in the nineteenth century, declared Kandy to have nothing of interest to attract a visitor (1975:165–6) and the distinguished German scientist Haekel at the end of the century found it a complete disappointment (1975:98–100). At mid century, after only a few decades of British colonialism, Tennent wrote about the degradation and delapidation going on, and Davy himself had noticed the extent of the destruction and commented: "in all probability not a vestige of the old town will remain and an English town will rise on the ground it occupies" (1821:371). Approximately a century later, Isherwood and Auden, who so admired the Kandyan countryside did, in fact, describe the town itself as "drab and clean and English" (cited in Goonetileke 1984 ed:59).

The modern tourism industry in Kandy has perpetuated these twin themes of despoliation and mixture in the minds of many residents, for in some instances tourist facilities have literally been built in or over ancient landmarks. The *Ulpenge* (Queen's bathing pavilion) on the edge of the Kandy lake and a few yards away from the Temple of the Tooth, housed during 1982 a Tourism Information Office as well as a batik shop. The Hotel Dehigama is built on the site of the *walauwa* (opulent residence or 'manor house') of the Dehigama chief. The Kandy Arts and Crafts Association had been housed temporarily in the *Kunam Maduwa* (House of the Palanquins). This admixture was far from acceptable for a number of people in Kandy. There was audible concern that some of the architectural quality of the city had already suffered too much (*Island*, 2 July 1982). In fact, during 1982, there was talk of declaring 'sacred' whole precincts of the town, with the consequence that commercial developments of all kinds would then be debarred, and, indeed, some existing activities relocated. Sievers makes the point forcefully that the religious aura in Kandy and cultural pride have already acted as effective brakes on a more extensive development of tourist facilities and activities in Kandy (1983: 96–7,127–8). Indeed, according to her, this widely felt incompatibility between modern commercial activity and the force of tradition in the town was of such strength that Kandy, in the 1980s, was only at the beginning of modern tourism development (1981:127).

Before exploring further Kandy's particular features as a tourist site, it is necessary to sketch a more general contemporary picture of the city and its rural hinterland,[2] in order to be able to see tourism activity in context. The Kandy region contains some of the deepest pockets of poverty in Sri Lanka (Gunatilleke 1978:71). Pieris (1982) paints a general scene of population pressure, inefficient agriculture and high unemployment. The picture of 'disintegrating' village communities in the Kandyan hill country, hemmed in by plantations, unable to expand, with unworkably small plots and increasing landlessness a basic feature, was certainly emphasised by Morrison, Moore and Lebbe in 1979 (Morrison *et al.*, 1979 eds), thus reiterating the findings of the Kandyan Peasantry Commission of 1951, and continuing a *leitmotiv* established in the previous century (Spencer 1990:142). Whilst it is important to avoid romanticising 'traditional' Sinhala village communities as harmonious and egalitarian (Samanaweera 1981:131–3), there is no doubt that social changes, many of them the result of population growth since the Second World War, have put added pressures on these rural communities. A sizeable rural proletariat seeking seasonal agricultural work in the 'dry zone' or working as road gangs throughout the island is now a permanent feature (Morrison 1979:110; Morrison *et al.*, 1979:20–2; Silva 1979:62), as is the very high incidence of unemployment, particularly youth unemployment (Peebles 1982:95).

Whilst it would be misleading to speak of a 'typical' Kandyan village, given that their caste composition, landholding patterns, relationships to temple authorities, and so on, vary considerably, it is nonetheless possible to describe their social composition in general as a complex admixture of traditional, feudal-like relations and more modern monetarised class relations (Morrisson *et al.*, 1979:11). The introduction of capitalistic social relations went hand in hand with the establishment of British imperial control over the island, so that feudal-type ties have been disintegrating for over a century (Silva 1979). On the other hand, it would be wrong to envisage the establishment of a completely new social order, for as Gunasinghe has convincingly argued (1990), it suited the British very well deliberately to keep alive certain 'archaic' social relationships which were already established and effective tools for exploitation. This has no doubt contributed to the fact that in the present day, traditional obligations and attitudes as well as the cash nexus both structure everyday social relations. It would also be misleading to see the vil-

---

[2] Providing a picture for the Kandy administrative district as a whole is relatively easy since there is available detailed socio-economic information on the region (Pieris 1982) and some good studies exist of some of the villages near Kandy (Morrison 1979; Gunasinghe 1990; Silva 1979). For the town itself, however, whilst there is historical and archaeological material published (Duncan 1990; Karunaratna 1984; Nanayakkara 1977; Seneviratna 1983), there does not appear to be readily available any detailed material on urban social structure.

lages as in any sense self-contained or self-sufficient, for the links between them and Kandy, and indeed with the state itself are multiple and profound. Many village activities are controlled by regional and national authorities and success in the village, it has been said (Morrison 1979:38, 41), very much consists of maintaining an effective network of extra-village ties, particularly with politicians. The lives of villagers are, in every sense, tied up with what goes on elsewhere in the island.

Kandy itself in the modern world is a busy, bustling town. It is still an important transportation centre for the hill country, and although political, economic and administrative affairs are now generally centred in Colombo, it does house the Department of Agriculture. Being a university city (the University of Peradeniya is on its outskirts), there is a higher than normal professional population, a feature enhanced by Kandy's attractiveness as a place for professional people to retire to. The urban municipal area being 10 square miles puts Kandy second only to Colombo in extent and the population of the entire Kandy administrative district averaging 1300 per square mile (sometimes rising to 2500) is the second most densely populated area in what is a densely populated country (Peebles 1982:23, 35, 79; Morrison 1979:76; Moore 1985:xv). The city grew substantially during the British period, a population of roughly 3000 in 1817 climbed to 16,581 by 1871 and to 51,000 by 1946 (Peebles 1982:35, 79; Roberts *et al.*, 198:193). While the rapid rate of population growth after the Second World War, largely the result of advances in public health and the provision of extensive welfare support, led to a doubling in size to 103,000 by 1982, it should be noted that Sri Lanka has not experienced that massive drift of people into the cities that have so characterised the demography of other post-colonial Asian countries (Higgins 1982:18; Moore 1985:22, 123–6; Spencer 1990:36). Broad welfare policies have enabled more people to remain in the villages than would otherwise have been the case, although such communities are under pressure (Gunasinghe 1990:19–22).

What is clear, though, are the intricate sets of relationships between life in the villages and urban activities. Many of the wealthier villagers in fact commute daily to Kandy to perform 'white collar' jobs. Additionally a reasonably efficient and inexpensive public transport system brings thousands of other villagers into Kandy each day for 'blue collar' work. Since the Sinhala language policy was introduced into schools in the 1950s, in fact, many more people from the rural areas were able to take up employment in the city for which they would previously have been ill-equipped, lacking facility in English. Each day, too, people come in to Kandy with agricultural produce to sell in the streets. It is also common for the more well-to-do in the villages to send their children to schools in Kandy where the standard of education is regarded as being higher than that obtainable in the villages (Gunasinghe 1990:72–3; Silva 1979:66). These relationships are not all one way. Many of the wealthy traders in the Kandy market own land in the villages.

Lower middle class people such as school teachers also often purchase land in the villages, not necessarily in economically viable parcels, but simply in order to acquire the status that goes with ownership of paddy land and personal control over tenants (Silva 1979:54, 59; Spencer 1990:103; Obeyesekere 1967:213). The middle classes in Kandy also constitute an important demand for metal and wooden craftware items which have been made for centuries in numerous villages around Kandy. Such items also sell in great quantities to international tourists, many of whom do much of their shopping for such items in Kandy. Both foreign tourists and locals in Kandy, in other words, help to keep some of the craft villages in the rural hinterland of the city viable (Gunasinghe 1990:69).

KANDY AS A TOURIST SITE

In terms of the tourism industry in Sri Lanka as a whole, Kandy is somewhat atypical in a number of respects. For a start, Kandy's seasonal tourist flows are somewhat out of kilter with those for the rest of the island. The great majority of Sri Lanka's international tourists have been from western Europe, many escaping for a two week annual winter holiday. November to March is the island's peak season and whilst Kandy gets its share of tourists then, it is also, because of the *perahera*, the focus of attention in late July/early August, which is otherwise the middle of the off season. At that time Kandy is swarming with tourists and accommodation is so scarce that prices rise astronomically. Kandy, however, is probably the one place to which all tourists in Sri Lanka go — hippies, budget tourists, 'package tour' groups, and even those merely on a brief flight 'stopover'. At the same time, it is a place where few stay very long. Kandy very much has a "*touristichen Durchgangscharakter*" (Sievers 1983:97); it is little more than a transit place for many with respect to their main destination somewhere else in the island, normally a beach resort. In this respect, little has changed since 1912 when Thomas Cook was arranging single day and day and a half trips from Colombo to Kandy (Cook & Sons 1912:13–15).

Package tour groups during 1982 would spend between half a day and two days in Kandy, quickly visiting the Temple, the Botanical Gardens at Peradeniya, perhaps a Kandyan dance performance, before rushing off to the ancient cities of Anuradhapura and Polonnaruwa, again quickly done in a day or two, and then on to a beach resort for a week to ten days or so. Many longer staying budget tourists, because of the cooler temperatures, like to relax in Kandy for a day or two away from the heat of the beach areas, or just to 'settle in' after their arrival at Katunayake airport and normally fairly rapid escape from the noise, heat and humidity of Colombo, before moving around the island. Tourist attractions are many: the Tem-

Photo 4   Kandy bus station.

ple of the Tooth, the Palace complex, the splendid Botanical Gardens, a fine museum, the artificially constructed lake built by the last Kandyan monarch early in the nineteenth century, Kandyan dancing, the elephant bath at Katugastota, the Uduwattakele forest sanctuary, tea factories in the nearby hills, a large number of attractive temples just outside the city. There is evidently a great deal to do and see, quite apart from shopping for batiks, jewellery, antiques, wood, metal and leather goods, or simply resting. Despite all these attractions and facilities, however, Kandy in 1982 was still a place for only a brief stay for most foreigners. Whilst the 'sacred' aura of the city inhibiting tourist development may have something to do with this, the short stays really are not surprising in view of the simple fact that the vast majority of foreign visitors come to Sri Lanka for sun, sea and sand, and Kandy being in the middle of the island is as far away from the beaches as it is possible to be.

Several older residents of Kandy told me in 1982 how as recently as the 1930s paddy fields were still very close to the city centre. Kandy, they claimed, compared to the west coast, was a somewhat "sleepy" town; some even used the word "backwards". Some who reminisced about such peaceful times suggested that with all the noise and commotion, every day was now like a *perahera* with large crowds bustling through the streets. Some put this down very much to the presence of tourists, even blaming the tourist industry for a change in Kandy's temperature.

They pointed to the hills outside the town, previously thickly wooded, but now cleared for hotel construction, and suggested that the disappearance of the trees had caused temperatures to rise significantly. Whilst, no doubt, international tourism has added to the bustling atmosphere of the city, the simple fact is that Kandy is a large city and the centre of a very populous region; the attempt to attribute all the noise and activity to tourism is quite misconceived. On the other hand, tourism has certainly has had several direct effects on the city. During the 1970s, for example, many shop keepers completely changed the kind of stock they kept to cater to the specific needs of affluent foreigners. Some jewellery shops became antique shops, for instance; several general clothing shops were transformed into batik outlets; and so on. In 1982, Kandy had over 40 gem shops, over 20 shops selling batiks, and over 30 selling antiques, quite apart from the outlets for such goods within the retail areas of the better hotels. This is an astonishingly high number of tourist-orientated establishments, and reveals the extent to which Kandy had become a tourist site.[3]

Whilst there was a considerable range of views as to what changes could be put down to the influence of tourism, Kandy, long before modern tourism began, had ceased to be a distinctly 'up country' city. As mentioned earlier in this chapter, in the decades after British conquest many people from different parts of the island moved into Kandy to take advantage of a range of new opportunities. During the twentieth century that process has continued. Many of the grander guesthouses and private hotels in Kandy, for example, are owned by people from the low country who purchased prime real estate in Kandy near the lake before tourism really got under way. Although some informants were adamant that the distinction 'up country'/'low country' was a British colonial administrative invention of no significance to the Ceylonese, the distinction between 'Kandyans' and 'low country' Sinhalese in terms of outlook, ability, temperament, and so on, was as real to many of my informants as the distinctions they made between Germans, Japanese and British tourists, and it is not without relevance, in fact, to the operations of tourism in the town. One often heard comments that Kandyans were somewhat "slow" in

---

[3] The tourist arena of Kandy included several of the villages nearby such as Embekke and Kalapura. Relatively hard to get to for tourists using public transport, many foreigners in 1982 would hire a taxi or arrive in a hire car. Tourists often expressed the view that once out of Kandy they would find villages where the local people would be little affected by tourism and so the prices would be lower. Unfortunately, as some found out to their cost, however, such places were not at all 'backstage' to a tourist economy, they were fully a part of it. Many foreigners would have done better to have purchased their souvenirs in the marked price outlets of Kandy than to venture into a terrain where the locals were more than competent to drive a hard bargain with a stranger, especially one rich enough to be able to afford to hire a taxi to get there in the first place.

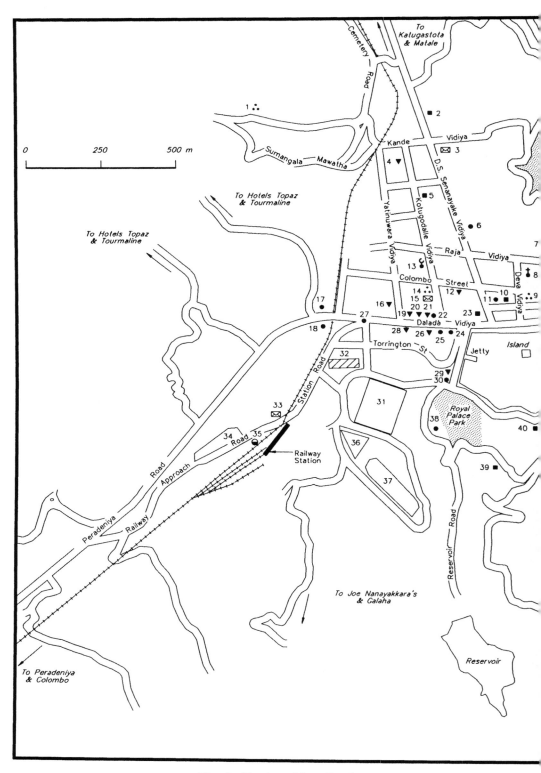

Map 4 Tourist guide to Kandy.

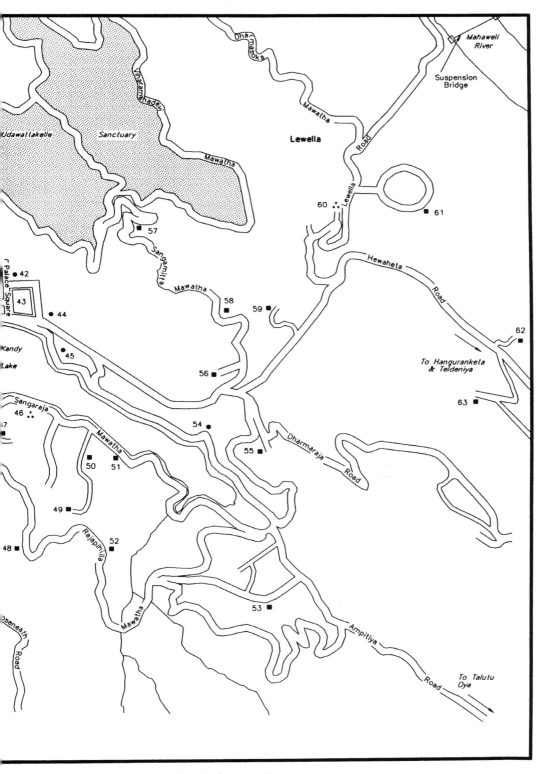

For Explanatory Key see next page.

■ PLACES TO STAY		OTHER	
2	Burmese Rest	1	Asgiriya Vihara
5	YMCA	3	Post Office
10	Olde Empire	6	KVG de Silva
23	Queen's Hotel	7	Vishnu Devale
39	Castle Hill Guest House	8	St Paul's Church
40	Devon Rest	9	Pattini Devale
47	Lake Round	11	Air Lanka
48	The Chalet	13	Mosque
49	Sharon Inn	14	Skanda Devale
50	Pink House	15	Seetha Agency Post Office
51	Hotel Suisse	17	Tourist Police
52	McLeod Inn	18	Police Station
53	Hillway Tour Inn	22	Bank of Ceylon
55	Mrs Clement Dissanayake's	24	Hatton National Bank
56	Hotel Thilanka	25	Cargill's Food City
57	Green Woods	27	Clock Tower
58	Jingle Bells	30	Laksala
59	Travellers Nest	31	Prison
61	Charm Inn	32	Market
62	Prasanna Tourist Inn	33	Main Post Office
63	Gem Inn II	34	Goods Shed Bus Yard
		35	Colombo Private Bus Stand
▼ PLACES TO EAT		36	Bogambara Bus Yard
		37	Stadium
4	Flower Song Chinese Restaurant	38	YMBA
12	Victory Hotel	41	Natha Devale
16	Paiva's Moghul Restaurant	42	Archaeological Museum
19	Impala Hotel	43	Temple of the Tooth
20	Bake House	44	National Museum
21	East China Restaurant	45	Kandyan Art Association
26	Devon Restaurant		& Tourist Office
28	White House Restaurant	46	Malwatte Vihara
29	Lake Front Restaurant	54	Buddhist Publication Society
		60	Gangarama Vihara

Explanatory Key to Map on pages 80–81.

contrast to other Ceylonese who were "sharp". Because of the longer exposure of the coastal areas to European influence, it was widely stated that low country people were more at home with foreigners. By contrast, Kandyans were often portrayed as proud, self-glorifying and unfriendly. Such an image of Kandyans as arrogant and rude was established in the written record in the seventeenth century by Robert Knox, the British sailor held captive by the king of Kandy (Knox 1911:101–3) and it still had wide currency among non-Kandyans living in Kandy in 1982 who believed that these traits rendered Kandyans so much less adept at tourism than people from other regions of Sri Lanka.[4]

Kandy may in several respects be less developed as a tourist site than many coastal resorts, but it witnessed during the late 1970s and early 1980s a veritable explosion of tourist accommodation, especially of unlicensed guesthouses operating outside regulations imposed by the Ceylon Tourist Board. Kandy also attracted a very large number of unlicensed guides, widely referred to as 'touts', who again were effectively beyond the control of both the national tourism and local government authorities. The so-called 'informal sector' — those activities which grow up along the margins of the approved and licensed activities — is huge in Kandy. As a popular travel guide book puts it, Kandy is the "guesthouse capital" of Sri Lanka and touts in the town are "pushier and in greater numbers" than anywhere else in the island (Wheeler 1980:95; 1987:135), a fact to which many foreign visitors at their wits end in 1982 could attest. Tourists would tell me with considerable feeling

---

[4] There appear to have been some cultural differences (in kinship, and the degree of 'feudal' development) between the coastal and inland areas of Sri Lanka prior to European penetration (Ryan 1953:11, 15, 201; Wriggins 1960:22), but the differences became much more substantial later precisely because colonisation of the two regions took place three centuries apart. The British had been accustomed to dealing with a separate Kandyan kingdom so when they took control of the whole island, the distinction was enshrined for all sorts of administrative purposes, making it even more real (Roberts 1979:44). The categories 'Kandyan' and 'low country', in fact, were only abandoned for such statistical and other official purposes during the 1980s, although intermarriage and geographical mobility have long made the question 'who is a Kandyan?' somewhat problematic (Roberts 1979:51). The antagonism between Kandyans and other Sri Lankans has often emerged in the modern political arena where Kandyans have felt themselves to be under-represented in the national bureaucracy. Indeed, in the 1920s, Kandyans, aloof from the revivalist and nationalist sentiments of the times, were even arguing for a federal state structure so that their separateness could be institutionalised (K.M. de Silva 1979:144; Moore 1985:211; Nissan 1988:258; Roberts 1979:45). The contrast between 'modern educated' and 'feudal illiterate' has frequently come to the surface in such situations (Seneviratne 1978:140–2). The appointment of a 'low country' man in the 1970s to the position of *Diyavardana Nilame* (the lay custodian of the Temple of the Tooth), who plays a leading role in the arranging of the annual Kandy *perahera*, was itself the occasion for some to express intense regional antagonism.

that they could not get 100 yards down any street in the town without someone coming up to them and asking: "What is your country?" Some commented that, having travelled in other Asian countries, Sri Lankans were more insistent than others when it came to harassing tourists and that Kandy was the worst place they had ever experienced. During my time in Kandy, in fact, I came across a number of tourists cutting their short stay in Kandy even shorter because they simply could not stand this incessant badgering.

A question immediately arises as to why Kandy should have been so noticeably worse than other tourist locations in Sri Lanka. Part of the answer must be the fact that virtually every foreign tourist in Sri Lanka visited Kandy, most very soon after arriving in the country when they are not yet sure of themselves, know little about price levels, and so on. Most of them are also there for a short period of time and so are rushing around trying to do too much, before heading off to the beaches. Size, too, probably has something to do with the problem. Colombo is large and sprawling. Many tourist resorts on the coast are spatially somewhat separate from other settlements. Kandy, on the other hand, seems fairly compact, but with a large number of small shops and guesthouses catering to those who travel at their own pace alone or in pairs, around the island. It is thus an ideal niche in which touts can try their luck and in which those with spare accommodation can try to pick up foreigners who do not know exactly when or where they are going because they have not formulated exact plans. The number of unlicensed guesthouses is certainly important here, for it is largely out of commissions for delivering tourists to such establishments that the guides make much of their income.

The size of the informal tourism sector throughout Sri Lanka was causing the authorities great concern during the early 1980s and statistics from a *Census of the Unauthorised Establishments in the Informal Tourism Sector* were released by the Ceylon Tourist Board in 1984 (C.T.B. 1984d). That survey showed that in 1983 as many as 18,810 people were employed in the informal sector compared with 22,374 in the formal (the hotels, guesthouses and other establishments operating with the approval of and adhering to the standards established by the Ceylon Tourist Board). The 3,129 unlicensed establishments included restaurants as well as places providing accommodation and with 312 out of this total, the Kandy region came second to Galle for the level of tourism activity being carried on outside the control of the national tourism authority. The Ceylon Tourist Board booklet *Welcome to Sri Lanka* for July to September 1982 listed for Kandy 11 hotels, 11 guesthouses and 34 paying guest accommodation establishments, yet everyone knew of literally dozens of other guesthouses operating within the municipality. Ali suggested to me that the number might be as high as one hundred and fifty. Although the informal sector is normally conceived as marginal, in Kandy, it was on an extensive scale. Guesthouses had "grown like mushrooms", as many informants put it, in the late 1970s along the roads leading into Kandy. Lewella, near the Mahaweli river to the east of the city, had become well known as a place where hippies could stay for very little in establishments which frequently provided no modified European facilities whatever. Previously an area of no marked status, it had become a hippy haunt by 1982 and a number of people of fairly modest means had been able to cash in on the presence of these foreigners. Those owning unregistered accommodation, of course, escaped municipal taxes and commercial charges for electricity and water which the licensed establishments had to pay. They presumably evaded income tax as well. During 1982 the antagonism of those bearing the taxes and charges of running legitimate businesses towards the unlicensed operators was clearly coming to a head in Kandy, as it was nationally.

The physical location of the Tourist Board's own information office in Kandy was somewhat symbolic of the difficulties in the relationship between the formal and informal spheres. Over the years, the Board's location had moved from the foyer of the Queen's Hotel, to the *Ulpenge* on the lakeside, to its location in 1982 as a mere desk on the front verandah of the Kandy Art and Craft Association building towards the eastern end of the lake. During 1982 yet another search was on for a site where the rent would be lower but its location was also a problem for another reason, notwithstanding the fact that many tourists visited the art and craft shop to buy metal goods and wood carvings. A site near the railway or bus station or at least in the city centre would have made much more sense than its locale somewhat towards the outskirts of the town. Its peripheral location was made the more absurd by virtue of the fact that tourists casually walking by the lake would normally first see prominently displayed a 'Tourist Information' sign on the *Ulpenge*. This sign actually advertised a business run by an entrepreneur with a number of commercial interests in Kandy, but was frequently assumed by visitors to be, in fact, the official Tourist Board information office. The result was that many tourists had their questions answered and their needs for accommodation and so on met before even finding out where the Tourist Board official was located.

Having mentioned the informal and formal sectors, it is necessary to remark that they do not operate according to completely different system of rules, although the authorities liked to pretend that this was so. On the pavement outside the Kandy Arts and Craft building one day, two traders with small quantities of wares to sell were competing energetically to catch the attention of tourists before they went up the steep flight of steps to the shop. Things got out of hand and the two individuals actually started throwing stones at each other before both moving off. The security guard employed by the craft shop and the Tourist Board official both made highly derogatory comments about the disgraceful display to which foreign visitors had just been treated by these "low types". I was quietly writing on the verandah throughout the incident and the guard, one of whose jobs it was precisely to keep undesirables away from the premises and to prevent tourists being hassled by touts, asked me to give him one of my biros. When I curtly refused his request he apologised and asked me whether I would like to see one of the crafts-men at work on the back verandah who was making the wooden bowls for sale within the shop. I followed him to the back of the building whereupon the crafts-man and the guard tried to sell me a bowl to undercut the prices within. On my return to the front verandah I spoke to the Tourist Board's information officer, a man to whom I had spoken on several occasions before, about the fighting incident, and he made some haughty comments about "ruffians" and then tried to sell me an expensive ticket for a seat to watch the *perahera*, as well as inquiring whether I could get his son into a good school in Australia. He complained bitterly that the entrepreneur around the lake who displayed the 'Tourist Information' sign inter-cepted tourists pretending to be someone he was not, fixed up accommodation for them and made commissions simply by phoning ahead to a guesthouse alerting them to the tourist's imminent arrival. The response of the entrepreneur to such suggestions was that the Tourist Board representative was merely jealous of his own success and that while paid a salary for simply handing out information and maps to tourists, he too tried to make commissions by doing business with them, but was evidently not very successful at it.

MODERN TOURISM GROWTH IN KANDY

Given its religious importance, Kandy has for centuries been a destination for travellers and pilgrims. Given its beauty and climate, it was also a well-estab-lished recreation area during the colonial period for civil servants, merchants, plan-tations owners, and their families. But from the early 1970s onwards, foreigners of a different kind — modern mass tourists — have arrived in Kandy in greater num-bers nearly every year, with many new facilities being created or modified to cope with the growing demand. In December 1975, the Tourist Board's booklet 'Wel-come to Sri Lanka' listed Kandy as having 13 guesthouses and hotels and 10 private homes where the 'Meet the Ceylonese' scheme was in operation. Since that time several large hotels have been built both within the city and on the hills just out-side. The famous Queen's Hotel was undergoing extensive renovations during 1982 in order to upgrade its facilities. A number of substantial private residences had also been converted into establishments with facilities suitable for foreigners, some indistinguishable from small hotels. In two cases, sizeable hotels had been built on land only yards away from the owner's opulent private residence. Although the original 'Meet the Ceylonese' scheme operative in the mid 1970s had long been abandoned, several smaller plush residences had converted rooms or built on extra rooms to the standards required by the Tourist Board to operate as licensed guesthouses.

In two significant ways, however, 1982 was different to 1975. Firstly, in the earlier year, the accommodation listed in the official brochures would very much have represented what was available in Kandy. Not so in 1982 because of the mushrooming of private homes operating as guesthouses without Tourist Board approval. Some such establishments had minimal tourist facilities such as mosquito nets and westernised toilets, but many were virtually unaltered. Nonetheless, in 1982 such homes provided accommodation for hundreds of foreigners visiting Kandy. Secondly, while in 1975 there was optimism, indeed even a 'fascination' about tourism, there was in 1982 a distinct streak of pessimism and some who had taken out substantial bank loans to extend their premises were very worried. In the mid 1970s international tourism appeared to have a rosy future, so such investment seemed sensible. By 1982, however, things were very different. In 1982, with the effects of the recent European recession being felt locally as noticeably fewer tourists arrived in Kandy, many were anxious about meeting the interest payments on their debts. One person highly critical of the level of taxation now imposed on what used to be a favoured industry, was thinking of bypassing the standard Tourist Board advertising to publicise directly his various tourist establishments in Europe in order to ensure that his accommodation remained in demand. Another whose hotel during much of 1982 was almost completely empty, was thinking of saving herself the crippling burden of land taxes by donating her hotel to charity for use as a hospital. Others running small guesthouses thought that they might have only two more years before tourism in Kandy came to a halt altogether.

Although sound statistical data for tourism development specifically in Kandy is limited, something of the local story of modern tourism development can be constructed from the biographies of a number of people who early on became involved in the new industry. Some of the pioneers were still in the business in 1982, while others had long since retired. Patterns of ownership and management had also become complex. Indeed several informants pointed out to me that it was often not clear at all who actually owned what. Some hotels were owned by an individual or at least a few members of one family. Some were owned by a family but were run by management companies with Colombo addresses. Some were Ceylon Hotels Corporation establishments, that is public companies with large numbers of individual shareholders living throughout Sri Lanka, but also sizeable investment by the government itself. A somewhat cynical journalist commented to me that having management carried out by professional firms from Colombo was now very popular because it served to disguise the extent of wealth concentration by making an establishment actually owned by a few people appear something like a public company.

For one wealthy retired lawyer, whose father's home was used for billeting troops during the Second World War, the idea of tourism was a natural outgrowth of that earlier experience of providing facilities for foreigners.[5] It became the more urgent in the early 1970s, according to my informant, when the S.L.F.P. Minister for Housing, whom he regarded as a communist, was thought to be planning the confiscation of luxurious homes from the very wealthy to make accommodation available to the less well-off. To convert a large home with many rooms into a tourist facility was one way of avoiding the less desirable alternative. A Muslim doctor, also worried about this new policy but additionally vulnerable by virtue of being a visible outsider in a Sinhalese city, gave the same justification for getting into tourism. Originally he and his family did all the work themselves, including accountancy. Over the years, however, the duties had become increasingly onerous and with the expectation tourists have of being supplied with alcohol and meat, he stepped back from direct involvement, placing his original home in the hands of a Colombo-based management firm. Later in the 1970s, two entrepreneurs who had made fortunes, the one out of fish trading and the other from the gambling industry, invested large amounts of money in hotel projects.

On a smaller scale, many of those originally involved in the 'Meet the Ceylonese' scheme in the mid 1970s had also dropped out. A well-known bookseller in the town explained to me how a decade previously he and his wife had had 'paying guests'. Food, drink, trips in their car, were all part of providing to foreigners a Sinhalese 'family environment', which the tourism authorities at that time were encouraging. He pointed out to me that all these extras were free and that there was no service charge. He told me that he had dropped out of the scheme because involvement had become too onerous and because tourism had become too commercial, although one could note here that the charges suggested by the Tourist Board for accommodation in the private homes of the relatively well-to-do in 1970 substantially exceeded, in fact, the prices often being charged by many in the informal sector in 1982 after nearly a decade of inflation. In this sense, even with no specific service charge, foreign guests were paying substantially for the hospitality and friendship they received in the earlier period. In one of the most opulent homes in Kandy, a retired lawyer whose home had long been providing tourist accommodation told me that all the guests were booked in by travel agents in Colombo and were handled by servants. He never mixed with the tourists himself and, in fact, did not even know how many guests were staying at his home at any time. A few examples, however, suggest a counter-trend away from increased commercialism

---

5 In 1944 Kandy was the Headquarters of the S-E Asia High Command under Lord Mountbatten, the Supreme Commander of Allied Forces in the area (Karunaratna 1984:90).

and impersonality. One woman felt so strongly about keeping the "personal touch" in tourism that, although she and her husband had operated a largish hotel for many years, she got increasingly disenchanted as the hotel grew bigger and bigger through a series of extensions. Finally she left to open an establishment which she herself occupied but from which she could engage in tourism on a "more homely scale", more in tune with "Sri Lankan traditions of hospitality", as she put it.

The story of a widowed, retired Christian school teacher tells another part of the story of tourism growth in Kandy during the 1970s. Early on she established a Y.M.C.A. just outside Kandy. Her motives were to provide the young traveller with a cheap place to stay in a family atmosphere, and to provide her children, forced since the mid 1950s to be educated in Sinhala, to have the opportunity to meet Europeans and to learn English. She too, partly because of her age, had virtually given up tourism by 1982 and receiving so few guests was refusing to pay the Tourist Board's annual fees for a listing in the 'Welcome to Ceylon' booklet. She also confided in me that most of her children had learned the ways of the tourist only too well. They could all speak reasonable English, but all save one were out of work and consequently hung around the house all day long, spongeing off her instead of earning an income. One of them reputedly supplied hard drugs to tourists in Kandy.

Some owners of the more luxurious private hotels were fairly candid about their original intentions simply to make money from the foreigner. Consequently they were quite prepared to state that Tourist Board rhetoric about preserving Sri Lankan culture was nonsense, because one either kept one's own culture or promoted international tourism, but certainly not both. By contrast, most stories of tourism involvement from those of more moderate mean portrayed their activities as if financial considerations were marginal. Individuals "discovered" that their homes were simply too large when their children had grown up and left. A Bank Manager told me that tourism was just "to give my wife something to do". One person commented that it was "just to occupy the servants". Others suggested that they accidentally got involved in tourism when they offered to help out neighbours who, from time to time, found that they simply did not have enough rooms available. Ambiguity in regard to the relationship between hospitality and commercialism is widely reported in tourism literature (Pearce 1988:132–3), so accounts of the kind above which highlight accidents and ambivalence are not at all surprising, especially given the value Sri Lankans place on generosity and hospitality. This is a culture in which certain kinds of commercial activity are distinctly frowned upon and are associated with specific ethnic categories. Thus, for every informant who spoke about simply making money from tourists, another would speak of "traditional hospitality" or liking "foreign friends". Some spoke of how tourists could experience real Sri Lankan life and how locals could learn about foreigners, while others scoffed at the idea that tourists were interested in experiencing other ways of life.

Although numerous people in Kandy commented to me on these issues, there were not always clear correlations between the replies and the kind of establishment in which a person was involved. For instance, I raised with several hotel managers the general issue of the relationship between tourism and Sri Lankan hospitality. In particular I inquired why, if tourists came to Sri Lanka to see a different culture, they stayed in hotels which were very much the same the world over. What was particularly Sri Lankan about the hotels they managed? Some managers claimed that they tried to create a deliberately Sinhalese atmosphere in their hotel, or that services were provided in "a Sinhalese way". Some claimed that tourism was a natural extension of the traditional courteousness of the local people. Others, however, baldly stated that there was nothing Sri Lankan about the hotels, but tourists, they said, did not come for local culture and certainly did not want to experience or share another way of life; they came for rest, comfort, safety and cleanliness and perhaps a minimal exposure to some exotic food, all of which could be obtained in a quality hotel. The function of a good hotel was to supply tourists with what they wanted and there was nothing particularly Sri Lankan about the way in which they did this. Such hotel managers added pointedly that one would not really experience "the Sri Lankan way of life", or "a family atmosphere" in the guesthouses either.

In the period 1975–1982, another feature of tourism changed noticeably in Kandy. The eldest son of the proprietor of the Y.M.C.A. just outside Kandy told me that he had been the first guide in the town. While still at school he used to meet tourists at the railway station at lunch time, partly for fun, but also to help out with his family's finances. Although still indirectly involved in tourism in 1982 by virtue of running a business supplying seafood to hotels and shops in a number of 'hill country' towns such as Nuwara Eliya and Kandy, he had long since abandoned a guiding role. In the very early years, he told me, tourists were pleased to be greeted at the station. This was a period before good guide books were readily available, so tourists did not know much about the town or where to find cheap accommodation. He would greet them and then take them by the local bus to the Y.M.C.A. It was not long, however, before others took on the same guiding role, and by the late 1970s, according to him, a frequent response by tourists to being cajoled at the station entrance by a number of guides all competing for their attention was simply "Fuck off!". "There was no longer respect in it", he explained, and so he had abandoned the activity whilst another kind of person took over, a frequent development as far as tourism is concerned and noted in many other countries besides Sri Lanka (Cohen 1988:18–19). Ali had watched the evolution of the guiding system in Kandy from the mid 1970s to the early 1980s when numbers had swollen, in his estimation, from a dozen or so to over one hundred and twenty. According to Ali, whilst some of the more experienced guides occasionally passed on their skills to others, most people simply tried their luck with little preparation. In the intensely competitive days of 1982 there was a great deal of anger and frustration on the streets of Kandy and Ali attributed some of this to the fact so many of the guides had no real idea of how to do the job properly and hence made little money from it.

By 1982, for many tourists, the five minutes walk from the railway or bus station to the cheap cafes in the centre of Kandy, had become an uncomfortable experience of continuous harassment and bad language. Not only were there the teenage street guides, there were also numerous young children trying to wrench away one's luggage in the station carpark to put it into a taxi boot. There were also several middle-aged professional people — school teachers, business men and notaries among them — in the station entrance vying for business among the groups of foreigners getting out of the train. In fact the station was not even their first encounter with such people, because some guides, perceiving how competitive Kandy had become, actually travelled on the train between Colombo and Kandy to try to secure their 'catch' before arriving in the town. It had become a regular feature of any journey by train into Kandy to witness several guides methodically moving from carriage to carriage, speaking to all the tourists in the hope that they could fix them up with accommodation. Because there were frequently several guides on each train, travellers often arrived in Kandy after the three hour journey in a tired and exasperated condition. By 1982, in fact, the 'catchment area' had extended even further. Guides from Kandy were trying to pick up their tourists on the station platform at Colombo, outside Colombo railway station, or even outside the cheaper hotels and guesthouses in Colombo as tourists started to make their way to the station. Felix, one of my guide informants in Kandy with eight years experience told me that on a number of occasions rivalry between guides had reached violent proportions. One guide some years previously had been pushed out of a moving train. Fights with broken bottles, sometimes leading to serious injury, had also apparently occurred in Kandy. He himself felt that there were now so many guides in Kandy that they had "spoiled" tourism in the town. Many a visitor in 1982 would, no doubt, have agreed.

The same guide told me that over the previous ten years or so, the nature of the tourists coming had also changed. His recollection was that tourists had earlier been very generous and that earning 100 rupees (approximately $U.S. 5) per day was not difficult. In 1982 there were too many guides, several travel guide books in a range of European languages were available, the Tourist Board told foreigners not to speak to the guides, and to cap it all, tourists were now poorer. He knew very well that a good many tourists were not particularly rich in their own countries, that their fortnight annual holiday was the result of saving hard all year, and that having spent so much on the air ticket many did not, in fact, have a great deal of spending money left over.

The malaise felt by the Kandy street guides during 1982 when noticeably fewer Europeans arrived was shared by others involved in tourism in the town. Many people wondered whether tourism in Sri Lanka had peaked and so numbers would now start to decline. A number of owners of small guesthouses who had tried to cash in quickly on tourism were not very sure about taking out loans to build an extension because they thought that tourism might be good for only another two years or so. A number of them felt that the Tourist Board's declared intention to concentrate more on high spending tourists would kill the industry in Kandy because so many tourists simply did not want to spend their time in hotels when they could quite comfortably stay in less expensive dwellings and so have more money to spend on other things. Several hotel managers, too, were somewhat doubtful about the future. Most still pooh-poohed the idea that the Maldives would become a serious threat which could take significant numbers of tourists away from Sri Lanka. Nonetheless confidence was somewhat guarded. Some commentators were suggesting that the extensive renovations proceeding at the Queen's Hotel were quite unnecessary because more luxury accommodation was simply not called for in Kandy. Many greeted the announcement late in 1982 that a 'five star' hotel would be built at Katugastota just outside Kandy with derision; even planning such projects in Colombo itself was misguided, given that there were strong signs that tourism was heading for a significant downturn. Some of the industries clearly geared to tourist demand had already peaked and were now clearly in decline, according to some onlookers. The story of batik manufacture is illustrative here.

Although batik making is actually an ancient art in Sri Lanka (Sievers 1983: 48), it had been largely forgotten. In its modern form, so I was told by a prominent batik designer in Matara, it had to be learned afresh from Indonesia. One successful muslim batik maker in Kandy explained how a decade before, when the idea of batiks was new in town, one could put virtually any price on a piece and still find a tourist willing to buy it. Profit margins then, with only a few people making batiks, were enormous, well over 100%, he claimed. He, trained as an engineer, had been able to buy a house outright within six years from the proceeds of batik sales. By 1982, however, it was a very different story, according to my informant. The price of batiks and the strong tourist demand meant that many people, some with precious little talent, had entered the market. There was now an over-supply and prices had fallen considerably. In fact, one large batik shop with a good local reputation was closing down during 1982, with the intention of reopening as a general 'white goods' and electrical appliances outlet catering rather more to Sri Lankan migrant workers returned from the Middle East than to foreigners. That market, the owner of the shop told me, was more assured than was tourist demand for batiks. With the European recession of 1981–2 noticeably affecting the number of tourist arrivals in Kandy, the price of batiks had become highly negotiable. In addition, there was simply no domestic demand for them.

My main informant as regards batik manufacture in Kandy painted a very grim picture of the future, believing that this market was now in irreversible decline. He still made batiks for one Muslim shopkeeper in the Kandy Central Market. Although he had exhibited his designs overseas, he was quite forthcoming that he would not want his works displayed in his own home. In his view batiks were garish and vulgar and he personally disliked them intensely. He presumed that Europeans liked them because their bright colours cheered them up during cold, depressing winters. He still had six young girls in his employ making batiks in his own back garden, but he was not optimistic, suspecting that he might have to reduce the number of his assistants still further. He also claimed that batik making, like other industries connected with the tourism industry, was one where foreigners really made most profit. Although cheap vegetable dyes and local cloth could be used, high quality work required imported cloth and chemical dyes from Germany. Such dyes were extremely expensive, he claimed, so the real profit makers from the Sri Lankan batik industry were the German chemical companies in any case.

SOCIO-ECONOMIC PERCEPTIONS

Whilst many informants suspected that foreigners were the real beneficiaries of international tourism in Sri Lanka in general, it was also believed that those economic benefits which accrued to locals were distributed in a very inequitable fashion. It was important, therefore, to explore in depth local perceptions as to who was making money from tourism in Kandy and also to inquire whether and in what ways this industry, with the effects it was having on various people's circumstances, was changing the town. Was the new industry sufficiently large-scale, for instance, for one to be able to say that there were significant socio-economic changes occurring in Kandy as a direct result? There are small coastal villages in Sri Lanka where the advent of mass tourism has brought very considerable change. Hippy communities in particular, it is often said, have had a profound effect on the behaviour of the young. In some areas land prices have soared, very much to the benefit of Colombo entrepreneurs and speculators. Kandy, however, is a large city, not a small village, and although tourism gives an income to those who work in hotels, guesthouses and shops and employment to taxi drivers, guides, prostitutes, craft workers, and so on, a view frequently put to me was that tourism had not substantially affected the town or the local community in any great way.

This view is possibly correct to the extent that many of the changes that have taken place in Kandy since the early 1970s are tied up with more general forces for social change in Sri Lanka and so are not specifically attributable to tourism. Probably changes have not taken place in terms of the distribution of wealth of a kind to say that the prevailing pattern of social stratification has been transformed. For a start, many of the profits from tourism go to share holders and entrepreneurs, not necessarily living locally; indeed, much of the profit flows to the central government or to overseas interests. But secondly, tourism is an industry notorious for the 'uphill' flow of benefits: profits normally flow in tourism to those who are already wealthy, and thus the overall effect of tourism is often to reinforce existing patterns of inequality. A few very wealthy individuals or families in Kandy were receiving income from hotels and large guesthouses. A hundred or more would be gaining from renting rooms in their homes, but few in these circumstances in such amounts as to significantly affect their social position. Hundreds working in menial jobs in shops, cafes and hotels owed their employment to tourism, but again, no large-scale changes were resulting, although in general the tourism industry paid wages somewhat above the norm for other blue collar and service occupations. Occasionally those in the informal tourism sector such as the street guides made windfall gains, but such income was unreliable, the money often quickly spent, and for most of the time such people were living a hand-to-mouth existence. Although several hotels had been built on land in the hills around Kandy, in the town itself there was very little spare land, so in this area, unlike some coastal areas, extensive transfers of land ownership, I was told, had not taken place. It was Ali's view that overall tourism had had no great transforming effect on Kandy and had not fundamentally affected the distribution of wealth in the locality. For many people tourism was just a way of securing a job; for those of modest means it might be an opportunity to "make do" or "keep up"; only those who had sufficient capital to invest in tourism were able to make large sums of money, but they invariably already belonged to the 'super rich' category.

When asking a range of people in Kandy the question "who makes most money from tourism?", I normally supplied a number of categories for my informants: foreign capitalists, Sri Lanka's elite, the Sri Lankan government, middle class house owners, guides, businessmen, shop owners, prostitutes, beggars. A tourist car driver and journalist who claimed to have made 116,000 rupees ($U.S. 5,800) commission from one large gem sale in Colombo in 1979 said that he was able to purchase a house on the outskirts of Kandy with the income earned during that one year, stated that the foreign capitalists were the main winners. He waxed lyrical about the fact that foreigners did not lend capital to poor countries for the development of such countries, but for their own benefit. The government could not prevent this process, he stated, for to do so would be tantamount to an admission that "for years we have been suckers". He was also aggrieved at the way the "kick back" system worked to the advantage of top management. He had once lost a driver's job with a large Colombo travel agency because he had refused to share his commissions with the director. He regarded it as quite unfair that an executive on a substantial salary should expect to take a cut from deals in which he was not directly involved. When I raised the general issue of commission with the director in question he claimed that his firm fairly distributed commissions to its employees and that he would never interfere in the relationship between a driver and his client. As was so often the case in my research, specific events yielded wildly divergent accounts, a result often reflecting, no doubt, the pecuniary interests of those doing the narrating.

The view that consistently came from senior hotel management in Kandy was that it was the foreign travel agents who received the lion's share from tourism, and for very little work too. Foreign investors, gem and batik shop owners also made good incomes, according to them. A director of a leading Sri Lankan travel agency commented that there was always negotiation over prices. Foreign firms could not simply impose prices for a package tour or impose a room rate on a hotel, but he did concede that the European firms had superior power when it came to fixing prices. A number of those to whom I spoke were convinced that the government itself had become the major beneficiary of tourism, by way of income tax, entrance fees, departure tax, business turnover tax, and so on. Many made the point angrily, alleging that the authorities were beginning to exploit the tourism industry, rather than encouraging it as had occurred at the outset. A senior member of the Ministry of State, however, was quite adamant that the government should make money, for it was out of such revenue that it could keep up its public spending commitments which benefited all Sri Lankans. One of the most poignant comments came from an Australian-born Buddhist monk resident just outside Kandy. He had no doubt that foreigners made the most with the assistance of the local ruling elite. According to him, the government was really saying to foreigners: "We are a poor country. We need your foreign exchange. Come, take the women. Rip us off".

Whilst the overall shape of the Kandyan community may not have been basically changed by the influx of tourists, simply asking the question "who makes the money from tourism?" produced a great deal of information about how locals perceived their own society. I was frequently told that Muslims in Kandy were more conservative than their cosmopolitan counterparts in Colombo and that they largely kept out of tourism, preferring more traditional business activities. Tamils, it was often said, very much kept themselves to themselves as a group, and many had difficulties in speaking English. One thing evident from the official Tourist Board booklets was that, at least in the approved accommodation sector, there was a predominance of low country Sinhalese names, and interesting explanations were given for the relative absence of Kandyans from the tourist trade. The low country Sinhalese perceived themselves to be fluent in English, friendly, and used to western ways. By contrast, Kandyans, particularly *Radala* people (the elite sub-group within the highest status *Goyigama* caste, who had been influential at the Kandyan court and some of whom had retained considerable influence under the British) were viewed as cold, snobbish, cruel towards their servants, awkward with foreigners, and unwilling to deal with the *hoi poloi*, such as taxi drivers and guides. Kandyans were "old-fashioned", lived in another era and simply did not understand the needs of the tourist. Nor were they particularly astute commercially, although some were described as exceedingly greedy. Land reforms this century have greatly restricted the amount of land held by this elite, but even without such legislative changes, much of their holdings are not in suitable places for tourism development, or their homes have not been modified to suit westerners. Meanwhile, prime sites around the lake in Kandy had been purchased a generation ago by low country people from under the noses of Kandyans not sufficiently sharp to appreciate their potential value, I was told. Like most 'images' of a society conveyed by one section of the population, this view of Kandyans contained a rich admixture of both truth and falsehood. By 1982 a number of prominent Kandyan families were, in fact, involved in tourism, converting their homes and investing considerable sums in the industry. And, in fact, one of the very earliest complexes of tourist accommodation was on land owned by the highest status local *Radala* family on the outskirts of Kandy right next to where the paddy fields began. Since the early 1970s various members of this family had catered for the whole spectrum of tourists, from hippies right through to those wanting the luxury of hot water in their rooms.

The stereotype of the aristocratic Kandyan inept at tourism is only one of a number of local caricatures.[6] Kandyan informants, of course, had a number of equivalent images of their low country colleagues. It was hard, in fact, not to see snobbery or envy lying behind almost every statement about tourism development in the city. For, instance, those in the approved sector, whether in private hotels or large guesthouses, commented in a very hostile vein on those running unlicensed premises, especially the poorer people letting their "unhygienic" premises to "lower types" of foreigner, where food was unpalatable, standards of cleanliness

---

[6] As mentioned earlier in this chapter, such stereotypes have a long history. Knox not only commented that Kandyans were rude, but also that they were crafty and untrustworthy (1911:101–3). Percival at the beginning of the nineteenth century stated that they were polite but insincere, and compared them unfavourably to the low country people who had been exposed to European contact (1975:153–4, 169). Tennent at mid-century observed that they were obsessed with rank, were less sharp than their low country colleagues and were suspicious of strangers (1859:222–3).

poor, and where belongings were, it was said, frequently stolen. Although such comments were frequently presented in moralistic terms about protecting Sri Lanka's image, tourism clearly generated an enormous amount of spite and resentment. One insightful informant, in reply to my query about whether tourism had made any significant changes to local society, said: "No, all it has done is give the wealthy something more to be fiercely jealous about". It is worth remembering that in this society, for all the Buddhist emphasis on positive emotions such as equanimity, compassion and kindness, jealousy (*irisiawa*) remains a very powerful trait in the Sri Lankan psyche (Warrell 1990c:19).

Only one informant, a bank manager whose wife ran their own home as a guesthouse, provided me with a systematic model of how the economic benefits of tourism were distributed. It was a fairly straightforward model of social stratification in which the greater opportunities for making money existed the further up in the social hierarchy one was. The basic social divisions were familiar western class divisions, although it must be recognised that in Sri Lanka class term such as 'middle class' more often refer to 'status groups' and thus refer to lifestyle, education, language, and such like, rather than to strictly marxian analytical notions (Nissan 1987:8; Roberts 1979 *et al.*, 1989:26–7).[7] The bank manager divided into two categories the elite of local society. The "super wealthy" were those who had made their fortunes in other business activities and who had used their gains there to finance the building of hotels or the purchase of prime real estate. Others in the elite, less wealthy than those of the previous small group, had professional backgrounds in law, medicine, and the like. Again, professional incomes over many years or in some cases over generations, had given individuals prime real estate and homes which could easily be extended or converted into quality tourist accommodation. Some members of this elite were Kandyan 'aristocrats' on traditional land near the city. One such family had even converted the site of their 'town house' into a hotel cum restaurant after several years lack of commercial success as a set of shops. With one highly noticeable exception (an individual who had made a fortune in the fish transport business before investing in a hotel), most would be described as of the westernised, educated elite. As mentioned earlier in this chapter, some were still directly involved in running their affairs, others had long since withdrawn to allow professional managers to handle their business interests.

One rung down the hierarchy in the bank manager's model were those who would normally be described as upper middle class. Here the tourism story

---

[7] Social structure has often been spoken of in Sri Lanka in terms of a mix of both caste and class (Ryan 1953:27), but the importance of caste nowadays is hard to gauge. Caste appears to structure very little in daily life, except perhaps marriage. Although 'caste consciousness' is certainly not dead, today it is often a matter of some considerable embarrassment (Spencer 1990:40).

changes somewhat. Into this category my informant placed people such as himself. With salaries of around 4000 rupees ($U.S. 200) per month, he and the few others who fell into this small category normally referred to themselves as "comfortably off" rather than rich. Tourism here was seldom portrayed as a commercial venture, but more as a hospitable, auxiliary activity, often fulfilling the goal of maintaining their position in society during a period of rapid inflation. It was said that occasionally, through exceptional success, particular families might be able to propel themselves into the lower end of the elite. In fact one family, through a combination of running a shop and adding tourism facilities progressively to their home, had managed over seven years to make sufficient money to plan the building of a small hotel nearby on other land that they owned; only the gloomy tourism prospects in 1982 were keeping them from pressing ahead with the project more swiftly.

Further down the salary scale came middle class professional people such as university lecturers and school principals; and beneath them the lower middle class — clerks, post masters, school teachers, etc. A number of people in this latter group were involved in tourism as a quite critical effort to supplement their government-controlled salaries during a period of inflation. Many a school teacher on a fairly low salary in the region of 1100 rupees ($U.S. 55) per month spoke with considerable jealousy and resentment about the "half-educated fellows" — manual and technical workers — who after working in the Middle East for a year or two, were filling their homes with diverse electrical and other consumer goods as symbols of their newly found wealth (see Gunasinghe 1984:40–1). One family in which both husband and wife had formerly been school teachers, now rented out two of their rooms to tourists. The running of the home was in the hands of the wife who, having no servants, did all the extra cooking required herself. The husband, still employed as a teacher, would try to pick up tourists from the railway station, usually late in the evening. He used his extra income from tourism to buy the raw materials for making concrete pillars in his back garden so as to extend his house in order to leave his son and daughter a more decent inheritance. He was very aware of the fact that given the high salaries earned by Sri Lankans on contract in countries such as Saudi Arabia, the "uncouth" family on the plot next to him had earned overseas in two years what it would take him over a decade to earn from teaching. It was a comparison which, given his facility in English and his educational attainments, rankled him deeply, considerably upsetting his notions of relative social status.[8] He and his wife frequently looked up the road towards their neighbour's large home, where commotion and displays of bad manners were fre-

---

[8] Occasionally tourism brings great wealth to some low status individuals via a massive demand for items such as masks. But it is still frequently an uphill battle for such individuals to transform their new found wealth into a communally accepted higher status (Simpson 1993).

quently in evidence. They said that the men who lived there were extremely rowdy and they also found it embarrassing that one of the women worked in the nearby gambling house, itself owned by one of the wealthy tourist entrepreneurs in Kandy. Their only consolation was the expectation that the *nouveau riche* family would spoil itself; already, they said, the violent arguments within the household were getting more frequent.[9]

The bank manager who formulated the model for me claimed that with one or two notable exceptions, the middle class just managed to maintain their status by gaining a little money from tourism. The situation at the bottom of the social hierarchy was very different. The lower classes were not, for the most part, in a position to make money from tourism, and those who did made little. Those who did not get any additional income, either directly or indirectly, from tourism, in fact suffered from the adverse effects of rising prices on their standard of living. At the top of the lower class division he placed village cultivators who grew their own food. Below them came bus conductors, security guards, and the like, and beneath them waiters, carpenters, tailors and manual workers in general. Next to bottom were the tea estate workers and at the very bottom beggars. Some people whom he labelled 'working class' did offer rooms to tourists, but hardly any had been able to afford to improve their facilities. He referred to one widowed, middle-aged woman living not very far away from him as "Queen of the poor". She tried her best to get tourists, but the quality of her food and the toilet facilities were quite unacceptable, so no one, apparently, ever stayed very long.

The bank manager's wife, like several others to whom I spoke, confidently claimed that the poor were not jealous of the money being made from tourism; they had no hope so were not dismayed by their inability to profit. On the other hand, both husband and wife and nearly every guide I spoke to, explained, sometimes quite humorously, how tourism had caused enormous jealousy between the fairly well off, even creating in some of them aspirations quite out if touch with reality. A senior employee of the education department in the locality was spending a great deal of money adding rooms and shower facilities to his home and seemed to be permanently preoccupied with how many tourists other establishments had. This was scarcely surprising given the relative inaccessibility of his home and the fact that neither he nor his wife would take any active role in catching foreigners in the town. They, in fact, had one long-stay foreign research worker living with them and when they discovered that I was attached to the University of Peradeniya they expected me to stay also, having sworn the person already there to secrecy about

---

[9] This new source of wealth from migrant labour is so unsettling the Sri Lankan sense of social hierarchy that some returning migrants are sufficiently conscious of the jealousy their new-found wealth will create that they engage in anti-sorcery rituals to keep themselves safe from mystical attack (Kapferer 1988:107–8).

the level of rent that he was paying. On every occasion I met the owner in town or his wife at the University I was asked where I was staying at that particular moment and how many tourists were there. When it became clear that I had no plans to stay at their establishment, I was asked if I could refer Europeans I met to them, provided such people were prepared to stay for a reasonable length of time. It was too much trouble, they told me, to make provision for foreigners who would stay for just a day or two.

Informants often suggested to me that while occasionally someone from an upper middle class position became very rich and just as occasionally a middle class person could, through the location of property or just good management, make a lot of money from tourism, it was very much those already wealthy who were best placed to benefit from tourism. In that sense, socio-economic positions were confirmed, the gaps between strata were widened, rather than the overall social structure being significantly changed by the advent of international tourism. Some individual mobility had undoubtedly occurred, but the higher up the hierarchy to begin with, the easier was further advancement. At the bottom, the impossibility of obtaining loans for improving facilities and so the impossibility of obtaining official registration, put a very definite limit on the involvement of the poor in tourism, although, as will become clear in Chapter 5, there are a number of roles available in the informal tourism arena which do not depend upon owning accommodation. That possibility and the complex indirect income and employment effects of tourism, make it all the more difficult to provide a solid answer to the question "who is making the money out of tourism in Kandy?" For a start, it is not possible for many employees to establish a distinctively tourist-derived income: taxi drivers, waiters, and the like, clearly cater to both foreigners and locals. Adding to the difficulty here is also the fact that in the sizeable informal tourism arena people were evading various taxes and charges; it would hardly have been in their interests to be too explicit about their income in conversations with me.

Whilst I have outlined above one fairly formal model for the socio-economic consequences of tourism for Kandyan society, it must be stressed that in the main I have set out in this section little more than a set of claims and opinions, some patently tied up with envy or camouflage, many of which may thus be wildly inaccurate, whether by deliberate deceit or not. At the same time, such responses, whether accurate, misguided or deliberate lies, are themselves valid social representations indicative of how local people perceive international tourism's impact on their community.

THE EVENTS OF 1982

A series of events in mid 1982 well illustrates how forces linked in a variety of ways to tourism development were having an effect on life in Kandy. Some of them were summed up in a somewhat sensational newspaper article entitled "Kandy after dark" (*Island*, 5 May) which concerned the way in which thieves and criminals "took over" around the lake after sunset. The lake had become the venue for thieves, pickpockets, drug dealers, prostitutes and touts trying to get tourists into accommodation or to Kandyan dance performances. Everything that this article stated went on around the lake after dark was fairly common knowledge. I myself made no systematic inquiries about the drug trade in Sri Lanka, for fear of attracting too much attention to myself, but one could not walk around the lake in the evening without several people asking if one wanted any *ganja*. There were also several guides in Kandy with a reputation for dealing in hard drugs, drugs very much linked to the tourist trade. Outside the Temple of the Tooth, the sacred heart of the city, on most evenings would be prostitutes of both sexes, both adults and children, and drivers in hire cars waiting for their clients to emerge from the Temple on their way to a liaison with a prostitute in a hotel or guesthouse on the outskirts of Kandy. There is no doubt that tourist money has contributed to the growth of prostitution in Kandy, but at the same time, it must also be recognised that prostitution catering to both the poor and the wealthy in local society existed prior to international tourism. Some people also stated that the generosity and gullibility of foreigners had directly led to a marked increase in begging in the town, which created a bad impression of Kandy for the tourists themselves, as well as being a general public nuisance. Many irked by this were actually urging the local authorities to forcibly remove the beggars and to advise foreigners not to give anything to them. Again, though, begging preceded mass tourism, and many local people regularly give money to the poor, even if not as much as some tourists do. Tourism may well have produced more beggars, but their existence cannot simply be attributed to the foreign presence.

The situation is different with those the authorities and guesthouse owners commonly refer to as "touts", who were widely regarded as the major menace to the operation of tourism in Kandy during 1982. The guides who worked the streets were mainly teenage or young adult males, and estimates of their numbers ranged from 100 to 300. Frequently hassled by the police and other authorities, their reputation among polite society and those engaged in the formal tourism arena is summed up in one expression — "wolves in sheep's clothing". These were the "semi-literate parasites" who would fleece tourists, get them into all sorts of difficulty, and even rob them without scruple. Early in May, in fact, the police had arrested three street guides in Kandy in connection with the brutal rape of a French tourist making her way to her guesthouse one evening. She had been left battered and unconscious just a few hundred yards away from the lake in the very heart of the town (*Daily News,* 4 May). One of the guides I spoke to regularly on my street corner base was one of three who had been held in custody over this incident. Another guide to whom I often spoke one day took me into the public library to read up on the story. He was incensed that the police should straightaway have pounced on the street guides as the obvious suspects. He thought his friend stupid for bragging to the police about the incident, for he had had nothing to do with the incident. After a few days, in fact, all three guides had been released when some strangers to Kandy were convicted of the crime. My guide informant predicted that this subsequent conviction would not appear in the papers accompanied by suitable comments about wrongly detaining local guides. He was right.

The nature of the street guide, as we shall see in Chapter 5, is somewhat different to this violent/robber stereotype, and the nature of the relationship between the guides, the guesthouse operators and municipal authorities has to be understood before the existence of this irredeemably bad image of them can be understood. For some in Kandy in 1982, however, the touts were jeopardising the very future of tourism. The *Sun* (30 June) even carried the headline: "Do touts control tourism in Kandy?" This article related how twenty two shopkeepers had presented a signed petition to the Deputy Inspector-General of Police in Kandy, insisting that he use his powers to wipe out the menace of the touts. The expression "guerilla warfare" was used and stories were told of how touts harassed tourists outside or inside shops, demanding money from the shop keeper after tourists had gone. Touts were said to be diverting tourists away from shops where they received no commission, so they were, in effect, exerting a stranglehold over their trade. The Tourist Police, the petitioners argued, were doing nothing to stop this situation. A letter in the *Sun* (27 October) asserted that the tout and beggar problems had been more or less effectively eliminated by the police in Colombo and asked why the same had not occurred in Kandy.

Specialised contingents of Tourist Police are often recommended in national tourism plans and one was established in Kandy in 1979, the other two locations in Sri Lanka where such a units were in place being Colombo and Hikkaduwa. In 1982 the Tourist Police in Kandy, some of them with no special training for tourist-related problems, consisted of an Inspector, a sergeant and three constables, all housed in a small building a few yards away from the main Police Station in the town. The main tasks of the special unit were to act quickly in any case of friction between tourists and locals. This might be to solve a rent dispute, investigate the theft of a tourist's belongings, follow up a complaint by a guesthouse owner about the behaviour of one of his foreign guests, to intercept a tourist leaving without paying rent, or to take swift action when a tourist had been pick-pocketed. The unit, in other words, concerned itself with problems from both ends of tourist-local relationships. According to the Inspector to whom I spoke, the essence of their work was speed, given that tourists were normally in any one place for a limited period of time and so would not welcome long delays in settling their affairs. Indeed, so much was the emphasis on instant action, that no statistical data were available to me about the number of cases that the unit had dealt with over the years for the simple reason, I was told, that no records were kept. If a matter could not be solved immediately and amicably, the courts would have to be involved and such matters were then handed over to the regular police authorities to deal with in the normal way, the Inspector informed me. When I raised with him the subject of the shopkeepers' petition he expressed considerable dismay. He conceded that there was a serious local tout problem, but he stated that in all the time he had been stationed in Kandy not once had any shopkeeper made a complaint to him about the guides. The petition was "out of the blue" and most unfortunate, since it clearly put his unit in a very poor light.

During 1982 the guides in Kandy were increasingly being used as scapegoats for nearly everything that was regarded as undesirable about tourism. Viewed objectively, however, they were only doing what other people were doing, namely using those strategies which their circumstances and assets permitted to tap into a new flow of resources. This was going on both inside and outside the tourism arena, for in almost all areas of life in Sri Lanka, informal systems grow up on the margins of approved activities. For instance, when a new regional office of Immigration and Emigration was opened in Kandy in 1982 to assist with the processing of contract labourers going to the Middle East, it was only a few days before the newspapers were reporting that touts were outside, using bribes, intimidating applicants, and forgeing passports. Con men were even working in the Temple of the Tooth, posing as official guides and trying to prevent some foreigners from going inside unless they paid for their services. Purists complained that the temple authorities themselves had already compromised themselves in regard to money and tourism. Occasionally tourists entered the Temple dressed in an unacceptable manner — men in very short shorts, women in revealing blouses and skirts. There was a strong sense among some locals that foreigners who did not dress appropriately should simply be refused entry because they did not respect Sri Lankan culture. Instead of an outright ban, however, the Temple authorities chose instead to hire out lengths of cloth to foreigners to wrap around their bodies to cover up the offending parts. Decency was preserved and the authorities made some money, a solution not acceptable to the critics. Indeed, a number of my informants stated candidly that behind all the rumpus about "low types" edging their way into tourism, there were wealthy and influential people, even those respectable ones themselves complaining about international tourism, who would personally be making considerable sums from the industry. The double standards often associated with tourism were well exposed by a journalist in Kandy who also worked as a tourist car driver (*Sun* 8, 29 September 1982). His newspaper articles were striking in that they essentially adopted a 'worm's eye' view of what was going on in Kandy. The journalist asserted that much of the condemnation of the guides by hoteliers and guesthouse owners in terms of preserving the reputation of Kandy or treating tourists with courtesy was sheer hypocrisy. Their rhetoric simply camouflaged their annoyance that the poor could divert money from their own pockets, he claimed. All the rhetoric coming from the reputable about kindness and understanding was a red herring: "the Ceylonese, rich and poor alike, have x-ray eyes; they look straight through a foreigner's jacket and see the wallet, not his heart".

Street guides lead an uneasy existence with the authorities. They certainly felt that they were unfairly picked on by the police, for whom they had little respect in general, alleging that the police themselves were involved in the same 'under the counter' activities as everyone else. One guide told me that anyone could walk into the local police station and buy what they wanted from the lost or stolen property held there, with the police on duty at the time simply pocketing the money. The police in Sri Lanka, it is true, do have a general reputation for brutality, political interference and corruption (*Daily Mirror*, 9 September 1982), and so it is not surprising that they should be accused of being very selective as to whom they apprehended. Why, guides asked me, is it that the people with wealth could carry on all sorts of nefarious activity and go around in the knowledge that they would not be interfered with? Why was it that if a guide went up to speak to a foreigner, they might find a plain-clothed police officer immediately come up to them and warn them that if anything happened to that visitor they would have to answer for it? Why was it that places like the elephant bath at Katugastota which had all the characteristics of a typical 'tourist trap', were left resolutely alone by the police? Originally this site on the banks of the Mahaweli river was simply a place where, at certain times of the day, working elephants would be brought by their riders to bathe. By 1982, however, mahouts, described in the *Sun* (26 September 1982) as "laws unto themselves", would wait all day in the one place with their elephants for any tourist passing along the road. Elephants were trained to sit directly in front of or right behind a hire car, preventing the car from moving off. Once on an elephant, a tourist might suddenly find himself at the rough end of a bargain when the mahout decided to charge an exorbitant fee for getting the elephant to let the tourist down. Stories were in abundance of petrified Europeans paying high sums of money just to get off an animal and be out of the place. I never once saw police in this vicinity and indeed was told that the situation was so out of hand that locals also avoided the road because they too would be abused by the mahouts who wanted to carry on their strong-arm tactics with tourists unobserved by others.

Touts were occasionally arrested and fined in court. Occasionally, as in the rape case, groups of them were held in detention, as prime suspects when mischief occurred. Annually, however, towards the end of July and before the large crowds arrived in Kandy for the *perahera*, the most notorious pickpockets and touts would be rounded up and put behind bars for at least ten days until the celebrations had ended and the crowds had dispersed. Thus, it was no surprise when on 27 July the *Daily News* announced the rounding up of fourteen people in Kandy who would be remanded in custody until August 10. Such a move was to ensure that the *perahera* went smoothly. The 1982 festival season in Kandy, though, did not proceed smoothly at all. For a start, the city of Kandy itself was not being portrayed in the national press in a particularly favourable light. The *Weekend* on 1 August, just as Kandy was beginning to fill up with thousands of tourists for the culmination of the ten day festival, carried a story entitled "Kandy Down in the Dumps". The President of the Kandy Ratepayers Association was complaining about the water shortage in the municipality, dirty cafes, bad roads, pollution in the lake, inadequate schools, and all the vices attendant on tourism. Kandy, the article stated, was "being used like a prostitute by some. The city earns valuable foreign exchange by selling Kandy as a splendid tourist attraction but Kandy gets none of the returns". The President of the Young Men's Buddhist Association complained how Buddhists could no longer afford to purchase seats to get a good view of the *perahera*, which was above all a pageant to honour the Buddha. The Mayor of Kandy, in the same article, complained that touts flourished in Kandy like flocks of crows, a powerful local image given that at dusk each day hundreds of screeching crows would gather in trees near the Queen's Hotel. Participants in the procession were complaining about their rewards and conditions and a major row exploded as to whether the *Diyavardana Nilame*, the lay custodian of the Temple of the Tooth (who was also the Sri Lankan Minister of Justice), had abused his power.

Perahera time in Kandy, particularly on the last two nights of the festival, is a time when the city is packed with people from the surrounding villages. Thousands of others make journeys from all over the island to see the spectacle. Special public transport is put on. Large contingents of police are brought in to control the crowds. Food prices and hotel prices skyrocket. Hotels are full and rooms sell to latecomers at very high prices, having been block-booked by travel agencies anything up to a year in advance. The procession itself, which starts out from and returns to the Temple of the Tooth, involves carrying the Buddha's tooth relic around the streets of the city and is one of the most spectacular Buddhist pageants in Asia. On the final night there can be as many as 1500 performers and 200,000 onlookers standing ten deep on the pavements the entire length of the route (Warrell 1990b:68). The tooth relic is Sri Lanka's "most precious national treasure" (Carrithers 1983:112) and reminds the population of the central message of the

Mahavamsa that Sri Lanka is the home of an ancient Buddhist civilization, that a strong state and a flourishing religion are interdependent so that if the one falters then the other will perish. *Peraheras* — the word simply means ceremonial procession — are numerous in Sri Lanka, but the Asala perahera of late July/early August quite explicitly commemorates the life of the Buddha (Warrell 1990b:78–9).

That, at least, is one cluster of meanings for this *perahera*, an annual event which has been interpreted in diverse ways by different scholars. For some, the *perahera* is not so much a Buddhist pageant as something unified by both Buddhist and Hindu themes; it is virtually a 'deification' of Sri Lankan national identity, a glorification of civil religion and so of the integration of diverse ethnic and religious groups (Swearer 1982:307–8). Although there does not seem to be any myth of origin for the procession, others very much see it essentially as a rite of renewal, embodying both cosmographic and cosmogonic features (Warrell 1990b:63–79). A historical perspective is clearly vital here, for over the last century and a half the event has changed its character considerably (Warrell 1983, 1990a: Duncan 1990:128–36; Aluwihare 1964). The procession before the British conquest of 1815 while the Kandy kingdom was intact; its truncated, almost non-existent, form during the latter half of the nineteenth century under the colonial regime; its revivification this century as Sri Lanka underwent various social changes; its place in the political antagonism between low country and high country people, and its importance in the competitive displays between various local influential families; its significance with the 1972 Constitution enshrining the duty of the state to foster Buddhism — clearly there can be no simple answer to the issue of *the* meaning of this ceremonial.

Interpreting the *perahera*, like any other cultural performance, also raises the question 'meaning for whom?', for there is clearly a multiplicity of voices in evidence here, to mention only those of the sponsors, the local and national authorities, the performers and the local audience. But today, apart from being a spectacle for masses of Sri Lankans, the *perahera* is also very much a tourist spectacle, a fact which many decry, believing that an essentially religious event has been degraded into something merely commercial. In 1982, as in previous years, in the audience, as well as pious Buddhists, Members of Parliament, members of Kandy's monasteries, senior members of the national bureaucracy, day trippers from Colombo, and people from nearby villages, would be thousands of foreign tourists, especially for the two last evening processions. What was once a matter of royal patronage has now become very much a tourist event, highly dependent upon foreign money to keep it going. The ailing national financial structure underlying the historic ceremonial is commented on every year, in fact. The rural temples (*Island*, 6 October 1982), traditionally suppliers of elephants for the procession, were saying that there was an urgent need for government funds to prevent their physical decay and that without subsidy they could not even afford to maintain elephants. In 1982 President Jaye-wardene (*Daily News*, 18 June 1982) had promised a donation of one million rupees to ensure that the pageant was of a high standard. He is also said to have been insisting that the procession should be according to tradition, with the modern and foreign elements which had gradually crept in over the years removed.

The personal involvement of the President in the 1982 *perahera* was nothing new. Originally the *perahera*, according to some scholars, had very much been a display of the links between religion and the state (Seneviratne 1963:176–8;1977:65), given that the authority of the Kandyan monarchy very much had a Buddhist legitimisation and one perhaps needing deliberate emphasis from the mid-eighteenth century onwards when the kingdom was actually ruled by the Nayakkar dynasty from south India (Dharmadasa 1979; Duncan 1990:32, 40). During the British period, connection between 'church' and 'state' was necessarily severed, but in the post-independence period, though not at the time of independence itself, the connection was re-established. Thus, whenever a new government is elected (Seneviratne 1978:121) there is always a visit to the Temple of the Tooth as part of the legitimisation process. However, despite such a contemporary import which means that the *perahera* certainly cannot be regarded as an anachronism, a western spectator will probably still sense a profound incoherence. Here in a self-proclaimed modern, secular, democratic, socialist republic is an annual event which is, in one aspect at least, the aestheticised microcosm of a feudal, caste-based kingdom (Seneviratne 1978:9). The procession is a parade based on a division of labour linked to a regime of caste, albeit not with the same ideological foundations as the Hindu *varna* system. The dissonance in modern Sri Lanka is striking, even if not to all onlookers (ibid:150; Ling 1980:578; Nissan 1988:259).[10]

---

[10] In comparison to many other Sri Lankan festivals, such as that held annually at Kataragama, which are essentially participatory, the *perhahera* is very much a 'spectacle' where presence itself brings merit (Daniel 1990:236–7; Nissan 1988:254). According to the *Mahavamsa*, the *perahera* is performed for the contemplation and joy of the spectator (Warrell 199b:65). In that sense, 'pilgrim' and 'tourist' at this event are much closer identities than some of the critics might wish to allow. There are, of course, in this country where the tradition of domestic pilgrimage is so well established and significant in broadening the moral community beyond village level (Obeyesekere 1979:290–1), many pilgrimage centres which are also tourist sites, although one might wish to invoke the concept of 'merit' in order to preserve some distinction between touristic and religious motivations for travel. It should also be noted that the rowdiness and frivolity which sometimes accompanies modern-day pilgrimages in Sri Lanka and which some put down to the corrupting influences of tourism and westernisation, may not be the result of such contamination at all, because these are long attested features of pilgrimage in the island (Pfaffenberger 1983). On the links between tourism and pilgrimage in general, see Smith 1992 ed.

Photo 5   Temple of the Tooth lit up at night.

Seneviratne comments that over the years the *perahera* has been performed increasingly in an "atmosphere of tension" (1978:164,169). Not only has one had the rivalry between the Kandyan aristocracy and the modern, low country, western educated bureaucracy (1977:68; 1978:140–3; Warrell 1990b:290), but even within the one procession between representatives of the opposing U.N.P. and S.L.F.P. parties (Seneviratne 1978:171). Tensions have also come from those called on to perform the more menial roles in the ceremony. *Rajakariya* (service for the king) has long been repealed, and other obligations based on feudal land law, including those to temple authorities, are widely ignored (Ryan 1953:57), but every year the ritual season requires flag bearers, torch carriers, musicians, dancers, and so on, which in previous ages were the ritual specialties of certain caste groups. The thrice daily temple services previously part of a system of obligations are now performed by salaried individuals and so it is nowadays for the annual procession. In 1982 (*Sun*, 18, 20 August), Kandyan dancers who had been expressing the fear that their art was being degraded by amateurs taking to the stage attracted by tourist money, also complained that the 20–35 rupees *per diem* payment during the festival season was inadequate, that they were not provided with adequate changing facilities prior to the procession, and that the treatment accorded to the temporarily released prisoners carrying flags at the start of the procession was better than that meted out to themselves. This comparison was particularly galling and many took offence at the fact that the flags carried in this Buddhist pageant were borne aloft by pickpockets and thieves let out of prison and rewarded with food parcels which the dancers did not themselves receive. Buddhists were angry at what they saw as tantamount to the use of conscript labour (*Island*, 27 July 1982); pious Buddhists should have been carrying the banners, they claimed.

The complaints from the dancers paled into insignificance, however, compared to another rumpus that arose during the 1982 festival season. Seneviratne's detailed study of Kandyan ritual ceases about the time that international tourism was beginning to be particularly important in Sri Lanka, so he does not discuss the *perahera* specifically in a tourist economy. He does, however, mention how the special ten day period was bringing much money to the municipality and how hotels were putting up private seats for spectators (1978:148). Clearly, even at that time (H. L. Seneviratne, pers. comm.), there was beginning to be some tension between various authorities in Kandy over tapping into money generated during the pageant season, and tourists were beginning to be involved in this, although at that time it is likely that 'tourist' would have referred very much to the wealthy from Colombo and planters from the Hill Country. Seneviratne mentions that it is the right of the *Diyavardana Nilame* to determine the precise route of the procession, which can result in financial windfalls for himself and the Temple by depriving some leading hotels of the best views. This is precisely what happened in 1982 when the route differed in several respects from that used in previous years, and it led to considerable hostility on the closing nights of the *perahera*, when the *Diyavardana Nilame* processed to loud jeers from many in the large crowd.

The change of route, like the pageant as a whole, meant different things to different people. For some, a fixed processional route was part of tradition. There was a route that the elephants themselves knew and some expressed fear that there might be a serious mishap consequent upon the last minute changes, no unfounded fear to the extent that on a few occasions in the past elephants had run amok during the *perahera* inflicting serious injury on spectators. Others spoke of a blatant abuse of power by the lay custodian of the Temple. When complaints were taken to the President himself, the reply was that determining the route was squarely within the authority of the *Diyavardana Nilame*. One could add, too, that it was precisely the nature of such honorific offices that their incumbents were traditionally supposed to make money from them rather than receive a salary. Some commentators argued that this was no less true today than in earlier times.

Some were less sympathetic to this line of argument, in particular a business man involved in tourism in Kandy who estimated that he, along with five others in a consortium, had each lost 30,000 rupees as a result of the rerouting. He explained to me that the controversy was not actually about what most seemed to think. Near the Temple of the Tooth there were two large grassed areas on which seating platforms were customarily constructed in order to give people a good view of the procession. One area of land belonged to the municipality and the other to the Temple. On one of these areas normally sat temple workers, monks and other dignitaries. On the other are seats erected for tourists, who for the final two days of the pageant season will pay very high prices for the best seats, in 1982 up to 800 rupees ($U.S. 40). The difficulties in 1982, according to this informant, really turned around the refusal by the consortium which won the bid to construct the tourist seating site to pay 100,000 rupees into the President's fund. The business man told me that this penalty was imposed because a dispute in 1981 over the rent demanded had not yet been resolved. My informant claimed that the demand placed on him was totally unjust because in 1981 the consortium had been different. The 1982 group of entrepreneurs had complained to the President that the rerouting proposed would mean that many of their clients who had purchased seats simply would not be able to see the procession since it would now not pass in front of where the seats had been erected. The President refused to become involved, pointing to the right of the lay custodian of the Temple to route the procession as he chose. The rerouting went ahead, with tourists who had already purchased their seats loudly complaining; for most nights many of the seats erected for them were empty. Meanwhile the seats near the Temple put up by the Temple authorities were full of visitors, and my informant was particularly galled because he claimed that the Temple authorities had been frantically phoning up travel agents in Colombo to place their clients in the seats belonging to the Temple.

Disputes over temple and other incumbencies are not infrequent in Sri Lanka, involving not only money but also control over personnel. But the *perahera* rerouting in 1982 became headline news in the national press. Given the powerful people involved it was not possible for me to delve too deeply into the matter, but clearly, from those I spoke to there were widely disparate interpretations, no doubt in some cases tied up essentially with my particular informant's pecuniary interests. Nonetheless, it is clear that the sheer size of tourism revenue now makes the organisation of this event a matter over which severe conflict can be generated. Both traditional and contemporary forces were tied up in this conflict: the *Diyavardana Nilame* using the authority of an ancient office versus a business syndicate over who would control the flow of money. Both old and new elements were also involved in the complaints of the dancers: traditional obligations had changed, new arrangements were required for the staging of the processions, but the dancers were also concerned that tourism money posed a threat to the authenticity of their art. It is clear from the records that the pageant has often been associated with rivalry between various sectors of Sri Lankan society, but in the contemporary tourist economy, new parties enter the piece, there is a new audience for the spectacle itself, and the stakes can be much higher.

The end of the festival season did not bring an end to controversy in Kandy. A newspaper headline in the *Sun* on 9 August, just a few days after the end of the *perahera*, claimed that Kandyan art was dying. Given that Kandy is a region famous for its dancing, metal and wood craftsmanship, this was not of minor significance. Towards the end of August there were calls for the establishment of a Kandy Cultural Council to better the lot of impoverished local artists and craftsmen. The call had added poignancy given that 1982 was actually the centenary of the Kandy Art Association (*Daily News*, 13 July), an association set up in 1882 expressly to reinvigorate local artistic traditions thrown into disarray in the decades after the British occupation. In 1982, the Association, run by a small board of public figures receiving honoraria, was still charged with the prime function of supporting Kandyan craft families by distributing profits to them. Craftsmen in surrounding villages would bring in their metal and wooden wares and prices would be offered by the Manager of the Kandy Arts and Crafts Association shop on the basis of the quality of each piece of work. Goods accepted would pass straight into the shop without the intervention of middlemen. Sales during 1982 were close to 500,000 rupees ($U.S. 25,000), much of the money being used to finance the building of a new Arts and Crafts centre in the city.

The Kandy Arts and Crafts Association establishment is well patronised by tourists. Prices are marked and the shop is often mistaken by tourists for the *Laksala*, the Government-controlled craft shop elsewhere in the town because of the 'Government Approved' sign prominently on display. In fact, it operated quite independently of the Government. A prominent Kandyan metal craftsman and retailer with his own small antique, craft and jewellery shop in the town disputed almost everything that I had been told about the operations of the Association. Where was there any published information about the distribution of profits to the craftsmen, he inquired? It was a nonsense to suggest that the majority of local craftsmen had joined the Association, he claimed. An attempt to form a trade union for local craft workers had failed some years earlier, but most workers still did not belong to the Association. Also, the idea of fair rewards through the deliberate exclusion of intermediaries was misleading, according to my informant.[11] The prices of goods were really controlled by the importers of sheet-metals and by the larger craftsmen who would distribute raw materials to the smaller craftsmen in various villages. The Association was, therefore, just another institution by which

---

[11] Pieris, in his study of Kalapura (literally 'Art town') just outside Kandy, a settlement created as a direct result of government policy in the 1960s to provide a better future to a number of impoverished Kandyan craft families, comments that it was not long before the community was effectively controlled by a few wealthy members and middlemen (1971:95–9).

the relatively wealthy controlling the system deprived the poor craftsmen of their fair rewards.

Having heard such views, I spoke to the Manager of the Association's shop again, raising such issues as I thought could be tactfully phrased. The official story did not change, save that the point was made that the Association was purely voluntary, that no one forced any of the craftsmen to join, so that if they chose not to do so, that was quite alright. I told Ali that I had been given two totally different accounts about arts and crafts in Kandy, and he responded proverbially: "There is a saying in Sri Lanka that no one can climb a tall tree to get at honey without his hands becoming sticky". At least two substantially different accounts for nearly every event, widely divergent representations of how tourism worked, a variety of discordant, ambiguous and ambivalent voices on almost all issues — this was typical of the data I constantly received. Given that fact, it was clearly important to explore more systematically the images of tourists and tourism held by different segments of society in Kandy. The results of that inquiry are set out in the next chapter.

CHAPTER FOUR

Images and Representations of Tourism in Kandy: A Study of Different Viewpoints

Within a few days of my arrival in Kandy in 1982, it became very clear that almost no one to whom I spoke was neutral on the subject of tourism. Whether directly involved, marginally involved, or completely uninvolved in tourism, nearly everyone had pronounced opinions on the subject. Some spoke in favour. Some reeled off a list of destructive consequences. Many made ironical, double-edged remarks.

The first person to whom I spoke was a retired Buddhist school teacher, in Kandy for a few days of relaxation. He complained about the prices now being charged for a room in the Queen's Hotel and about the polluted state of the lake in the middle of the city. When I asked him how international tourism had affected Sinhalese culture and values, he responded that Sinhala culture had long ago been damaged when the British allowed Muslims and Tamils into the country. He remarked, somewhat furtively, that President Jayewardene himself had Muslim relatives, and that the politicians waxing lyrical about Buddhist values were in many cases Christians, who wore traditional white apparel simply to pander to the masses. Eighty per cent of tourists, he declared, came to Sri Lanka for sex. The following day, I spoke to a clerk, a Sinhalese Christian, who was having difficulty learning Tamil, which he was attempting because the government had stressed that all communities were part of the one nation. He declared that tourism was good for Sri Lanka, bringing employment and foreign exchange, and he was not unduly troubled by the adverse consequences. He did not condemn prostitution; that was simply a part of human nature. Nor did he have anything to say against the hippies: "This is a democracy; they have a right to a cheap life". Another person I engaged in casual conversation spoke in a heated way about how, since the advent of tourists, it was almost impossible for a local person to get decent service in cafes in the town. He often had to sit for ages without an order being taken, he informed me, because waiters would ignore locals, hoping for large tips from foreigners. A cafe owner acknowledged this as a problem and informed me that he had told his staff that they were not to ignore local customers; but he also pointed out the fact that foreigners did tend to spend much more money, so they had to be given the best service.

113

A jeweller, who had spent several years overseas, claimed that the notion of the *dharmista* society was just "an opium" for the people. Tourism was a collaboration between the local ruling elite and overseas capitalists who required local partners to set up their enterprises. Luxury hotels were often investments whereby the very wealthy could hide the fortunes they had made from drug and gem smuggling. A Buddhist professor at Peradeniya University, an S.L.F.P. supporter, claimed that tourism would become an election issue because the people were suffering from, not benefiting from it. U.N.P. policies would drive the country towards civil war, he predicted. Tourism was creating more stratification in society which was creating deep unrest among the poor. As for relations between nations, tourism was leading to mutual contempt between people of different cultures, rather than creating peace and understanding. A metal craftsman, member of an elite Kandyan family, admitted that tourism had bad effects, but being a poor country, Sri Lanka desperately needed foreign exchange. His own livelihood now depended very largely on tourists spending money, so he would never say anything in public to criticise foreigners, even if some of them were up to no good. A Muslim doctor who had opened one of the earliest guesthouses in Kandy declared tourism to be the centre of a "multiplicity of repulsive forces". All the talk of friendship was nonsense, he claimed. Tourism was a commercial business, a neo-colonial enterprise which had set class against class. The Principal of a local secondary school for girls was totally opposed to tourism. Tourists "behaved like animals"; they had "no respect for their bodies and no respect for Sri Lankan culture". They encouraged the young to become lazy. When I asked about guesthouses in Kandy, she, in front of a fellow school teacher who ran a guesthouse, declared: "I'd rather starve. One has no self-respect having tourists in one's house. It is better to have no foreign exchange than to depend on tourism".

The above remarks display a range of attitudes to tourism and tourists — from clear economic gain to a form of cultural debasement — which could probably be illustrated from any Third World country which has become an important tourist destination. But curiously little detailed and systematic research has been done on the obviously important topic of how local people view this new industry and how they speak about and represent tourists. This chapter, using data gained from research in Kandy, explores in some depth two areas relating to international tourism and representation. Firstly, it examines images of touristic behaviour in general, then looking at the various national caricatures held of tourists from different countries. Secondly, it examines the ideas about tourism held by distinct categories of people in Kandyan society.

The topic of 'representation' might appear to be somewhat arcane, but it cannot be considered of marginal interest for tourism is, after all, very much about images. The travel industry constructs images of other countries and cultures and tourists then go to consume those images. Thus, Sri Lanka, a country beset for many years by fundamental economic and ethnic problems is portrayed as a veritable paradise on earth and full of friendly smiling faces. But constructions of meaning are two-way in tourism as anywhere else (Farrell 1979:127), so just as the industry constructs images of the destination country, so the locals are constructing a set of ideas about the tourists and the countries they come from. In other words, there is very much a "reverse ethnography" (Marcus 1980:56) present where, unlike in conventional anthropology where 'we' construct 'them', here 'they' construct images of 'us'. Local-tourist encounters are often fleeting, and besides, because being out of everyday contexts (Wagner 1977), tourists are not particularly good 'culture carriers' from whom one can make insightful inferences about the sorts of society from which they come. It is not surprising, therefore, that local notions about foreign tourists may frequently be as fanciful as those created by the tourism industry itself. Such imagery inevitably involves elements of caricature, but it also needs to be recognised that it may be extremely insightful. After all, many locals make their living by catering to the needs of foreign visitors and so they must possess some accurate grasp of what they are dealing with. In addition to this, however, stereotypes create expectations which then produce their own reality (Evans-Pritchard 1989:91, 98; Boissevain and Inglott 1979:483–4). How one is categorised as a tourist really does affect what rules are applied to one and how one is treated (Brewer 1978).

The second area for detailed attention in this chapter involves the issue of how differences of social position produce highly divergent voices in regard to tourism (Dogan 1989:225; Husbands 1989). One commonly reads in the tourism literature statements about how a particular 'community' has responded to or views tourism, but there is plenty of evidence to suggest that a community can display quite marked variations in response, so that generalisations can be highly misleading. This chapter thus explores the representations of tourism found in three quite distinct sections of society in Kandy. Firstly I set out a 'Town Hall' perspective, very much the voices of the well-to-do and local municipal officials as expressed in an afternoon seminar held in the Town Hall in Kandy. Secondly, I examine the ideas about tourism of teenage school children in Kandy. It is often said that tourism has markedly adverse effects on this age bracket, but, again, little systematic research has been done to obtain their own views. My raw materials here were over one hundred essays written by senior pupils in three of Kandy's secondary schools. Thirdly, I analyse the views of people living and working on the streets of Kandy, many of them substantially or marginally dependent on incomes from tourists. My information here comes both from casual conversations held over seven months and, in some instances, semi-directed interviews conducted in the streets of Kandy.

TOURISTIC IMAGES

Many languages and cultures in Third World countries have no indigenous concept which can be adequately translated as 'tourist'. Naturally terms for 'traveller', 'pilgrim', and so on, are widely found, but the connotations of the term 'tourist' rarely overlap adequately with such notions. Hence in many destination countries, a European term (depending on colonial background) is used rather than a local term. This itself raises a question about cultural meaning, for if there is no indigenous conception of the sort of activity called 'tourism', people will need to create rules for interaction with a new type of social being, and will also need to construct representations about their behaviour and motivations. All cultures have rules relating to 'guests', 'strangers', and the like, but again, international tourists may be put into a category on their own, so that the moral rules relating to these others may not apply. On the other hand, tourists need to be fitted into local social classifications by some means, either by assimilation to some pre-existing category, for instance other types of Europeans known from the colonial past, or by creating a new social field (Evans-Pritchard 1989; Sweet 1985:10, 22–3, 86).

It has been said of Sri Lanka that "the presence of rich whites during the colonial era is immediately evoked by the tourists (Goonatilake 1978:16) and that the colonial period has left a "deep-rooted dislike and distrust for the white man among the people … Tourism is introduced into this atmosphere of unfriendly and hostile feelings" (Samarasuriya 1982:82). Such views strike me as somewhat exaggerated, although it must be conceded that such attitudes, where they exist, would likely not have been communicated in a forthright manner to a foreign researcher such as myself. Ali told me that most people held no such antagonistic feelings, that hostility towards European tourists based upon such historical ties would be confined to only a few aristocratic and snobbish Kandyans. This too, I think, is somewhat misleading given the sizeable class of politicians, intellectuals, economic nationalists (Roberts 1979:61) and traditionalists in Sri Lanka for whom denunciation of things western is *de rigueur*. I personally saw no evidence that historical factors interfered with how, for instance, Dutch or Portuguese tourists were viewed, although there are precious few of the latter in Sri Lanka. British tourists, it is true, are frequently depicted in a manner somewhat different to other European tourists such as the French and Germans (Ahmed 1989:355). They are viewed as being proud, remote and reserved, just as the British during the colonial period were depicted, but it might well be that this is how a considerable number of British tourists do in fact behave, rather than being a historical trace. One historical factor does seem to exist about American and Australian tourists, though, namely that the fondness with which many Ceylonese remember American and Australian troops during the Second World War (a memory of friendliness and generosity, in stark contrast to the remoteness of the British) seems to spill over into a widespread liking for tourists from those two countries.

Whilst it is probably a mistake to draw too close a link between attitudes towards tourists and specifically colonial racial antagonism, we must recall that international tourists are, by definition, 'foreign' and therefore are inevitably touched by general symbolic associations which Sri Lankans make about outsiders in general. As has been stated in Chapter 2, in Sri Lanka there is a large glossary of derogatory and pejorative epithets about foreigners (Roberts *et al.*, 1989:2–21), all the way from *sudda* ('whitey') to *karapotu* (cockroaches). There is a very strong inside/outside opposition which leads to outsiders being seen not only as low and vile but also as threats to the stability and well being of a somewhat vulnerable Sinhala society. Westerners particularly are often seen as disorderly, energetic and exploitative people who come to Sri Lanka, take what they want and then quickly leave. An overlap is obvious here between tourists and westerners of an earlier era, just as there is in the writings of Anagarika Dharmapala, Piyadasa Sirisena and others of the Sinhala cultural revitalisation movement at the end of the last century, who portrayed westerners as wild, licentious, carnal and hedonistic (Amunugama 1979; Obeyesekere 1979; Roberts *et al.*, 1989:10–14). Burghers, symbolically suspect because of their mixed ancestry, were often portrayed as *'kana bona minissu'* (Roberts *et al.*, 1989:8) — literally 'eating drinking people' — and this image of indulgence without a thought of tomorrow is again certainly part of the tourist stereotype. In fact, we can go back to some of the very earliest Sinhala writings about the Portuguese and find ourselves in very modern territory. The Portuguese centuries ago were said to "rest not a minute in one place" and to "give two or three pieces of gold and silver for one fish" (Roberts *et al.*, 1989:2). Such statements are commonly made of tourists in the present day.

We need to be careful, though, in discussing such images of tourists to be cognisant of the fact that Sri Lankans do not have simply one homogenous category 'tourist'. Most of my informants, in fact, employed three. There were the 'tourists', typified by those on 'package tours'. Quite distinct were 'travellers', a category which referred to a range of individuals making their way alone or in pairs, with no rigorously pre-set route or timetable, many of them staying as 'budget tourists' in the 'informal' accommodation sector in order to stretch their funds to make longer stays possible. For most informants, the 'hippy' was a third distinctive type, rather than a sub-species of 'traveller'. The hippy has a definite, if contradictory, image in Sri Lanka, and a number of people likened them to the aboriginal people of the island, the Veddahs. These *kalave minissu* (jungle people) were bearded and unkempt so there was a physical likeness to hippies, but the parallel was also a moral one. The aboriginal people were said not to know the rules of decent society and hippies are also widely regarded as barbarians who break all the rules of decent society.

The stereotype of the 'package tourist' is no less flattering than that of the hippy. Most such groups in 1982 were in Sri Lanka on a annual two week holiday which might include one or two days in Kandy before making for a beach resort. To the street guides waiting on various corners in Kandy, these tourists presented a somewhat sorry spectacle. They were likened to caged animals being mustered into gem and batik shops, then onto their hotels, and then to the dancing, without any time to breathe. Felix once asked me what point there was in coming to Sri Lanka to spend one's time in an air-conditioned bus: "they do not meet the Sri Lankan people and they do not even experience the weather", as he put it. He wondered if they relaxed at all because they were so obviously in a constant hurry, just as if they were still in their own countries. He pitied these "herds of sheep" who were not allowed to walk about as they pleased to find out about prices, for instance, but were just taken to selected shops where they would pay very high prices and where their foreign tour guides would collect very large commissions, unbeknownst to them. Ali likened them to people being escorted around "in the condition of prisoners", and a man working in a tourist information centre said that they were like prisoners "let out on parole" who did not understand anything that was going on around them. Frequently, when a tourist coach arrived in Kandy, it would go around the lake once and then depart without even allowing the tourists to get out. On many occasions this spectacle of rows of white faces pressed hard against rows of coach windows gave rise to loud jeering from onlookers. One of the commonest images associated with tourists is that of people in an almost inhuman rush. In one gem shop in Kandy where six young assistants worked, each in charge of one particular type of precious stone, the owner would be disappointed if an entire coach load of tourists (that is well over four customers for each assistant) could not be dealt with and out of the shop in a twenty minute period, during which time some customers would spend very significant sums of money. While the staff were trained to deal with the customers in this way, several told me that they regarded the behaviour of the foreigners as "crazy". Ali described the people who travelled in coach parties as "something like thumb-suckers and something like dogs". "If you try to help them", he said to me, "they will tell you angrily to get out of the way, but if they do not find what they are looking for they come back and barter; then they are polite and child-like".

Behind a normally polite facade, many local people had very disparaging things to say about tourists. For instance, a large group of German tourists entered a well-known craft shop in Kandy one day and given their haste and the confined space, a number of articles were knocked over and broken. The two assistants watched po-faced as this went on, but as soon as the party left, they burst out laughing and then in Sinhala referred to them as a herd of clumsy elephants. Animal imagery, in fact, is very common in tourism (Fussell 1980:40), so too are the images of haste, anxiety and clumsiness. All are testimony to the often very close attention which people in tourism destination countries pay to the behaviour and even bodily shapes of their visitors. Informants, for instance, could spell out for me in great detail how tourists from different nations would stand, sit or talk; how their clothes and physiques were different. The business man running the Tourist Information service by the lakeside in Kandy bragged to me that when tourists were still fifty yards away he could guess their nationality by the way they walked, what poses they adopted when they stopped to talk, the colour of their clothes and the way and speed at which their lips moved. I was amazed at how frequently he was correct, putting together all manner of minor details which I either did not know were significant or simply did not notice myself.

Ali and Felix were also very anxious to demonstrate to me their skills in this regard. On a series of afternoons on the street corner where I did much of my observation, they would try to guess the nationality of tourists when they were some distance away, and then inquire of the tourist which country they came from when they actually passed us. Felix and Ali did not always agree on the country of origin, but their rate of successful prediction was high given that there were well over a dozen significant tourist nationalities from which to choose. My efforts to find out which clues they used in each particular case produced a heterogeneous set of features: physical build, type of bag being carried, colour of hair, type of walk, style of clothes, shape of face, colour of clothes. Very early on during my time in Kandy I had witnessed a striking version of their practical skill. Ali, Felix and I were watching a middle-aged tourist, walking fairly briskly and responding resolutely but politely to various entreaties from people hawking wares on the pavement. From his general demeanour and accent I said that the man was English, but Felix disagreed asserting that he was Australian. Having familiarity with both nationalities, I explained that Australians were an easy going, somewhat rough and ready lot, and that the formal politeness we had just witnessed was typically English. Felix then justified his guess. The English may well be well-mannered at home, he argued, but in Sri Lanka, they were so used to "kicking us around like a football", they behave arrogantly and are very rude. "Maybe the Australian is rude at home", he went on, "but when abroad, he is very friendly and polite". Felix's guess, in this instance, turned out to be correct.

Images of tourists in terms of nationality were far richer than those based on any other criteria. Thus, a tourist answering the question "what is your country?" which plagued foreigners in the streets of Kandy in 1982, provided locals with a great deal of strategic information. From the reply, they immediately have notions as to what you are after, how you will behave, how rich you are. There is not a great deal of research done on national stereotypes in tourism (van den Berghe

1980:375, 384), but what evidence we have suggests that it is simply not true that all tourists "blend into an amorphous mass" (Nolan and Nolan 1978:2). There may well be generalised sets of ideas about tourists at large, but there are also very well developed particular national stereotypes as well as typologies of other kinds (Brewer 1978; Pi-Sunyer 1978:152–4; Sweet 1989:69). I became aware of the richness of these national portraits on my very first effort to find out about pricing in the tourist arena. My informant said to me: "I have three prices: one for locals; one for foreigners; and one for Germans".

Although I discussed national images at great length with a number of shop keepers and guesthouse proprietors in Kandy, street guides were my most valuable source of information. Ali, who dealt with foreigners both as a guide and as a pavement hawker, probably provided me with the richest set of national portraits. For him, Germans were "50% o.k. but the rest are the worst of all tourists and have no respect for our country". He said they were "barrel-shaped, with thick necks and tummies and round faces". In his view they took more drugs than the French. Some just liked to see the country, but others liked to buy batiks and gems. The French, for Ali, "were thinner and shorter than Germans with a curvy body shape". They spoke "slowly and not loud like Germans; they like to buy brassware and antiques". The English he regarded as always well-dressed and politely spoken and remarked that "they do not bargain very much". He added that "they like guides because they are in a hurry". For him, Americans "speak very differently to the British and you cannot understand what they say; they do things in an expensive way". He regarded some Australians as hippies who "do not like guides very much and try to do things their own way". Swedes were "very similar in speech and behaviour to the English", but he added that they liked to adopt Sri Lankan children. Danes were similar to Swedes; they did not spend very much and were interested in seeing the country, especially the ancient cities. Of Italians he observed that "some were rude and dishonest". "They have black hair like the Ceylonese, they are tall, have long faces and their accent is different to other people". He also added that "they bargain a lot and always try to lower the prices asked". Russians were "very fat, especially the women". He stated that "they always come in groups and cannot speak English. They try to bargain a lot with the goods they have brought from Russia". Spaniards had "round faces and long black hair". They bargained a lot and were neatly dressed. The Swiss were good characters and wanted to be left alone. The Japanese, for Ali, were "short and have round faces and short hair. They are neatly dressed. They do not say what they want until you are friends. They have a great interest in sex and gems". Indians came for the duty free shops and to buy what was expensive in India and some liked to see the Hindu temples. "They are hard to do business with as they ask for very low prices. They try to live in a simple way and spend little. Some are rogues who bring goods to sell here and take other goods to sell back in India".

It is difficult to know exactly what status to grant this set of representations.[1] To the extent that other people I spoke to held similar stereotypes, clearly they are not simply personal ideas. On the other hand, their collective status must be qualified by the clear recognition that other informants, including other guides, had very different stereotypes for some nationalities. Clearly it is often in the nature of caricatures to be subtle blends of both fictitious elements and penetrating insights, but in the case of these national portraits some seemed to be quite reasonable pictures built up out of repetitive observations, whilst others seemed to be constructed out of single, striking and really quite atypical occurrences which had become blown out of all proportion. Even so we still need to recognise that those images which are built up out of the close observation of human behaviour are still essentially guides to very practical strategies of interaction with foreigners rather than intellectual constructs. For instance, in Kandy's Central Market one of Ali's younger brothers, a wealthy Muslim shop owner, said that he deliberately priced articles according to the nationality of customers, which he judged by accent and clothing; the jewellery worn, quality of cameras carried, and so on, additionally enabled him to judge the personal wealth of any customer. He always charged higher prices for rich tourists and tourists from certain countries. With the English, he always stated one price and stuck to it, because, he claimed, the English got confused by bargaining. French couples, according to him, always bought goods for each other or for their children, so he always steered them to what goods he had of that kind. He had a strong dislike of Italians whom he regarded as noisy and rude. He had had one experience of an Italian actually stealing goods from his shop and he always found them very harsh in bargaining. He did not know until I told him that in some European countries like Italy bargaining was a regular way of buying and selling. He was under the illusion that Italians were just copying the Sri Lankan custom and, of course, did not know how to do it properly. So, when Italian tourists approached his shop he would always raise his prices dramatically because he knew that the opening gambit by the Italian tourist would be to halve the price that

---

[1] This formal method of presentation clearly disguises the essentially practical nature of these images for their holders. They are general notions employed in specific situations for interacting with foreigners. I must also add that my research was conducted solely in Kandy, and mostly in the informal sector. National stereotypes existing in hotels may well be different, and the images reported by Ahmed (1984) in his study of middle class, English speaking Sri Lankans in Colombo are certainly not the same as those I received. There may also be considerable regional differences in imagery. Most of my informants, for instance, had a low opinion of Italian tourists, yet in Matara, perhaps because of local development projects going on there financed by different European nations, Italians were apparently held in very high regard (Due, pers. comm. 1982).

he stated.

The manager of a well know Arts and Crafts shop in Kandy told me that he explicitly taught the national characteristics of foreign tourists to his shop assistants as part of their basic training and, like Ali, he was more than pleased to provide me with his 'system'. Italians "shout and are rude. They like to buy large metal animal objects. They bargain as if they are in a fight". Germans, by contrast, were "Large and friendly. They buy quickly. They walk about aimlessly". Of the Japanese, "they are friendly but it is difficult to establish relations". For him, the English "need time to think. They like to talk about various object for sale, they use the object to get friendly. They like natural not artificial things. They walk purposefully and methodically. Even when on holiday they are well dressed. They are snobs". Americans, by contrast, were "like babies. They are very demanding. You talk to them about anything until they buy an object. They like large purchases which they have to post back overseas". Russians were "mean, but have very little currency so they try to purchase things for half price". With Scandinavians "a few of them try to bargain by asking if we can reduce the price a bit". He thought that Australians liked to "buy a lot for their houses. Half are friendly, half are reserved". Of Spaniards he claimed that "they come in charter groups. They are in and out of the shop in fifteen minutes. They are noisy and fast".

This informant claimed that one could tell the nationality of a tourist from how they walked and what articles they picked up and examined. A number of explicit strategies then came into play. Some nationalities one left alone to browse; others one engaged in conversation. Americans one actually followed around and pressured a little. Such examples may seem far fetched, but they are actually employed. If one were to suggest that these local images often correspond very imperfectly to tourist behaviour, we must also acknowledge that tourism researchers themselves do not know a great deal about national tourist differences (Smith 1978:276). That being so, paying close attention to such local images of tourist behaviour might well yield important insights. We might even discover that people engaged in tourism in a practical way are considerably more observant than those who merely write academically about it.

THE VIEW FROM THE TOWN HALL

A series of events during 1982 discussed at length in Chapter 3 revealed the high potential for conflict within the tourism arena in Kandy, and the municipal authorities were centrally involved in a number of them. Two weeks after the end of the *perahera* season, therefore, I went to the Town Hall to arrange an appointment with the mayor to discuss tourism in the city. Not only did we briefly discuss tourism then, but the Mayor agreed to set up an afternoon seminar for later in the year during which I could express some of my ideas and a number of local officials and people involved in the tourism industry in Kandy could speak to me.

The Mayor's office sent out numerous invitations for this event to officials, hoteliers and guesthouse proprietors and for several weeks before the seminar was due to take place, I sensed a marked increase in wariness from my hosts in the guesthouses in which I stayed during that period. It occurred to me at the time that once the seminar was publicly announced, I might be thought to be a spy for the municipal authorities, checking up on guesthouse operators as to whether they were paying taxes, municipal dues, and so on. A number of guesthouse owners told me quite pointedly that they would not under any circumstances go to the Town Hall to discuss tourism with the Mayor. Some even went out of their way to get me to promise that I would not mention that I had been staying with them. In one guesthouse the owner spent an hour happily telling me about her family's involve-ment in the growth of tourism in the town over the previous fifteen years, but then the following day, via another foreigner staying there, she informed me that she regretted telling me anything. Indeed, the way it was put to me it was clear that she wanted me to leave immediately.

Although this sort of reaction came initially as a shock, in retrospect it is quite understandable. Someone doing research largely in the informal tourism sec-tor was asking about matters where people would not really welcome close scru-tiny. I visited one family with whom I had briefly stayed in 1980, saying that I was writing a book and wished to learn about the growth of tourism in Kandy. In 1980 they had been very happy to talk about tourism in Kandy, but in 1982 I arrived three times with appointments to be sent away each time with a different excuse. In another guesthouse, one notorious in the town for sex and drugs, I never once found the owner present. His wife always found an excuse to leave the room imme-diately and I was then consistently referred to a teenage daughter who claimed to know nothing about tourism in Kandy. Clearly, if there is any truth in the idea that tourism has something to do with cultures learning about each other, the sort of knowledge I was after was seen as a threat by many of those I came into contact with.

The tourism seminar held in the Town Hall in Kandy on 29 September 1982 was very poorly attended. Apart from the Mayor and myself, there were a handful of municipal officials, the police were represented, there was one hotel manager, a few individuals running expensive guesthouses — all told fewer than twenty peo-ple. The Mayor's concern was very much a local, administrative one — how to "clean up" tourism in the town, how to deal with such "evils" as beggars, touts, hippies, etc. All save one speaker whose main concern was to address the problem of how Kandy could better market itself as a tourist destination, concentrated on the *hoi poloi* elements whom they saw as ruining tourism and the city. As the Mayor said in formally opening the proceedings:

> There are certain things that people criticise, so we thought that we will dis-
> cuss all these matters and then come to some understanding so that we will be
> able to solve certain problems, especially where our city is concerned. We feel
> that our city should be safeguarded from various complications, rising out of
> tourism. A little while ago we were discussing a problem. You see, I said the
> influx of tourists to the city, there are attendant evils, they are all talking
> about evils, but not about making money or something. I have no objection
> to anyone making money ... yes, I must tell you frankly ... because these are
> times for people to make money, so why should I deprive people of making
> money. But I am only worried about the city, the cleanliness of the city, and
> also various other factors like infiltration of bad habits into our community.
> The young people that are getting misled, sort of misguided, their drug hab-
> its. You see these are the attendant evils of tourism. And also the beggarly
> population. We didn't have so many beggars, but now there are large num-
> bers of beggars because they think it easy money. Normally they'd make no
> more than, say, 10–15 rupees a day, but now they are making very much more
> than people who run these guesthouses because only a few people come. So
> these are problems which we have to solve in the interests of this town
> because it may be that good tourists are a sophisticated type of people who
> might not come a second time. First time they will come. Second time they
> will come they will say it is a dirty city, it is not a good place. So it's a bad
> impression mark on our city, on our country. So we have to safeguard it, all of
> us, you see, sort of safeguard the interest of the country which we live in. So
> we have to sort of have some solution for this problem. In fact, we have dis-
> cussed this some time ago — the police, social service department — but
> nothing came out of it. I suggested to take about 300 or 400 acres of govern-
> ment land and have some sort of camp-like thing, take these people, keep
> them there, feed them and give them clothes, give them some sort of training
> and something, maybe industry, maybe agriculture, but nothing is happening.
> And there will be a number of able-bodied fellows. Maybe police should
> round up these fellows and take them to places like Gangodawila. But they
> were there for one week, next week they came back here. It's very difficult to
> control. So that's one evil that we have.[2]

These mayoral comments set the tone for almost the entirety of the seminar which thus became a 'local version' of what at the national level was emerging with the Specified Tourist Services Code and in Operation Overstay, namely the wealthy and influential trying to squeeze out small-time operators. The small gathering obviously was not and was not meant to be representative of all interests in tour-ism, nor of all sections of Kandyan society. It was a gathering mainly of the well-

---

[2] Besides taking extensive notes during the seminar, I also recorded the entire proceedings.

to-do and officials and for obvious reasons excluded those in the informal sector. In that sense the Town Hall gathering was very much an instance of what one section of society says about another which it has deliberately rendered voiceless. For me it was also personally a somewhat uncomfortable experience of one class of Sri Lankan scapegoating another for all the ills attendant on tourism development, as well as, in the case of some contributors, a clear display of perceptions of tourism confined solely to their own financial self-interests.

When the Mayor had finished his introduction he invited me to speak, which I did for some ten minutes, trying to give a balanced socio-economic view and also trying to introduce some national concerns. Whilst my audience was attentive, my contribution clearly did nothing to divert the outpouring of resentment which then ensued from one speaker after another. A retired public servant and operator of a guesthouse opened with the following:

> My first impression is that in tourism in Sri Lanka it is the driver who is king. In fact I had the experience that the driver expected to be treated before the tourist and I had to tell him to take his tourist away. Why does the driver behave like that? He gets V.I.P. treatment before the tourists. Are we catering to the local men in handling the tourist trade or are we looking after the tourist making his stay in this country happy and enjoyable? Why do they come to this country? They don't come here just to spend their money. They come to see places, they come to meet people, they come to understand the culture, the history, and the social conditions of our country ... My tourists have told me that on their first day they want to discuss matters relating to our history, to our culture, to our social problems, to the racial, communal problems and all the propaganda that is being done all over the world. They get a clear picture only if we engage in intelligent discussions. Most of the tourists that come to my place are those who belong to the educated and professional classes who are interested in that type of thing and they themselves have complained that they are at the mercy of guides and car drivers. Very often they are taken to places where they are not wanted and they are being forced to see some of these places, unregistered places. No checks are done. Now, Mr. Mayor, I think you are aware of about 300 places entertaining foreign guests, but if you go through the brochures of the Tourist Bureau, I don't think you have thirty on that brochure.

Having pilloried the tourist car drivers and unlicensed operators and also introduced the issue of different sorts of tourists — he specialising in the educated, professional variety — he went on to complain about the taxation policy in the tourism industry before returning to the unlicensed operators and their tout accomplices:

> I must say that the city fathers should not tax everybody who is registered as a guesthouse owner in the same way. You take a guesthouse with about two, three or four rooms. You may not get guests throughout the year. It is really

unfair to ask these people to pay the same commercial rates as these big hotels with package groups coming through. There has to be some sort of grading, even on the matter of liquor licences. I run a private guesthouse. I don't give liquor but they come in and say: "Can I have a beer?" Now to get a beer license it costs me a very big sum. License fees are very high and maybe you will not recover that amount for selling liquor for the whole year with the license fee. In fact I wrote to the Minister of Finance that there should be a separate basis for licensing smaller units, but I don't know the exact fees. These are some of the problems on which I wish to focus attention. Then also there is the question of standards, minimum standards of health, sanitation, all that should be maintained. Now if you go down Lewella, every second house is a guesthouse, and you will find tourist rooms being let for 15 or 10 rupees a week, I don't know, but are we going to get that type of tourist to this country and how are we going to develop by this type of thing? And if there is prostitution, if there is use of drugs and all that, the tendency is for most of these to occur in those places than in decent hotels and guesthouses and private accommodation units, because certain standards have to be met. There has been a deterioration. Anybody can get tourists. And then there's the guides. Now Dr. Crick referred to guides. I prefer to call them touts. You get into a train in Colombo Fort. You will find half a dozen to ten fellows. They are going canvassing and being a nuisance to the tourists. I have seen them being shooed off, so there is no proper licensing. And the tourist should be informed on arrival at Katunayake that if any fellows come and accost them, to call for the license, identity card. That is the only way to check these undesirables from being a nuisance and then taking them to all these places of doubtful repute. These are the problems. I would also suggest that you instruct your officers to be very careful and take notice of these houses that entertain foreigners for payment for lodging and food. I know several in my neighbourhood. Why should we pay the higher taxes and rates and pay licenses, and they get off 'scot free'. The law is always against the honest man, so how can we do tourism if we allow this type of thing? And as you yourself mentioned, we don't want beggars to come to this country, even if they want to see this country. We want decent type of people to come. We should gain by their visit, not only financially. We should come into contact with them, exchange ideas and all that. There has to be some mutual benefit, but by getting these people on the dole and these type of chaps who go to places of doubtful repute, I don't think it is the type of tourism that we should encourage.

The Mayor responded to the comments about budget tourists by recalling something that I had said to him weeks earlier, namely that it was difficult to judge whether foreigners were 'hippies' or not simply from their appearance because there were many wealthy, highly educated tourists who liked to dress very casually and lead a simple life while on their vacations. On the subject of unlicensed operators, however, the Mayor roundly denounced them as immoral for avoiding various taxes and charges. He also added that he felt that because of the activities of the touts, some of the illegal operators were doing considerably better than those doing tourism in an above-board way. At his point I endeavoured to give a broader and more positive picture of the street guides, including the obvious one that if the point of tourism was to make money from the foreigner it was to be expected that all sections of society would endeavour to join in with whatever skills they possessed. I also endeavoured to counteract what seemed to be the prevailing view that somehow tourism was the cause of the beggar problem in Kandy.

Exchanges of views about beggars and unlicensed guesthouses continued for several more minutes, with various officials arguing that very definite controls needed to be instituted so that the streets could be cleaned up and people made to pay appropriate taxes and charges. The Mayor admitted that numerous people had informed him that people were evading their obligations, but he stated that it was impossible to search every house. Besides, many people had foreign friends who visited them. He also stated that the Tourist Police unit was drastically under-staffed. He wanted the police along with municipal officers to remove the beggars and give the able-bodied training courses so they could become productive. Security guards, he added, would be needed for the camps where they would be placed because otherwise the beggars would simply drift back into town. He also acknowledged that many beggars were actually in the employ of businessmen who would bail them out as soon as they were arrested.

The Mayor then shifted his attention to the guide problem, stating that Kandy had "very poor specimens" who did not even know the history of the city. He reported on his several attempts to set up with police cooperation interview panels to screen guides, but stated that seldom did suitable individuals come forward. A number of people then made spirited attacks on the street guides of Kandy, most of them denying that these individuals had any right to be referred to as guides at all. This continued for about twenty minutes before I mentioned the fact that although the Tourist Board in Colombo trained 'guide lecturers' there was also talk about a less arduous training program for people who wanted to be 'regional guides'. A municipal official responded very favourably to this idea, stating that it would clearly be in everyone's interest to have respectable local people offering a guide service in Kandy. He went on to suggest that tourist operators in the town might all like to contribute financially towards training such people. This suggestion was met with widespread derision, some operators stating that they did not need the help of any guides, others stating that since guides made money from their activities it was quite inappropriate for them to have to contribute towards their training. One person asked why he should finance a guide who could then take tourists to someone else's establishment. At this point I made another attempt to portray more favourably the role of the street guide, pointing out how numerous guesthouses and shops in the town relied on their help and also suggesting a number of ways in which they assisted certain kinds of tourist. My contribution fell on deaf ears, so I was considerably relieved when someone who up to that point had been silent made a comment which allowed the seminar to take a completely different course. The contribution was made by a retired car salesman from Colombo who had purchased a large house in a good location near the lake and who had converted servants' quarters into several rooms for foreign guests.

> I feel up to a point we have confused the subject. We came to discuss how to develop tourism in Kandy, to make the place more pleasant for tourists, and at the same time make it pleasant for all of us. Dr. Crick and others have explained the problems that the tourists are going through. Tourism began in 1966. In that year we had around 70,000 tourists, but right now, for last year, we had 370,000, and an interesting point is that all these tourists come to Kandy. Hardly a tourist misses Kandy. Our problem is how to keep the tourists longer in Kandy. We find that they stay hardly a night here. There are different types of tourists: the type who goes to hotels, the type who is in search of guesthouses and good homes, and the hippies who stay the longest. The Tourist Board keeps on making calculations and predictions to get more and more numbers. This year the target is 400,000. This year early on was a failure, but by the end they hope to catch up. By the end of 1984 we expect to get 500,000. But most tourists are sent to Kandy just for a day and then go back. This is not profitable to the Municipality or anyone else. They just stay for lunch and I don't think hotels and guesthouses make money on lunches or food; it's a service we provide. It is room rent that gives us the money. The large number of tourists arranged through agents stay hardly a night. Quality guesthouses get tourists coming by car. They stay one night, sometimes two, but mostly when they come by car, the driver has arranged the trip in such a way that he's coming through a tourist agency or certain private car owners who drive tourists. They make it a point to keep their tourists all the time on the road. There was one day a tourist, for example, who came in the evening. They started at Hikkaduwa. This driver told them that they could see Kandy, Sigiriya, Polonnaruwa, and they can get back for the night to Hikkaduwa. The car was driven at such speed that when they came back to Kandy, they said: "We must stop. We can't drive any more". This is what we want. We want to keep the tourists in Kandy, failing three, at least two nights. So let us plan out some itinerary of interest for tourists, to keep tourists in Kandy longer. Suggest that people think of Kandy as the base for their holidays in Sri Lanka and not Colombo. Take them to Nuwara Eliya and back to Kandy; to see the ruined cities and back to Kandy. We have in Kandy lots of things to see, ruins and old temples. We have not developed Kandy as a base for tourism. We have got altogether about 800 hotel rooms and 1600 guesthouse rooms per day in Kandy. Keep people here longer. The guide system will come along when we keep the tourists longer.

The Mayor was quick to seize upon the positive sentiment behind these comments and invited the people at the seminar "not to think of individual interests but collective responsibility". He went on to urge:

> the hoteliers, guesthouse people and those with small guesthouses to get
> together into a small body. They can have a committee to see how to improve
> the industry, get the right type of people, more money to the country,
> improve the guide service. All that can be done. Anything pertaining to the
> Municipality, the committee can see the Mayor or Commissioner ... Tourism
> is to be encouraged. We should all be making money, putting up hotels. Dr.
> Crick has told me that foreign agencies put up hotels, bring their own tour-
> ists, and the money goes back to their own countries so that our country is
> not benefited. So our own people get complicated but not benefited.

I stated at that point that the Tourist Board had been making strenuous
efforts since 1966 to ensure that Sri Lanka gained from international tourism. I also
made the obvious point about Kandy as a tourist site, namely that since the vast
majority of foreigners came to Sri Lanka for sun, sand and sea, Kandy could never
hope to hold onto tourists as beach resorts did. I also added that there were limitations in the extent local plans could affect the behaviour of most tourists since most
came on 'package tours' where their itinerary was all mapped out in advance. After
those few comments, the Mayor brought the proceedings to a close, going over the
'evils' once more, but also staying with the positive and practical idea that there was
valuable work for a local committee to do:

> There is a bad side as well as a good side, but I have tried to eliminate the bad
> side as much as possible. But the good side we must improve. So, I am not
> able, but I would like you gentlemen to form a small committee and get Dr.
> Crick again for further discussions. To organise ourselves to get a little more
> money, that should be the policy. Get the maximum money. Of course, do it
> in a systematic way so that everybody will be benefited. You can advise me
> on the guides and I can advise the government on how to get these people
> trained. A small committee can talk to Dr. Crick before he leaves and the
> Minister in charge of tourism. And on the government side I will see what I
> can do about the beggar problem and other evils.

After the Town Hall seminar was over, I had further conversations with two
of the guesthouse owners who had been present and one of the police representatives. With one couple who ran a guesthouse, my views on whether beggars were
the result of general social conditions rather than tourism was queried repeatedly as
we departed from the Town Hall. My views did not persuade them and they
departed handing me a large stack of cards advertising their establishment which
they asked me to give to tourists I met. They also hinted that the Mayor himself had
a house rented out to foreigners and that he had not registered it with the authorities. The Tourist Police I spoke to some days later, and I had a fruitful series of conversations with the guesthouse owner who had raised the issue of the development

of a positive tourism plan for the city. He certainly felt it unfair that people such as himself should be paying very high electricity and water bills when a large number of others were escaping all such charges by doing tourism secretly. He also declared that "we must not allow the lowest categories in our society to deal with the lowest in theirs". But he was also candid that much hypocrisy had been in evidence during the seminar. Whenever one spoke to the well-to-do about the evils of tourism one always heard the rhetoric of Sri Lanka's image being "spoiled", of "selling our culture for a mess of pottage", and so on. But the guesthouse owner conceded that commercial self-interest really underlay most of these fine phrases. One of the reasons he remarked that guesthouse owners were so insistent on prostitutes being removed from the streets was so that they themselves could then supply them to their guests. For some, he said, this, rather than supplying food or accommodation, was the real source of their tourism income. He was not at all optimistic that his colleagues would form the committee the Mayor had called for to promote the cause of tourism in Kandy because they were all fiercely competitive and jealous of each other; they would therefore not wish to cooperate. And indeed, by the time I left Kandy at the end of October, no steps at all had been taken to set the wheels in motion in this regard.

THE VIEW FROM THE SCHOOLS

It is often stated that the younger generation is particularly vulnerable to international tourism development. Teenagers and even young children drop out of school, they start begging from foreigners, and some even take up prostitution; they are frequently regarded as displaying the worst symptoms of the so-called 'demonstration effect'. While such repercussions are widely reported, detailed empirical research on the younger generation's own views about tourism is scarce (Graburn 1983:3). That being so, one specific goal of my research in Kandy was to obtain detailed information about the attitudes towards tourism of a school-age sub-population. For this purpose over one hundred 16–18 year olds in three secondary schools in Kandy wrote answers to a set of ten questions about tourists and tourism supplied to them on a question sheet identified as coming from the Department of Sociology at the University of Peradeniya. Below is set out a digest of their responses, occasionally illustrated by direct quotations. It was never intended that an exercise on such a small scale should yield evidence about how ethnic or gender differences affected attitudes to tourism, and given that the teachers who oversaw the essay writing itself appear to have chosen pupils very much from middle class family backgrounds no very clear results show up as to how social status influences view about tourism within this age group. However, given well over two hundred pages of writing produced by over one hundred individuals, there is good evidence about how a group of teenagers in Kandy about to leave school felt on a number of key tourism issues.[3]

In response to the first question posed, "Are you in favour or against tourism? Say Why", approximately half of the 105 pupils involved in the essay exercise were overwhelmingly in favour of tourism, 40 gave responses of a rather ambivalent kind and only 10 were completely negative. As regards the factors stated in favour of tourism, over half of the pupils mentioned the gaining of foreign exchange, with 27 pupils specifically mentioning 'development' and only marginally fewer the increase in employment. Whilst, clearly, tourism is perceived above all as an economic phenomenon, a highly significant number of pupils (26) mentioned benefits stemming from international cultural exchange, the importance of Sri Lankan culture being better known to outsiders and the value of knowing about other cultures. Clearly, then, this age category shares to a degree the official 'peace and understanding' view espoused by the national tourism authorities. On the negative side, the most frequently mentioned adverse effects were 'corruption' and the 'loss of culture' (25 instances of each). Twenty pupils specifically mentioned the drug problem. Other problems mentioned were: crime and smuggling (5 instances), diseases (7 instances), homosexuality and prostitution (7 instances). Of course, given that a large proportion of the pupils clearly had somewhat ambivalent views, many statements combined an appreciation of economic gains with regret about the cultural costs. As one pupil put it:

> Ours is a country where very high religious and cultural standards are maintained. With tourists coming into Sri Lanka these standards are bound to deteriorate. It is true that we earn a lot of foreign exchange and that new avenues of employment are created by way of tourism, but it is sad to see that in the guise of economic development moral standards of Sri Lanka are deteriorating at an alarming rate.

Or as another put it more pointedly: "if our country is ruined in many ways, what is the earthly use of that income?"

In response to this dilemma, several pupils thought that the answer clearly

---

[3] This school essay project has been extensively discussed from a methodological point of view in Crick 1993. The three schools involved were: Trinity College, Dharmaraja College and Kandy High School for girls. Question sheets were prepared in English, Sinhala and Tamil. The teachers who supervised the writing of the essays were not involved in either producing the original question sheets or in translating the Sinhala and Tamil essays for me. Trinity College, the private school yielded 24 essays, all by males, all in English; Dharmaraja College yielded 19 in Sinhala and 12 in English, all by males; Kandy High School for girls yielded 20 in English, 20 in Sinhala and 10 in Tamil.

lay with the government's and the Tourist Board's duty to make laws to protect local culture and to insist that foreigners respect such laws. Others, however, adopted the same scapegoating devices as the adults who had attended the Town Hall seminar. One stated:

> One reason for my being against tourism in Sri Lanka is that it has created an undesirable lot of people such as guides. These people fleece the tourist and also the guesthouses by demanding large tips.

Another chose to pick on 'low types' of tourist:

> Sri Lanka should restrict tourism to good affluent people, and not the hippy types who bring drugs. The government should pass a bill saying that there should be no hippies in Sri Lanka.

A third picked up on the 'second class citizen' theme:

> In most places tourists are given first place. It is true that tourists should be tolerated not ignored, but in the same way they should not be given priority in every manner. This at times brings jealousy and violence among the public.

As regards the question 'Why do tourists come to Sri Lanka?', two thirds of the pupils stated that Europeans came because of Sri Lanka's climate and beautiful scenery. Just under half mentioned more cultural or educational motives, such as an interest in the history, religion and architecture of Sri Lanka. Forty-eight mentioned holidays or leisure specifically, but several combined this general theme of relaxation with one very much of 'escape':

> In European countries everything is done by machinery, and their life is also something like a machine. But those who are tired and fed up of mechanical lives do not have natural places to relax, so they come as travellers to Sri Lanka to see its natural, beautiful places.

Thirty-one students specifically mentioned Sri Lanka's low cost of living as the reason tourists come, and 20 mentioned business reasons. Eight wrote of the hospitality and friendliness of the Sri Lankan people. A small number mentioned that tourists came specifically for a variety of nefarious activities, with drugs (12 mentions) being the most widely cited. Again specific types of tourist were frequently mentioned in this connection:

> It is not the rich type of tourist who do this type of thing, but it is the lowest class of tourist.

I had expected in response to the question 'In what ways are tourists and Sri Lankans different?' that the majority of students would point to the obvious affluence of foreigners, but in fact only 13 did so in such explicit terms. Forty-two mentioned differences of culture, habits, morals, religion and behaviour, and apart from this general area of cultural difference, 29 mentioned language differences, 27 differences in skin colour, 26 clothing differences and 17 differences in food. As compared with 9 who spoke in positive terms about the individualism and freedom of tourists compared to their own conservatism, 23 spoke positively about their own cultural traditions as contrasted with the selfishness or immorality of tourists. For one pupil:

> Tourists do not think about society the way Sri Lankans do. Tourists are not interested in family life, but in Sri Lanka this is the essence of life.

For another:

> They do not have the habit of helping each other, they mind their own business. On the other hand, the Ceylonese are much kinder and always helpful to others.

For a third:

> Tourists only think of living for the day, they don't have a day called 'tomorrow'. There is nothing called 'the future' in their life.

One pupil reflected on both the cultural and health differences in a very pointed fashion:

> Most Sri Lankans are poor and well-cultured, whereas most tourists are rich and uncultured.

A question about national caricatures brought a set of images fairly similar to the sorts of portraits I had received from guides and guesthouse owners. Four pupils actually challenged the question itself by stressing that differences were individual rather than national, but only 7 claimed that all tourists were alike. By contrast, 57 claimed that there were very marked differences between tourists of different nationalities, despite many also claiming in response to Question 9 that they had not personally known any tourists. Many of the pupils were willing and able to sketch brief 'national portraits'. Twenty students, however, whilst admitting the existence of national differences, stressed that the major distinction was between 'western' tourists largely from Europe and 'eastern' tourists from India, Thailand and Japan, whom many saw as not producing the same harmful effects on Sri Lankan culture that Europeans did.

All 105 pupils had something to say in response to the fifth question 'What are hippies? Why do they come to Sri Lanka? What do they do in Sri Lanka?' and on first glance a strong and consistently negative image comes through.[4] Nineteen pupils used expressions such as "low types", "low caste", "unclean", "uncivilized", "white beggars", "coolies", "parasites" or "outcastes". Eleven students said that hippies had no culture and no standards. Eighteen linked them to nefarious smuggling activities and 10 saw them as dangerous carriers of disease. Fifteen associated them with nudism on beaches, prostitution and homosexuality. Nine described them as "aimless" wanderers and 11 pointed out that they took on any jobs simply to prolong their stay in Sri Lanka. The three features most characteristic of the hippy were clearly that they are relatively poor and so come for very cheap holidays (52 mentions), that they are involved in the smuggling and use of drugs (51 mentions), and that they are shabbily dressed and dirty (35 mentions). Twenty pupils went to great lengths showing how hippies had ruined Sri Lanka's culture, with 4 specifically mentioning their baleful effect on the young. A further 3 stated that they should be thrashed and expelled from the country. For one pupil, hippies had:

> become a threat to the noble Sri Lankan race. These indecently clad hippies
> are actively trying to take the glorious social background of the Sinhala race.

On closer examination, however, there are some very real ambiguities in the characterisation of hippies by this age group. Some pupils stated that hippies were scruffy and poor while others suspected that they might be quite wealthy. For some, they had no culture or civilised standards, but for others what distinguished them was that they had high ideals. Some associated hippies with living in large communes, while others saw them as loners. Some pupils declared that there were several types of hippy in Sri Lanka; some were bad, but some were good and had come for education, meditation and to learn about Buddhism. Twenty pupils wrote that hippies were trying to escape the pressures of western industrial society and 6 gave very positive characterisations of hippies. They were people who had rebelled against their own culture and had idealistic notions about the proper way in which to live. Five even described them as being closer to Sri Lankans than other types of tourist, even seeking out the company of ordinary Sri Lankans. As one pupil put it:

---

[4] Although the places commonly associated with hippies in Sri Lanka are beach areas like Hikkaduwa (on the west coast) and Kalkudah (on the east coast), there were a number of areas in Kandy and several guesthouses with a reputation for housing 'hippy types'. The Lewella area, just outside the city had, I was frequently told, a number of unhygienic establishments where those who could not afford a room simply slept on the verandah. For a fuller discussion of the symbolism of hippies based on the students' essays, see Crick 1989c.

they are a set of people who look forward to an unlimited freedom, enjoy nature as they have been suppressed and shaken up by industrialisation, and live in the midst of the commoner and learn the culture, customs and habits, likes and dislikes of these people. A lot of the hippies are doctors and engineers and also those who have got disgusted with the world because of religious issues and political disagreements. These people have given up their good living and now mix freely with the commoner and live with them.

In response to the question 'In what ways are tourists good for Sri Lanka?', economic matters were clearly to the fore. Seventy pupils mentioned the gaining of foreign exchange, 37 mentioned increased employment and 30 mentioned development. Quite a considerable way behind was the increased understanding of other cultures (15 mentions), the increased popularity of Sri Lanka in the global community (12 mentions) and the preservation of cultural heritage (4 mentions). The question 'In what ways are tourists bad for Sri Lanka?' produced the following responses: loss or corruption of culture (68 mentions), drugs (55 mentions), diseases (29 mentions), sexual immorality (21 mentions), smuggling (15 mentions), inflation (10 mentions), Sri Lankans being treated like second class citizens (4 mentions), environmental problems (3 mentions). In response to a clearly related question 'What problems do tourists cause?', the comments were somewhat different. The drug problem was mentioned by 47 pupils, followed by 26 who wrote about nudity, prostitution and homosexuality; loss and corruption of culture through copying foreigners was mentioned by 23 and 24 specifically mentioned the danger to the younger generation through imitating the ways of the tourist; 21 mentioned diseases brought by tourists; the smuggling of antiques and gems was mentioned by 18. Less frequently mentioned problems attributed to tourism were: inflationary pressures (12), nefarious activities (8), the shortage of accommodation (7), environmental problems (6), Sri Lankans being treated as second class citizens (5), the problem of hippies (5), increased numbers of beggars (5), the growing problem of drunkenness (4), the nuisance of the guides (3) and loss of Sri Lankan children through adoption (2).

The last two issues the pupils were asked to write about were rather more personal. The first asked: 'If you have known any tourists, write about what you remember about them and their relationship with you'. Very few wrote at any length in response, in fact only 82 students out of 105 wrote anything at all and of those 38 stated that they had not known any tourists personally. Of the 44 who wrote that they had known tourists, however, 39 did so in overwhelmingly positive terms, 5 in rather mixed terms, and none at all in a purely negative way. The very last question, however, drew very lengthy replies. The question was: 'When you leave school would you like to have a job dealing with tourists (i.e. working in a tourist shop, a hotel, driving a tourist vehicle, being a guide, etc.)? If you would, say why. If you would not, explain your reasons'.

Whilst the majority of pupils who had met tourists described them in positive terms, when it came to choosing a career in the tourism industry, most pupils were negative. Fifty-one said firmly that they did not want a job in the industry, 2 were undecided, whilst 36 expressed a desire to have a tourism-related job. There was a recognisable difference in how males and females responded to this question. Of the 50 female pupils, 32 were against a job in tourism, with only 11 definitely for. With the males, 19 were definitely against whilst 25 were in favour, of whom 12 were from the private school, suggesting, perhaps, that the more well-to-do regard tourism as an attractive and lucrative career. That certainly was not the predominant view. As one pupil expressed it:

> The Sri Lankan community generally looks down upon the people involved
> in tourism. Mostly because of the rumours we get to hear about tourists.

Whilst this comment is probably fairly accurate, clearly the school pupils were worried by far more than the cultural problems widely perceived to follow in the wake of tourism. Some plainly did not believe that tourism would last very long in Sri Lanka, and as one put it graphically:

> You cannot rely on this sort of job. At any moment, if the tourists do not
> come there is no job either.

Given that the responses to this final question were so detailed and revealed interesting disparities of response in both status and gender terms, the comments will be set out now on a school by school basis. With the private school for boys, while 12 were in favour, 5 were against a tourism career. In actual fact five of the 20 pupils came from families already involved in tourism (1 whose father was a hotel manager, 1 whose mother worked as a hotel receptionist, 2 whose parents owned guesthouses, 1 whose father rented out a house to tourists). The pupil whose parent was a hotel receptionist did not want a career in tourism. All the others with family members in this industry did, with a striking preference for hotel management. The reasons given for wanting a job in tourism were: money (5), meeting people (5), possibility of extensive travel (3), learning about other countries (2), showing Sri Lanka to foreigners (1), liking tourists (1), the possibility of improving the tourist industry (1).

With the state school for boys there was a marked discrepancy between the English and Sinhala medium students. Of the former, 3 wanted jobs in tourism and 7 did not. Three students came from families already engaged in tourism (guesthouse ownership, personnel management, hotel worker), and interestingly, only the one with a parent working in a hotel wanted to join the same industry. The other two claimed that tourism was destroying Sri Lanka's culture or that tourism simply would not last. Of the reasons given for wanting a job in the tourist trade, meeting people, learning about other countries, and level of income were each mentioned once. For the Sinhala medium students, 7 did not want a job in tourism whereas 10 did. One pupil had a father working in a batik shop and he too wished to work in a tourist shop. One had a father running a guesthouse and he wanted to make money as a guide and then go abroad. The types of tourist jobs aimed for by these students were rather different to those aspired to by the respondents at the private school. In the state school, 3 wanted to be guides, 1 to work in a shop, 1 in a hotel and 1 to be a tourist car driver. Reasons given for wanting such employment were as follows: money (5), to tell others about Sri Lanka (4), opportunity to learn about other countries (3), opportunity to go abroad (3), desire to improve tourism (2), opportunity to learn other languages (1), opportunity to meet people (1), the industry was good for the country (1), liking tourists (1).

In the state school for girls, a very different pattern emerged. For the English medium students, 14 were against a job in tourism with 4 in favour. The only career specifically mentioned was work in a travel agency (1 pupil). The four responding favourably cited the following reasons for their choice of job: meeting people (3), the industry is good for Sri Lanka (3), learning languages (2), learning about other countries (1), the possibility of travel (1). The reasons given for not wanting a job in tourism were as follows: problems caused by tourists (4), tourism was ruining the culture of Sri Lanka (2), dislike of mercenary motives (1), language difficulties (1), parental disapproval (1). The Sinhala medium female students were the most opposed to tourism. Only 2 expressed a desire to work in a tourism job, citing the possibility of learning about other cultures (2), improving international relations (1) and opportunities to go abroad (1) as reasons. Two of the pupils had close kin in the industry (one had a father who was a hotel manager, the other had a relative who worked as a guide), but neither wanted to go into the tourism industry themselves. The reasons cited for this were: other careers already in mind (3), tourism was ruining the country (3), loss of respect (2), problems for females working in hotels (1), unreliable future (1), parents would chose their career (1). The Tamil medium students were more positive than negative. Five pupils wanted a job in tourism, guiding being the specific occupation cited by two. Reasons given for wanting jobs in tourism were: learning about other cultures (3), the income attainable (3), opportunity to get abroad (2), opportunity to learn foreign languages (2), desire to teach others about Sri Lanka (1), tourism brings benefits to Sri Lanka (1). The four respondents who were definitely averse to a job in tourism cited the following reasons: parental disapproval (2), need to protect Sri Lanka's culture (1), tourism brings no benefits (1).

Had the research time at my disposal been greater my sub-population could have been extended to a second and much younger age group and also included some rural schools which would inevitably have yielded a wider class cross-section. Under those circumstances class, gender and possibly ethnicity might have shown up constantly as variables within a generalised picture of how the younger generation views tourism. As it is, though, the material gained richly illustrated what it was meant to. Clearly, those about to leave school echo much of the ambivalence and concern of their elders about this relatively new industry. But, given that in the early 1980s tourism was one of the few expanding economic sectors, clearly some were sorely troubled about which way to go. With some the negative wins out, with others optimism remains albeit combined with caution. Two final quotations from the students' essays well state the two positions:

> When I leave school I do not want to do a job in tourism. We cannot rely on the job lasting for a long time, nor can we do an honest job. By talking to them very kindly, to please them, we cannot do an honest job because our own people just want to get money from them. We do certain things, including cheating them. Even without a proper command of English, we can come to observe the tourists, study their bad habits and the way they live their lives, and in this way we become corrupted too.

> After leaving school, if I pursue the same field of study as I am now in (commerce), it will be inevitable that I have to deal in tourism as it is one of the main streams of income to our land. But, given a choice, I'd rather not have a hand in the ruination of our land. True, it is a lovely experience to get to know people of different nationalities and through them, their country and so forth, but the typical tourist of today is a self-centred person whose purpose of visit is solely pleasure, using hard drugs which are freely available. As a result, if there are ways of curbing these nefarious activities I would like to have a hand in that, and then have a job dealing with foreign visitors. But this is a very unlikely situation unless the government stamps down some really tough laws and finds some officers of law who deal with the law instead of bribes.

THE VIEW FROM THE STREETS

The final section in this chapter sets out the views of a variety of people who make their living on the streets of Kandy. Some of them like the guides were highly dependent upon tourism for their income, whilst others were only marginally affected by the presence of tourists. Essentially, though, these are all voices absent from the Town Hall seminar. Over several months I had spoken casually to many of these people, but often only to exchange pleasantries, to buy fruit, to get shoes repaired, and so on. In the wake of the seminar, however, I decided to elicit their views on tourism far more systematically, asking them all the same basic questions: whether they liked tourism, whether it was good or bad, who made the most money from tourism, and whether tourism had changed Kandy significantly. In the case of street guides (those characters normally referred to as 'touts'), I had many more free-ranging discussions and got to know four particularly well. I therefore present at the end of this chapter four brief 'street guide biographies' so that the views expressed by these individuals are particularly contextualised. Such biographical sketches will also serve as a good prelude to the more analytical discussion in Chapter 5 of the informal tourism arena in Kandy, in which the street guides are central actors.

Before I started my series of directed interviews in the streets of Kandy, I asked Ali whether the sort of people I wanted to talk to thought a great deal about tourism, whether they would see Kandy as being significantly changed by it, and what views they might have about the way in which its benefits were distributed. Ali claimed that the poor were not angry or jealous and did not think about tourism very much. They were resigned; jealousy would be pointless. It was not that they would be embarrassed to express their feelings on this to me, he claimed. When I began to seek their views systematically, Ali proved to be only partially correct. I initially asked a fruit seller whether he thought tourism good or bad, and he replied that he had no views about tourism at all; his sole concern was to earn enough each day to feed his family. Somewhat depressed by this, my first response, I wondered whether I would get the same response from others. Just then, one of the most conspicuous guides in Kandy, the one commonly referred to as the "crazy guide" because he looked permanently drunk and drugged, wandered by with this torn shirt billowing out behind him. I was not going to ask him his views since I had had, over the months, only the most dismissive and rude encounters with him, but Ali and Felix thought that I should speak to him. The guide, stopped by Felix, demanded to see what notes I was taking, and then said to me: "My friend, you will sell your book for royalties and so you must pay me for the information that goes into it". And with that he proceeded on his way.

Luckily, not all interviews were like this. An old beggar woman, frequently found just a few yards down the street from my main observation post, said that tourism was good and that it had not changed Kandy. She said that most money went to the rich, especially the shopkeepers; she was not jealous because it was pointless. I then spoke to an elderly man whose occupation was selling a few trinkets from a small metal box that he carried around with him. Tourism was good, he said, because it helped the country to develop; but Kandy had not changed. He said that the rich benefited most and he did not see the government doing anything to change this. He said the shops got most profit, but the rich proprietors were jealous of him for making a little money in front of their establishments.

It soon became known that I was systematically interviewing people and rather than discover that people had no views or avoided me, a small queue formed as people lined up to express their views. A prostitute who often waited on the corner where I did much of my observation said that tourism was good for her business, that Kandy had not changed and that there was no bad side to tourism. The hotels got most money, but she was not angry that the rich made more than her. A taxi driver explained how he kept 25% of the day's takings, giving the rest to the owner of the car. He admitted that tourism had spoiled some beach areas but claimed that Kandy was unchanged. The shops and hotels made most money, according to him, but the government would not distribute the benefits to the poor. He said that taxi drivers could make a lot of money by supplying drugs and prostitutes to tourists. A young female traffic warden said that tourism was good as she was often given above the required parking fee by foreigners. She was allowed to keep 75% of the 40–50 rupees she collected each day. Tourism had no bad side, she said, and Kandy was unchanged. The tourist shops made the most money. A security guard outside a jeweller's shop said that tourism was good and also agreed that the town was not changed by it. One of the pavement hawkers who had a small pile of mats for sale liked tourism because he occasionally got a small income from tourists passing in the street or getting out of a coach on their way to a hotel. Tourism had no bad side. Hotels and shops made most money, whereas street sellers just earned enough to live on. He claimed that he was not jealous of the rich, or of the other street sellers, because many were friends from the same village.

Another female beggar said that tourism was good, that it had no bad side and that Kandy had not been changed. It made her angry that the rich benefited most, but the government would not change its policy. Hotels and shops benefited most. The police, she said, helped the rich and the prostitutes. A necklace seller said that tourism had not changed the values or outlook of people in Kandy. The rich benefited most, but the government allowed this and would not change its policy. Prostitution was bad, she said, but women had to earn a living. A young female guide, only thirteen years old, and with a conversational command of three European languages, said that Kandy had not been changed, that tourism was good because it enabled her to earn a good living. She did not like the job of being a guide, but had to support her father. She hoped to go to university so that she could do something better when she was older. A shoe repairer said that tourism was good. Tourists occasionally came to him when their shoes needed work to be done on them and he allowed them to pay whatever they liked, unlike with locals where he stated the price for a job. He felt that the Tourist Board and the police should be stricter with the tourists, but local people did not have to follow the tourists' ways of behaviour. He did not like the "rascally guides" and how they made their living. The poor made little from tourism compared with the rich. Kandy had not changed, in his view. A small boy selling necklaces said he made about 50–75 rupees per day. Kandy had not changed, he said, and there was no bad side to tourism. He hoped that when older he could be a room boy in one of the hotels in the town. He said that the rich made most money from tourism and that that made him very jealous. He had been fined three times for selling goods in the street and would like a license so that he did not have to go in fear of the police; the police were friends only to the rich.

After a lengthy string of interviews spanning several days which took place mainly on the corner where Ali worked, I moved to speak to several people working in a slum area only yards away from the main tourist thoroughfares down a very narrow alley. An elderly woman selling betel in the alley said that tourism was good for Sri Lanka. It enabled people to sell goods and had no bad side. Kandy had not changed, nor had peoples' attitudes and values. Most money was made by the tour guides and prostitutes, but she was not jealous of their success. A shirt seller said that many tourists smuggled drugs and were often drunk, but there were no real problems. People benefited from selling goods to foreigners. He did not have any views as to who made the most money from tourism. An elderly prostitute said that tourism was very good. It brought money to Sri Lanka and it was beneficial to meet people from other cultures. It had no bad side. People had not changed their values or behaviour and Kandy itself had not changed. Guesthouses, hotels and the middle class made the most money. Another prostitute explained how tourism was good. For locals she charged 40–50 rupees, but with foreigners she could charge 500 rupees ($U.S. 25), with 100 of this going to the guide who brought the customer. Most money, she thought, went to the rich and the government would not change this. Being angry about this was pointless, because it would not lead to any change.

I proceeded from the slum to the Central Market in Kandy. A taxi driver outside the market said that tourism was good, that Kandy was not changed and that there was no bad side. He earned about 750 rupees per month, whereas the owner of the vehicle he drove earned about 300–400 rupees every day. He thought that gem and batik shops, along with guesthouses, made the most money; again jealousy of the wealthy was pointless. The government would do nothing to change the situation. He also added that the police were the friends of the rich. Inside the market I spoke to a number of shop assistants who had often seen me and to many of whom I had spoken before. One shop assistant said that tourism was very good. His boss was very rich, so he had a job earning about 500 rupees per month. Kandy had not changed, he said, and he was not jealous of the rich. One bad side to tourism, he explained, was the commissions that they had to pay out to the guides. A tailor working in the market whom I knew well and whose house I had visited several times said that his life and family depended on tourism. There were many benefits which came from tourism, such as extra work for himself and artists. There were some bad sides, such as drugs which the Europeans brought with them, but Sri Lanka's beliefs and values were not affected. The rich made most out of tourism. He worked hard all day for just 40 rupees. He was not jealous of the rich, but was sad that "the poor man, however hard he works, can never rise up. They are still in the same position".

I had no preconceptions before starting any of this concentrated interviewing as to what the replies were likely to be, but for me there was a touching irony that these street people, most of them not making a great deal out of tourism, should be so much in favour of tourism, think it good for Kandy and at the same time suggest that Kandy itself had not been really changed and their own values had not suffered. By contrast, many wealthy individuals making substantial sums from tourism were not only very jealous of each other, they were also trying to drive the poor out of the industry; at the same time they were personally prospering from the industry, they waxed lyrical about tourism's attendant evils. Perhaps those on the streets simply did not have the time, given their immediate concerns of making ends meet, to go in for 'cultural pollution' rhetoric, which indeed, is often seen very much as a middle class self-indulgence. The difference of attitude was certainly brought home to me the day after the Town Hall seminar. Whereas some who had attended used the occasion to distribute to me their cards asking me to tell tourists about their establishment and to mention it in the book I was writing, none of the street people who lined up to express their views tried to profit from the encounter. Indeed, Ali told me that a pavement vendor around the other end of the lake had asked him to thank me for taking the trouble to inform the Mayor that the poor also had the right to make some money from tourism.

I do not know whether Ali embellished this incident in any way to flatter me, but it is important to qualify the frequently stated view that the street people were not jealous or angry, were resigned to their fate and so simply accepted the way things were in tourism as elsewhere. Towards the end of 1982 the municipal authorities in Kandy were contemplating not only cracking down on touts and beggars, but were also planning to disrupt the activities of the sizeable population of street vendors who made their living on the pavements. In early October it was rumoured that a public procession headed by an important Minister through the streets of Kandy on his way to inspect the nearby Mahaweli dam project would be the occasion for a thorough 'clean up' of the streets in the town. There was outrage when news of this plan became public knowledge. Ali informed me that many of the street vendors who occupied the pavement between the lakeside and the central bus station were rehabilitated criminals, and being able to sell trinkets, fruit, cloth and so on, was a way of preventing their return to a life of crime. Pickpocketing, Ali told me, had dramatically declined in areas of Kandy where these people worked, because they had a stake in keeping a good reputation for their stretch of territory. A deputation was being formed in mid-October to tell the Mayor of the crime wave which would break out if the street people were forcibly removed. There was also the suggestion that all those adversely affected would vote against the U.N.P. government in the forthcoming election, a message which would certainly have hit home, given that the Mayor was an active U.N.P. supporter.

None who knew the street guides of Kandy in 1982 would have entertained for a minute the idea that they were content with their lot. Over seven months I got to know a number of these characters on a daily basis. Some were very suspicious of me and I had a number of abrasive encounters with several. Some of them I did not speak to at all. Indeed, my developing relationship with some of the guides itself became part of the system of rivalry which existed between them, for to form a close tie with one or more automatically put me out of favour with some others. I got to know four individuals particularly well and the remainder of this chapter sets out their views about tourism and tourists by way of brief biographical sketches of them. I doubt if one could call any of them 'typical', for the very reason that anyone who spent so much time with me, especially since I was not in Kandy for the things tourists are normally there for, could not be typical. While one needs to bear in mind the fact that I will be discussing four individuals who were more friendly and talkative than the norm, their different circumstances and plans still give a good idea as to the sorts of individuals who were trying to make a living as unlicensed guides on the streets of Kandy in 1982. The sketches below certainly cast doubt on the accuracy of the stereotypes which the municipal authorities and the well-to-do in Kandy held of the street people. They also raise doubts about the suggestion made by some researchers (Bochner 1981:27; McLeod 1981:37) that 'mediating persons' (mediation in the broad sense is what much guiding consists of) have a specific set of personality characteristics.

Prema, my first example, was a boy of seventeen but who looked much younger. He lived in a flimsily constructed wooden shack with his elder brother's large family in a Kandy slum literally yards away from a rubbish tip. He was an unassuming youth who had been following tourists since the age of five, at which time he did little more than literally walk after them begging for money. He could not read or write, but he knew a few phrases in Spanish, French and English. It was his ambition when older to own a barrow and sell fruit and vegetables near the central market in Kandy like his brother. Prema's services as a guide were fairly limited. He did not deal in drugs or sex. He did not escort tourists to accommodation either, because it was too troublesome, he told me. If he took a tourist to a guesthouse and subsequently the tourist caused trouble it would be his own reputation that would be ruined. What Prema did was take tourists around shops in Kandy, especially the gem and batik shops where he would earn a commission on sales. In the early years, tourists, he claimed, were much more generous and friendly. His biggest ever commission of 3500 rupees ($U.S. 175) from a gem sale was well over

Photo 6   Selling fruit near the Kandy Central Market.

half a year's salary in any job he was ever likely to have. Prema would have liked to have a municipal guide's license so that he did not have to fear police harassment, but he said he could not afford the annual fee. Latterly trade had been very bad and sometimes he had to go for three months without earning anything. Whilst he did not starve because other members of the family were earning money, he was embarrassed not to be able financially to support his parents or help his older brother.

An unusual aspect about Prema's guiding was the relationship he had with some of the foreign tour guides who accompanied the coaches full of tourists on 'package' holidays. Normally the 'formal' sphere in which these groups moved and the 'informal' sphere of the street guide were quite separate, because such tourists were normally deposited *en masse* into certain select shops for limited periods of time and so were not seen casually strolling through the streets. But over the years, Prema had built up a friendship with a few of the French and Spanish tour guides and he would eagerly await their arrival because they occasionally put some work his way, either telling him to go shopping in the market with one or two of the passengers or else helping out the official guide with the group as a whole. Apart from those occasions, Prema did not get a great deal of business in 1982. Indeed, it seemed that even his regular overseas tour guides were letting him down. Prema was, from what I saw of him, a good-natured teenager, but he was certainly angry about the way rich people made the most money from tourism. He was also jealous of the large amounts of money that the company guides, often foreigners, made. Despite his difficult circumstances, though, he did not once ask me for any money. Presents from overseas he treasured and on several occasions he brought me letters from England or France that he himself could not read.

A guide of an altogether different type was Siri. Eighteen years old, Siri was physically very small for his age and I am sure that his success as a street guide had something to do with his boyish, non-threatening appearance. Siri had been to a reasonably good secondary school in Kandy, although his English was quite poor. He had dropped out of school early to do tourism and was now using some of the money derived from guiding to pay for private English classes (which he attended somewhat spasmodically), to improve his command of the language so that he could do tourism better. He bragged about having three bank accounts where he put all his income from tourism. He also complained that because of his age, his father had control of the bank books so he could not get access to his money.

Siri did not need to do tourism. He lived in a reasonable home and his father had a secure job in a well known Kandy shop. Siri came across not just as a 'scatter brain' but as emotionally somewhat disturbed. Indeed, if anyone I knew well in Kandy symbolised the adverse consequences of tourism on the young it was he. Each day Siri's view about his own future changed. He also loudly bragged in public about "shady deals" he had pulled off and about women he had slept with. The other street guides thought that as a smallish boy he might occasionally be in sexual demand by middle-aged women somewhat anxious about sex with an adult, but most people thought he was simply lying about his sexual encounters. More than anyone else I knew, he 'acted out' the deviant sub-culture image that surrounded the street guides. But, however much of it was theatrical, by the time of my departure, Siri was sitting in cafes with his sleeves rolled up showing people the scars which demonstrated that he was injecting drugs.

For Siri, tourism was very much a matter of fast, easy money, thrills and 'bright lights'. Sometimes he would clown around in the streets wearing a French beret, stopping the tourists and uttering nonsensical French phrases with no serious attempt to do any business. He boasted on a number of occasions of having been involved in a motorcycle crash and often used to wear the trousers, torn and still covered in blood, which he had had on when the vehicle went off the road. He struck me as rather cowardly, but he bragged about the flick-knife he kept in his sock, and the small aerosol can of fly repellent that he also kept about him to spray into the eyes of anyone trying to rough him up. On many days I saw him in full swing, trying to get the attention of tourists, arguing with them and driving some of them to abusive retorts. When they swore at him, he would swear back at full volume in front of everyone else. Clearly, too, there was considerable conflict with his parents. He would often return home in the early hours of the morning and on several occasions he told me that he was leaving Kandy and would never see his parents again. In a few short years his involvement in drugs, sex, fast living and shady dealing had reached a point where return to anything like a normal life had become quite impossible (Garcia 1988:112).

Siri never showed me the notebooks in which he said he kept records of how much he had earned from doing tourism over the years. He had started doing tourism when twelve, between leaving school each day and before starting his homework in the evenings. He claimed his biggest windfall was 42,000 rupees ($U.S. 2100) on a sale of gems to three Japanese tourists in Galle. I once asked him why he did not dress in a better way if he had so much money and why he did not have his hair nicely cut like most of the other guides so that he could attract women. "First of all you must find their mind", was his way of explaining how to grasp what to do in any tourist encounter; his appearance, he claimed, was of little consequence. And one is bound to say that in 1982, a slack year for many on the streets of Kandy, he was still doing well, and was often out of town for days at a time on business. It was he that year who interfered with a group of Italian 'package' tourists, greatly annoying other guides in Kandy and the travel agency concerned. Normally street guides leave such coach groups alone, but Siri approached a group as they were paying 75 rupees to see a Kandyan dance performance saying that he could get them tickets for 35 rupees. He went on to tell the tourists that their tour guide was taking a large commission every time they purchased anything. The tourists then became very angry apparently, asking their official guide whether this was all true or not. Complaints then went back to Colombo and there was, for a time, a suggestion that the tour company would cease to route its clients through Kandy if they were not going to be effectively insulated from the activities of the 'touts'.

Over the years Siri had had his share of trouble through his tourist encounters. He was one of the guides held in custody in Kandy for the rape of the French woman near the lake. Ali and Felix thought it was typical of him to start bragging in front of the police. Siri never spoke sensibly about the trouble into which tourism got him. He saw tourism as a way of earning big money. "Look at me. I have a wrist watch on my arm. Next year I will have a tape recorder, you will see". Typical of Siri, too, he was trying to sell the watch. It had been given to him by a German tourist who claimed he did not have enough cash to pay him for his services. Instead he told him he could have the watch. Siri soon realised that the watch did not work and he tried to sell it to one of his ex-teachers. He even tried to sell it to me. No other guide with whom I regularly spoke would, I believe, have attempted to palm such an article off to me in this way.

Siri evidently had countless plans about his future. In the seven months that I knew him, his views about what he would do with his life went through a number of changes. Totally contradictory ideas about his future just seemed to drift into and out of his head. On occasions he was going to use his accumulated savings to set himself up in a roadside boutique just outside Kandy in order to sell general wares. On others, he was going to purchase land in Kandy near his parents' home on which he would build a number of cabanas for tourists. He would oversee the running of the establishment and do all the cooking himself. On some days he would speak about his tourist friends who wanted to buy land in Sri Lanka and own a guesthouse. Siri was to arrange this and run the guesthouse for three years with the foreigners coming back for annual holidays. They would take all the profits and then transfer the guesthouse to Siri's ownership. In September 1982 he was talking about doing "big monkey business" in Pakistan. He would use his savings to buy a plane ticket, pick up a kilo of cocaine and then take it to France to sell, becoming rich for life. I pointed out to him that a young Sri Lankan travelling from Pakistan to France would clearly be an object of suspicion. His only response was: "Maybe I will be caught, but if I go to prison it will only be for twelve years, and I can still work when I get out".

Siri was not one of the specialist drug guides in Kandy, but it was clear that he was getting increasingly tied up with the trade. He disappeared once for a round trip of the island with an English couple who wanted to see the spots in Sri Lanka where drugs were manufactured and traded. His food and accommodation had been paid all the way and he was loudly telling the story in a popular cafe in Kandy, behaving in a way quite unlike the "drugy guides", who were naturally somewhat secretive about their work. Both Felix and Ali commented on how crazy Siri was to be bragging in the open about such dealings. They told me that they thought Siri would be dead before he reached twenty five years of age. On bad days he would complain that he had only three friends in Kandy. When I first heard him say this he did not mention the other guides on the corner with whom he often used to hang out, but was referring instead to the drug specialists with whom only a few weeks earlier he had said he would have nothing to do. One day I met Siri in a street in Kandy where I had never before seen any guide at work. Indeed it seemed a ridiculous place for anyone to stand if trying to catch tourists. I asked him why he had shifted to this spot and he said that although tourists did not get out of buses there, he would know minutes before anyone else in Kandy how many foreigners were arriving from the north. I asked him if he was still thinking of setting up a guesthouse and he said that he hated tourism and was going to use his money to make a film to show foreigners how evil tourism was. The sudden change of plan, plus its lack of realism, seem typical of him.

Felix, my third example, was a Sinhalese Christian in his mid-twenties who had been doing tourism in Kandy for about eight years. He remembered 1977 as his best year for making money. He had been educated in a good school on the out-skirts of Kandy, and although he had learned English at school, he now spoke it somewhat hesitatingly. He was from a good Negombo family on the west coast but his father, a businessman, had died several years previously. Although he had an aunt living in a village near Kandy where he stored some of his best clothes and where he occasionally stayed, for the most part he slept rough in Kandy itself, it being a very long walk to the village when he lacked the bus fare. Felix, for some years, had been a security guard for a hotel, but he claimed that the income was not enough to live on. He had subsequently planned to join the navy but told me that politics intervened so that he was prevented from doing the necessary training course. For political reasons, too, he had been unable to get regular employment in Kandy since. Tourism, he said, was a "bad business" for which he had "no heart". One could not do the job "with an honest heart", and if he could only find employ-ment which would bring him in 500 or 600 rupees per month he would gladly throw it all in. "I hope one day God may look on my face in a friendly way", he once said to me.

But there was no such beneficence apparent for Felix in 1982. 1981 had been a bad year for him and he hoped that the 1982 *perahera* season would bring him luck. It did not, and for days at a stretch he had nothing to eat. I started sharing meals with him in a local cafe as he told me his various experiences in tourism, and this sparked off a whole host of rumours about what we were doing together. Felix was a handsome man and had quite a reputation as a "lady killer". For him to be spending hours with me, especially quietly talking at a cafe table, led some of his acquaintances to believe that he had "bent". The street guides knew that I understood some Sinhala, so on occasions their musings about what Felix and I were up to were conducted in Tamil so that I would not understand what they were saying.

There is no doubt that Felix enjoyed some aspects of his guiding role. He enjoyed sex with European women and had become very fond of three or four over the years, although still making the point that in nearly all cases this was still very much a matter of making money. In his time he had had some nasty incidents with guesthouse owners and also a number of fights with other guides. In one guesthouse incident his tourist 'catch' wanted him to accompany her inside the house, but the owner refused to allow this. In the shouting match at the door the owner pulled out a gun, according to Felix, at which point he left. Felix had also had his clashes with the local authorities. He had more than once been taken to court. On one occasion he was let off. On another, he was fined 15 rupees, which made him angry because, as he said, the Sri Lankan people were free and so one did not require a license to talk to foreigners. Felix was certainly very hostile towards the authorities. He admitted that some guides were robbers, but pointed out that it was quite unfair, because of the activities of the few, to assume that all the guides were bad. He estimated that 75% were honest, and only 25% were rogues. "Guides are good people", he told me, "it is the work in tourism that makes some of them bad". He was not happy that the Ceylon Tourist Board brochures and the various guide books on Sri Lanka spoke so harshly of guides, because they performed valuable services for tourists. Felix was very angry at the way the rich took what he estimated to be 90% of the profits out of tourism, while the poor guides like himself not only had to struggle to earn money but were also hassled by the police. "Guides do not get much money", he claimed, "they do it just to get enough to eat. In three years there will be no guides as tourists have travel books, understand the commission system and are increasingly poor, so that they do not spend anything. Tourists mistakenly think that guides earn a lot; that is why they do not speak to us".

I first met Felix in the second week of my stay in Kandy. I was at that time just establishing an observation base in the streets and he started asking me the same sort of questions that I was asking him and his colleagues. He asked me what I thought about tourism, whether I liked Sri Lanka, and he was evidently quite happy to give me information. He was grateful when I pointed out errors in his English because this would enable him to speak to foreigners more impressively. He told me that tourism was beneficial because we were all learning about each other's cultures. From the beginning, though, Felix was also somewhat guarded. He would tell me what I wanted to know on most subjects but would not allow me to record any conversations with him for fear that others would get hold of the information he provided and use it against him. He knew very well that other people would be paying close attention to what I was doing on the streets and told me never to mention his name. He would never tell me anything about the drug trade and prostitution he would speak about only in the most general of terms. If I wanted to learn about the links between hotels, prostitutes and taxi drivers and how the whole system worked, I would have to "sample it for myself", as he put it.

Over the years, Felix had developed a fairly sanguine view of Europeans. He was certainly envious of their money and, in the beginning, he had been very keen to learn new ways. He realised, though, that he had learned some bad habits over eight years. Kandy was becoming a European city, he said. He, having mixed with Europeans, knew that he had a taste for hotel comforts, beer and foreign women, which a poor person simply could not satisfy. He realised, too, that having had such experiences with foreign women, it would now be impossible for him to marry a local. Like many of the younger street guides, he was hoping that one of the relationships he struck up with a tourist might lead to an air ticket and work overseas. Nonetheless, he no longer idolised tourists. He was happy for tourists to come to Sri Lanka, but he disliked those who simply came and displayed their wealth in front of local people. For him, as for some other informants, the big difference between tourists and Sri Lankans was that Europeans lived by a timetable. Sri Lankans, apart from the very rich whom he claimed wanted to be like Europeans, had no "plans". Tourists not only had a timetable at home, when on holiday they were still hurrying around and behaving in the same way. Sri Lankans were crazy, he said, if they thought that Europeans led a happy life. Even on the subject of women he said that while sex with Europeans was enjoyable and "free" (in the sense that one could sleep with whom one wanted), it was still better with one partner.

Felix himself was not one of those whom tourism had ruined in the same way as Siri. Rather, he was somewhat sad. As the 1982 *perahera* season in Kandy came and went, he grew more and more despondent. He was putting much faith in getting a job on the massive Mahaweli dam development project some miles outside Kandy. Every time a certain English expatriate engineer came to Kandy, Felix was very civil and did some special favours for him, including trying to arrange a marriage with a local woman. At one point he told me that the engineer had promised him a job and so he waited for the word to start work. No word ever came, though, and Felix was very upset when one day the engineer walked through Kandy and did not so much as acknowledge him. He was even more distraught on finding out that his friend had already hired the crew that he wanted.

Felix had several pronounced chips on his shoulder. Ali used to say that Felix had sex with so many white women because he felt so resentful and, for reasons I could never pin down, he was very hostile to the English, speaking of them as treating Sri Lanka "like a football". He was too young to have had direct experience of British rule in Ceylon and I could never find out why he was so anti-British. Felix knew me as an Australian writing an academic book about tourism in Sri Lanka. He understood that I had different interests to most other foreigners in Kandy and never tried to do any business with me. Indeed, despite his often desperate circumstances, he never once asked me for any money. On the other hand, once when he did manage to do some business with a tourist, he sought me out in Ali's house and presented me with an enormous pile of fruit in return for all the meals we had shared together. I did actually help Felix out by having him accompany me to certain guesthouses so that he could earn some commission. He also accompanied me on many occasions to guesthouses knowing that I was only going there to ask questions of their owners. On some occasions this involved his sitting for half an hour with the guesthouse owner berating the way tourism in Kandy was being strangled by touts. Afterwards, I had Felix's commentary on what the guesthouse owner had said. Often it was that the owners were lying about the levels of commission which guides received and that they were trying to cover up how much money the guesthouses were making. It was very noticeable that Felix would not accompany me to certain guesthouses. He would hang around outside and out of sight until I emerged. I could not get him to explain to me his reluctance to go into some, so I put it down to past conflicts he may have had with the owners. He now very much specialised in accompanying tourists on shopping expeditions and going on trips around the island, especially with attractive females, he told me. He said he rarely took tourists to accommodation any longer because it had become just too troublesome.

Felix certainly carried a good many grudges and his sense that wealth did not necessarily make one happy did little to mollify his great resentment at being poor. One day, through the streets of Kandy, walked a strikingly attractive and opulently dressed young French woman. Instead of immediately moving in her direction, as I thought he would, Felix became very sad and depressed. Felix said that there was no sense in his trying to catch her because "she could have her pick of who she wanted to go with". To go to bed with her one would have to have enough money to buy her a meal, drinks, and entertainment first. Felix simply did not have the resources for this. "God makes man. Man makes money. Money makes everything", he said to me. "People look at me and think I am rich", he said, "because I have good shoes, jeans and a foreign shirt. But I look at myself and think: shoes — the German; jeans — the French girl; shirt — Dr. Malcolm; all gifts".

Like all street guides, Felix received presents from some tourists which he proudly sported. And it was a very special day for him in 1982 when, after he had made friends with a young female tourist, she invited him to meet her parents and to go swimming in the pool at the Hotel Suisse, a hotel which would normally have turned him away. He shaved off his beard, his hair was trimmed and he appeared wearing my shirt and various other pieces of finery foreigners had given him. He had even been out to his aunt's village to collect his leather boots. I asked Felix before I left Sri Lanka what would happen to the street guides in Kandy if tourism ever suffered a serious decline and he said that they would simply have to look for work in other cities or would turn to robbery.

The first time I saw Ali, my last example, he was selling a range of goods from the pavement on a street corner which subsequently became my key observation base in Kandy. I walked right past him then on my way to the central market at the end of my first week in Kandy. Ali was shouting out the wares he had for sale but I did not stop to inspect what he had. Later that afternoon I passed the same spot on my way home to my guesthouse and Ali remembered me from the morning and said, as I passed: "Oh, I see that you have bought yourself something. Can I have a look at it?". His good command of English, plus a hesitant, polite curiosity was what first caught my attention. I was somewhat wary of such overtures, but Ali went on to become my chief informant for the seven months I spent in Kandy.[5]

Ali was not a street guide in the sense that Felix, Siri or Prema were. He did not have years of guiding experience behind him and was chiefly a pavement hawker, selling a range of leather, and occasionally cotton, goods. Like some others on the streets, though, he occasionally tried to "do a little tourism" and in 1982 because business was so bad, he was actually thinking of abandoning his normal business activities for a more permanent involvement in guiding. As a street vendor and relative novice to guiding, Ali was on the very margin of the tourism arena in Kandy. Other characteristics too set him apart from most other guides. For a start, he was a married man in his fifties. He was also a Muslim of deep religious convictions. He used to tell me how, if he ever cheated anyone, it would rebound on him, because he would, in turn, be robbed. Ali also clearly understood the kind of book which I was trying to write, whereas nearly everyone else presumed that I was writing a travel book and so insisted that I mention their establishment by name. But more than this, Ali had a reflective nature which attracted me. At times he spoke to me as someone involved in tourism, while on other occasions he spoke not as a guide but as someone who had to deal with guides; on yet others he seemed to be a somewhat detached observer, simply watching what was going on around him. Locals, too, saw him in these several lights: for some he was a new competitor on the block, whereas others affectionately referred to him by the Tamil term for 'uncle'. He did, indeed, keep an avuncular watch over some of the younger guides lest they get themselves into serious trouble. Of course, the new role inevitably got

---

[5] I have explored my relationship with Ali at great length in Crick 1989b and 1992.

Ali himself into trouble with some rivals who were jealous of him. A thug one day threatened that if he wanted to act as a guide then he would have to hand over some of his money or be beaten up. Ali was visibly shaken by this episode but put a brave face on it, showing me the solid silver belt he wore around his waste which kept his sarong up. Guides, he said, were "all mouth".

Although during 1982 sleeping on a mat in his younger brother's house, Ali had actually been educated at Kandy's most prestigious private school, though he was not keen for other people to know this. He waxed lyrical about life under the British as the son of a wealthy merchant attending an exclusive school, portraying Ceylon as a land free from the ethnic tensions which had recently beset her. He was proud of having met Lord Mountbatten during the war and of mixing easily, at that time, with white women. His father had been an extremely wealthy merchant and his three younger brothers were all wealthy shopkeepers, in Kandy, Colombo and Badulla. Ali had originally wished to study medicine at university but had left school to help out in his father's business. Since that time there had been a succession of retail, clerical and supervisory positions. A fire had destroyed most of his possessions and he was then forced to sell goods in the streets to earn a small income. Despite having ended up on the streets from a privileged start in life, he was generous with the little money he had. As a Muslim he used to donate a proportion of his income to the poor, of course, and he also told me that a small pension he received was paid directly into a local children's welfare association. There was, I felt, something endearing about Ali, even amidst the obvious colossal fall that had taken place in his life and in spite of the many personal problems that he had.

On my first encounter with Ali, I had informed him that I was in Kandy to write a book about tourism in Sri Lanka. He immediately told me that he knew something about the subject and declared himself willing to help. He also stated that he would tell me nothing about drugs, because if he did he would be killed. He also asked a number of searching questions in the early days about what sort of book I was writing. Would it be critical of tourism? Would it stop Australian tourists from coming to his country? Would the guides in Kandy suffer as a result of what I published? I told Ali that I had a number of criticisms to make of the tourist industry in Sri Lanka, but that I would try to be fair. I also stressed that I was not writing a tourist 'guide book' but an academic work which tourists would not read.

While doing my daily rounds through the streets of Kandy early on in my fieldwork, I started to spend some time on the corner where Ali sold his wares. From there, a place close to the central market, shops, banks and hotels, I could see a lot that was going on in the town and also watch how he did business with tourists. I told Ali that I did not want to upset his business operations and he said that I would not. In fact, on occasions, I was able to divert business his way. Occasionally, for instance, tourists asked me to help them with accommodation, and I used to accompany them to the hotel or guesthouse, sending Ali in advance so that he could earn some commission. I also went with Ali to guesthouses I intended to stay in, and sometimes on shopping sprees, so that he could earn something. The deal was that he had to tell me how much commission he had been given. Indeed, sometimes he even offered it back to me. By establishing such a relationship, I could take on the role of a tourist with a guide and so was able to find out a lot about how tourism worked in Kandy. On some occasions, he was absolutely indispensable, as when I went into the slums in Kandy to speak to the prostitutes; I would never have attempted that alone.

Through the seven months that I was in Kandy, Ali persisted with his two occupations of selling goods from the pavement and trying to catch tourists. Actually, both activities were "doing the tourism" in a way, since the goods he had on display were almost entirely purchased by foreigners. Hence, although seemingly engaged in two activities, Ali really was not diversifying in a fundamental way. During 1982, including the *perahera* season, tourism was very bad in Kandy; for Ali, if there were fewer foreigners to sell goods to, so were there fewer to catch. Occasionally, when Ali found a tourist who wanted lodgings he would pack up his wares and disappear for the afternoon. Sometimes, he would be gone for just an hour or so leaving me or a shoe repairer to watch his goods. Very occasionally he would be absent for several days if he had been lucky enough to interest tourists in a longer trip. On one trip to the jungle with a small group of tourists, he returned exhausted and saddened because they had all been disappointed with what they had seen. He apologised to me for taking them on such a trip, and also refunded their money. One relationship which he hoped would pay handsome dividends failed to deliver the goods. He escorted a middle-aged American woman around Kandy for nearly a week, taking her into numerous gem shops and doing everything she requested, including sleeping with her, which he told me he had to do "with my eyes shut". After several days with her looking but purchasing nothing, she left Kandy with a fellow American who took her to buy gems elsewhere, no doubt pocketing the commission himself. Not only was Ali summarily dismissed with just 100 rupees and a packet of cigarettes, when he went to the Queen's Hotel to pick up what he thought would be a fairly hefty commission, he was informed that they had changed their rules and he was given only 13 rupees instead of the hundred or so he had expected.

Given the large number of street guides in Kandy during 1982 and also the relative scarcity of tourists, catching a tourist became very difficult. And precisely because things were tough on Ali's corner, many of the guides were driving very hard bargains. They would arrive with a tourist, negotiate a commission for themselves which, given Ali's normal profit margin, meant his virtually selling his goods at cost, or else forcing him to push his prices up to retain a reasonable profit margin but making his goods that much less attractive in the process. If Ali refused to deal under these conditions, the guides would just tell the tourist that they could find much better quality goods in the central market or elsewhere. Tourists, too, were being very mean, according to Ali. In the worst months, Ali, simply to gain some cash, did sell some goods below what he told me were cost price. Weeks, indeed months, went by with Ali on the street corner for seven hours a day without a single sale or without "catching" anyone. He began notching up marks on a pole to record the number of days without any business. Given that he lived with relatives there was always food available, but it hurt his pride when he could not contribute to the household. Things were made worse in the wet season with the daily need to collect up his wares and rush for cover to escape the downpour. On some days when the weather looked too unsettled he disappeared at noon and did not return. Added to the economic difficulties, was a sense of desperation one could see growing in the guides which then turned into intense frustration for the tourists. Many a tourist walked fiercely straight past Ali's display, neither looking at him nor acknowledging his presence when he spoke to them. Even his good English and joking behaviour failed to get attention. "Hello. Welcome to Kandy. So nice to see you here ... Look, real banana skin wallets. I am so sorry to have troubled you ... I would really like to own your knapsack". Nothing was making the tourists stop and look. Despite the run of bad luck and the increasingly uncivil atmosphere on the street corner, only twice did Ali lose his temper in my presence. Like Felix, he was sad and resigned rather than angry with those passing by. He once did get hostile with an arrogant Indian tourist who offered a ridiculously low price for one of his items. Likewise with a German whom Ali asked in desperation: "Do you think we are babies?".

Over the months, my relationship with Ali grew increasingly complex and involved: casual conversation led to a translating job and tape recording sessions. When I left Sri Lanka Ali accompanied me to the airport. He cried as he thanked me for what I had done for him and his family. Despite spending much time with him on the street corner, I had not wished to become embroiled in his personal and financial difficulties. However, when he told me that his young wife and child had returned to her village and that she had to be admitted to hospital, I felt I could not remain aloof. In a public hospital, Ali told me, he would have to provide generous gifts to the doctors and nurses to see that she received good treatment. Ali was ashamed to ask his younger brothers to help him financially, he told me, so I provided what he needed. To this day I remain unsure whether this whole incident was a quite appropriate display of the kind of reciprocity that should have grown between the two of us or whether it was an archetypal instance of a foreign tourist being 'milked' by a local. Clearly those social relationships between locals and foreigners which are created by tourism frequently involve much ambivalence and ambiguity. The activities of the street guides are richly illustrative in this respect, and there is no way that my relationship with Ali could have completely transcended this. Besides, as I have argued in Chapter 1, there really is an overlap in identity between tourists and anthropologists, so if Ali's behaviour is testimony to the fact that he treated me as some kind of tourist then I am scarcely in a position to protest.

Ali, Felix, Siri and Prema all derived a significant amount of their income from tourism, but taken together they hardly confirm the negative stereotype of the guides held by those at the Town Hall seminar. Clearly all four have been affected by tourism, but their circumstances are not the same and the ways in which they have been affected are very different. But it is important to end this discussion of street views of tourism in Kandy by making the point that though tourism had unquestionably become important to many people in the streets, for many involvement was very marginal and the effects on their personal lives negligible or even non-existent, as many of those who gave testimony in my street interviews made plain. A memorable incident which took place on a wooden bench at the city end of the Kandy lake makes this plain.

Early on in my research I thought that it would be interesting to sit on this bench for protracted periods of time each day reading a newspaper and conspicuously writing down large quantities of notes in a book. This was a place where many tourist-local encounters took place, especially between foreigners and guides. I imagined that it would create some interest, given that it was not a type of behaviour normally displayed by tourists in Kandy. The strategy worked well and on my very first time, literally within minutes of sitting down, a youngish guide walked past me, watching carefully, went on for a few yards more, stopped, turned around, and then walked past me again to get a good look at what I was doing. He repeated the operation and then for about five minutes floated about in the vicinity, finally taking off without speaking to me. I presume that he was assessing whether it was safe to strike up a relationship with me, but given my somewhat atypical behaviour, finally thought the better of it. During this five minute period, however, I was becoming acutely conscious of an increasingly uncomfortable source of heat just behind me. An old man had stepped up from the road and had gathered a few twigs together, had put a small pot on top of them and had commenced to boil a few pieces of chicken, which I thought had already 'gone off'. His fire in the earth at the base of one of the trees around the lake was only inches away from the seat on which I was sitting. The stench of the chicken was almost unbearable, but I had to move when the back of my legs began to singe. It was an instructive episode because while I was deliberately attempting to draw attention to myself in order to learn something about tourist-local relationships, for the old man cooking his meal, my sitting there was of no interest whatsoever. He ignored me totally, neither asking me for money nor asking me to move out of the way. No doubt like the fruit seller with whom my street interviews commenced, if one asked some people in Kandy what they thought about tourism, they would say that they had no interest in foreigners whatsoever and mean every word of it.

CHAPTER FIVE

Roles, Relationships and Representations in the Informal Sector: Street Guides and Unlicensed Guesthouses in Kandy

THE INFORMAL TOURISM SECTOR

The concept 'informal sector' has been employed with a range of senses by authors writing about economic and social change in the Third World (Tokman 1978). Whilst doubts have sometimes been expressed about its analytical utility because of this very imprecision and some have also drawn attention to an empirical overlap between the formal and informal sectors of an economy, for others it has considerable value in referring to that wide range of roles of somewhat dubious legality which soak up much of the 'underemployed residue' one finds in the service sector in countries undergoing rapid urbanisation and modernisation (Davis 1978:303). With reference specifically to tourism, for instance, whilst people are employed in the formal sector in the hotels as room boys, waiters, receptionists, and so on, outside on the pavements there are hawkers, black market profiteers, beggars, pimps, prostitutes and thieves who try to interact with tourists. In the formal sector are guides trained by the Ceylon Tourist Board or possessing municipal guide licences, whose activities are to conform to certain standards; in the informal sector are numerous individuals, normally referred to as touts,[1] who try to escort and advise tourists, who are trained by no-one and who are regulated by no set of rules. Likewise, alongside the formally registered guesthouses which have to meet certain standards set by the Tourist Board and whose operators pay taxes and charges appropriate to running a commercial operation, many people try to offer rooms to foreigners, but without substantially improving their facilities and probably not declaring any income either. Informal sectors commonly operate with no

---

[1] Touts pestering tourists seems to have existed from time immemorial; there even exist records of such individuals dating from the Greco-Roman period (Casson 1979:264). I normally refer to such people as 'street guides' or 'unlicensed guides' rather than 'touts'. For a start, the individuals commonly refer to themselves as 'guides' or 'guiders', but in addition, 'tout' is such a derogatory term that to employ it would mean tacit acceptance of the one-sided view which the authorities and well-to-do have of these people.

government sanction or registration procedures (Bromley 1979; Wahnschaft 1982:431); in some countries, the activities within them are strictly illegal, falling outside the regulations that protect the formal, approved sector (Davies 1979:91, 101). While some might regard such activities as 'marginal' in the sense of being on the fringe of approved and regulated operations, the informal sector can generate considerable employment and income, little of which shows up in the official statistics of the country concerned.

Most Third World governments have offered distinctly one-sided support to tourist development, assisting the expensive, graded accommodation-based variety of development and either failing to encourage, or actively discouraging, more grass roots developments where those of fairly modest means can profit (Wahnschaft 1982:449). Consequently, many of the roles available to such people fall outside the law and those available to some sections of the population — women are an obvious example — can also be highly demeaning (Samarasuriya 1982:33, 46, 77–8). As Samarasuriya states of Sri Lanka, to tourism planners and policy makers the poor are normally just a nuisance (1982:6–7). In this sense, as a development strategy, tourism tends to be a conservative choice where the economic gains that stay within the lesser developed countries tend to flow into the pockets of local elites. Thus within view of facilities established for the enjoyment of affluent foreigners, the poor have to do the best they can to tap into this new flow of resources.

Not surprisingly, those in the formal sector are often highly antagonistic towards those engaged in such unauthorised activities, whose lives are thus often subject to official harassment, on top of the insecurity inevitable in such activities in the first place. For instance, to mention only the unlicensed guides, in many parts of the world, hotels provide brochures for their guests, warning them about touts who may badger them during their stay. According to one: "Fiji welcomes you as a friend and the government of Fiji and the management of the hotel deplores these menacing practices and tactics and hopes that you will refuse to be exploited and taken for a 'sucker' by these people ..." (Cleverdon 1979:73). In Sri Lanka, tourists are certainly warned about unscrupulous touts by Tourist Board literature. Some guide books explicitly mention Kandy as a tout's paradise: "Touts are pushier and greater in number in Kandy than anywhere else. If you know where you want to go then ignore them, they'll only push prices up for you. Some places will even turn you away, saying they have no vacancies if you arrive with a tout" (Wheeler 1987:135–6). Some guesthouse operators in Kandy actually request tourists to phone them from the station because they would prefer to pick them up themselves or even pay a taxi fare than for their guests to arrive with a guide (Wheeler 1987:136). Some guesthouses will even state that they are full as soon as they realise that a tourist is accompanied by such a person (Noble *et al.*, 1993:129).

Impressions are all-important in tourism and, clearly, badgering, menace, deception and exploitation jar with the images created by the tourist industry about Sri Lanka — 'friendly, smiling people', 'relaxing in paradise', and so on. The tourism authorities normally attempt to maintain the overwhelmingly positive images of the tourist industry and of the country itself by attributing all the ills to very discrete categories of local mischief-makers and even to specific types of tourist, who are then hounded, with varying degrees of energy, out of the tourism industry or out of the country. Such manoeuvres, however, stem from grossly inadequate and highly biased understandings of international tourism. In Sri Lanka in 1982, for instance, while many would agree that unlicensed guides could tarnish the country's image, that some unregistered guesthouses were unclean, and that hippies indulged in drugs, it was also a commonly held view that highly respectable people with political connections and police protection were investing fortunes in hotels to launder profits gained from various types of nefarious activity. Some guesthouse proprietors would loudly denounce the touts and yet allow their own servants to be used by foreign guests as prostitutes. Informants also told me of the well-developed 'racket' whereby employees of the Ceylon Hotels Corporation would quickly transfer into a private vehicle tourists who had booked a Hotels Corporation hire car, thus making commission from the owners of the new vehicle. An entrepreneur running a tourist information service in Kandy had no qualms about telling me that "the first rogue in Sri Lanka is the Tourist Board".

Much that goes on in tourism is not what it seems. For instance, one beggar in Kandy regularly spent most days in the one spot collecting donations of money and food parcels, which he would hide behind his back. At the end of the day he would sell the food and then engage in his main occupation; he was, in fact, a fairly wealthy money-lender who owned several cars. Such deceptions as this, however, do not exist exclusively in the informal sector, for this area and the approved sector are not entirely distinct. Outside one prominent hotel in Kandy, for instance, frequently stood a woman who appeared to be trying to sell necklaces to passers by on the pavement. What she also did was receive signals from the coach drivers coming into Kandy to learn the quantities of drugs required by people on that particular vehicle, which would then be supplied to the tourists inside the hotel. Well-established links also existed between hotel staff, taxi drivers and guides for supplying the tourists with prostitutes, if not always in the hotel itself then at establishments just outside Kandy.

Images of shady dealing and double standards are perhaps part and parcel of the tourism industry worldwide, not only within the Third World. But particularly strong negative stereotypes exist about and among people in the informal sector. Street guides in Sri Lanka, for instance, would allege that, for all their talk about hospitality, guesthouse owners were greedy and only pretended to be friendly. Guesthouse owners would claim that guides were "wolves in sheep's clothing"; not guides at all but really "misguiders", or merely "commission agents". Wealthy owners of approved guesthouses accused the owners of unlicensed establishments of tarnishing the reputation of Sri Lanka. Street guides would also malign each other's reputations in the struggle to survive. However, with the relationship between guides and guesthouse proprietors, it is important to realise that adversarial rhetoric camouflages a symbiotic tie. The street guides and unlicensed guesthouses need each other, just as some shops are also highly dependent upon their activities. Possibly the images here are so negative precisely because these are relationships of mutual, if reluctant, need.

Although some have represented the informal sector as a niche rich in entrepreneurial opportunities (Henry 1982:460), it is important to remember the array of forces stacked against the poor. Few ever emerge from the informal sector having made fortunes (Skar 1985:156,163), and most lead lives, not only of intense competitiveness amongst themselves, but also of interference by the authorities. As one monk put it to me, society is a machine which creates waste products and demands human sacrifices: the prostitutes, beggars and touts are simply that. Whilst such a resolutely negative view is quite understandable, when examining the informal sector we should also recognise the creative skills and inventive strategies by which people in it turn what few assets they have to use (McGee 1979:56, 61; Hannerz 1985:149). Before describing such strategies, particularly those employed by the guides, it is necessary to discuss briefly the behaviour and needs of those tourists who become involved in the informal sector, for without understanding their circumstances it is not possible to grasp the street guide's 'middleman' role (Taft 1981:53; Bochner 1981 ed.) — a role essentially aimed at skimming off profits by fostering ties between tourists and other locals (van den Berghe 1980:381). We also need to depict clearly the situation of those who run the unlicensed guesthouses if we are to understand the activities of the street guides.

Two features of the tourists' situation particularly lend themselves to intermediary operations (van den Berghe and Keyes 1984:346–7). Firstly, touristic encounters tend to be superficial and transitory. Even on holiday, most tourists are in a hurry; this is certainly how Sri Lankans perceive them. Many, spending no more than two weeks in Sri Lanka, stay only a day or two in any one place, although much longer stays are the norm at beach resorts. Even the so-called 'travellers', making their way at their own pace around several Asian countries, are constantly on the move. Necessarily, then, tourists interact with many people only once. In such transactions, norms that are part of durable relationships are inappropriate. A sales assistant in a batik shop in Kandy informed me, for instance, that given the speed with which coach loads of tourists passed through the town 500% profit margins were sometimes obtainable. In establishing such margins, the assistant reckoned that he had to make up for the eight months off season. He also had to allow for a 40% commission to be given to a local guide, or 50% to a foreign guide. But his basic reason was that if tourists rushed about instead of first looking around to learn the value of items, that was their fault. Several of the street guides made the same point, adding that foreigners would think them stupid if they did not attempt to make as much money as possible.

Secondly, most relationships between locals and tourists are decidedly asymmetrical. While tourists have economic resources to spend, they usually possess very little cultural capital in the sense of knowledge of the local language, price levels or local customs. They therefore find themselves in a succession of encounters where they do not fully understand what is going on. By contrast, most street guides may lack substantial economic assets, but they are rich in cultural capital, especially in a practical understanding of how to meet the needs of the many tourists who, choosing not to experience a foreign country via a 'package tour', need to decide on a daily basis where to eat, where to stay, where to go to next, and so on. The street guides are in an excellent position to profit from this kind of foreigner's lack of knowledge, understanding or planning. This is particularly so given the widespread existence of negative stereotypes of tourists (as of outsiders in general), which in some ways legitimise manipulation and exploitation. As has been found elsewhere in the world, especially when tourist development proceeds to a point where there is widespread adverse community resentment, tourists who are so often seen as thoughtless displays of affluence may have an "informal tourist tax" (Chesney-Lind and Lind 1986:86) imposed on them in the form of systematic deception, theft and other more violent crimes. However correct it may be, at the systems level, to view destination countries as normally coming off worse than the affluent tourist-generating countries, at the inter-personal level, for the tourist at least, it may very much seem as if the tourist is the victim. For a country like Sri Lanka where many see the past four centuries as a series of episodes of being plundered by foreigners, much in the informal tourism arena may very much be seen as instances of the "revenge of the native", in Manning's (1982:14) graphic phrase.

One can grasp something of the roles and relationships in the informal sector by viewing it as an arena where a range of strategies are employed to channel whatever 'free-floating' resources are found there. The chief asset of the guesthouse owner, for instance, is clearly the possession of a home in an accessible location and normally with certain kinds of facilities. The channelling of resources mainly occurs within this context, where part of the cultural capital will normally be a reasonable command of English and probably some other middle class refinements and comforts. Although a few of the unlicensed guesthouses in Kandy were rented by their operators, most such services were provided in owner-occupied homes. The assets of most street guides were of a very different order. Their arena of operations was not the home but the streets and the cafes. Most spoke, at best, broken

English and few had much knowledge of Sri Lankan or even local history, and in that sense they are quite different to the licensed Tourist Board guides (Cohen 1985:15), part of whose training consists of taking courses in Sri Lankan history and culture. However, Kandy's unlicensed guides did possess much local 'know how', that is knowledge about drugs, prostitutes, cheap places to eat in and the best budget places to stay in — information which could not be obtained in Tourist Board publications or in most travel guide books.

Above all, guides have two basic assets: their wits and plenty of spare time. Street guiding is very much a matter of living off one's wits, seizing opportunities as and when they occur, without going too far. While the well-to-do often referred to touts as "lazy idlers", they are perhaps more accurately viewed as the "spurious leisure class of the unemployed" (Hannerz 1969:105). For over two decades, Sri Lanka has had a very serious problem of youth unemployment (Fyson 1987:57), made considerably worse by the high quality of primary and secondary education available in that country. Most street guides in Kandy had no regular job. They thus hung around in the streets and cafes, sometimes all day, looking for something to do. But what might appear as mere idle time was, in fact, a major asset. One has to 'hang around' to catch stray tourists in the informal sector. Having nothing else to do is vital in this 'hit and miss' game, to enable one easily to latch on to a foreigner's plans at a moment's notice.

As mentioned in Chapter 4, guides have a set of general conceptions about tourist motivation and elaborate national stereotypes. One also needs to recognise their insightful, if essentially pragmatic, understanding of human nature, their ability to quickly read a social situation, and their skill in turning it to their advantage in the face of competition from others in the streets.[2] As Siri and Felix put it, one has to "catch the eye" and engage in "tactics talk". Many a tourist is wary of being cheated in a foreign country, and so many react gratefully upon hearing "Hello friend", a common conversational opening used by the street guides. The term 'friend' here, however, is highly ambiguous (Wagner 1982:93; Cohen 1986), and tourists are frequently unsuspecting of the commercial consequences which may flow from such an overture (Cohen 1982a:246; Farver 1984:259). As Felix told me, when a tourist goes into a shop with a guide and the guide introduces the foreigner to the shopkeeper as "my friend", this is not a signal for the shopkeeper to be generous to the customer, but quite the reverse, namely an instruction to price an item in the light of the commission that has to be paid to the guide. 'Friend' in other words is just part of tactics talk in engaging with foreigners.

Having acknowledged such ruses by the guides, one also needs to recognise

---

[2] According to Smith (1980:26), it is because of such skills that they often make good anthropological informants.

that in Sri Lanka as is widely reported elsewhere, for those who run guesthouses there is often a profound ambiguity about the relationship between making money and providing hospitality (Stringer 1981:363–4). Host-guest relationships in this sphere are often construed as 'friendship' (Sweet 1989:70–1) and in Kandy, guest-house proprietors would often talk of "Ceylonese hospitality", "liking foreigners", and the like. Buddhist morality does indeed greatly valorise generosity and despises meanness, but upon leaving such establishments tourists frequently found every piece of courtesy itemised on their bill. Such mercenary calculation would commonly be regarded as completely sullying real friendship in Sri Lanka.

THE UNLICENSED GUESTHOUSES

The growth of tourist accommodation in Kandy has been described in Chapter 3, but it is now necessary to delve in depth into the matter of how the unlicensed guesthouses actually operate, the sort of people who run them, what services they provide to tourists, and what relationships exists between them and the street guides.

A number of owners of large licensed guesthouses expressed views exactly like the great majority of hotel managers in declaring that running a tourist establishment was simply a commercial enterprise. In the informal sector, however, such accounts were not forthcoming from the proprietors. They spoke instead about the money they earned by doing tourism as "a way of keeping up", "a way of staying comfortable", or "a way of affording a few luxuries". They stated that Sri Lankans were a naturally friendly people and all had a story of how they had put themselves out for a tourist, or given some service for free. Indeed, most of them had an 'origin myth' by which their becoming involved in tourism was represented almost as an accident, or as an act of kindness for a neighbour, or out of consideration for the children. Tourism was "a hobby", "something for the wife to do", "it enables the children to hear English spoken"; children had grown up and large empty rooms were discovered which could be put to use; or one had to help a neighbour when they could not keep up with the demand for their accommodation.

Such accounts obviously downplay or gloss over commercial calculation, but it was clear that for a number of moderately well-off people in Kandy in 1982 tourism was a tantalising opportunity to acquire extra income. One recently engaged young couple employed in a bank were deliberately adding an extra room to the house they were having built so that they could offer accommodation to tourists. They had no idea what facilities should go in such a room, what rent to charge or even how to get tourists, but nonetheless had already committed themselves to the extra expenditure. They were clearly hoping that I would explain to them how tourism operated in Kandy and volunteer to be the first "friend" staying with them, at the same time telling them what they should charge me in rent. I only ever heard once what I regarded as a convincing account which tied tourism into traditional Ceylonese hospitality, and this was a very elderly man whose son ran a guesthouse. Being hospitable was for him simply a part of Buddhist values, and displaying kindliness was a way to ensure a good rebirth. There were many changes going on which he did not approve of, including his son's neglect of him. He often helped in the guesthouse and compared the lack of consideration he was receiving with the fact that his son did not pay sufficient attention to his guests either. For him, service to tourists and Buddhist morality were one and the same thing. No other informant, in my opinion, convincingly made this connection during my seven months of fieldwork.

It is important when looking at the guesthouses in the informal sphere in Kandy to recognise that they are by no means all the same in regard to their facilities or the range of services they offer their guests. Some proprietors try to monopolise a tourist's time, others do not mind whether their guests eat there or in cafes in the town. Some even make a point of deliberately not involving themselves in the activities of their guests when they are not in their rooms. Some are very much seen as "family homes", where certain types of tourist are avoided, where guests may not bring back local women and where the single tourist may even be turned away because of the problems which might follow. On the other hand, some guesthouses had reputations for catering to tourists who took drugs and some were even well known for allowing their own servants to be used by tourists as prostitutes. In some, 'hippies' were allowed to stay at very low rents provided they spent some time trying to bring the type of tourist who would pay for the more expensive rooms. In at least one guesthouse, so I was told, a tourist had set himself up for a long stay, dealing with drugs not only with the knowledge of the proprietor, but living there rent free in return for commissions on sales of drugs going to the owner. Some guesthouses will not allow guides on the premises; others have guides living there, more or less in the employ of the establishment. There was even a place near Kandy, I was told by the guides, where three European women had set themselves up as prostitutes. In return for free accommodation and food which would prolong their stay in Sri Lanka, they sold their services to wealthy locals. One other guesthouse, run by a young Sri Lankan couple, had been purchased for them by a bisexual German who had established sexual relationships with both of them some years earlier, and who wished to create a permanent base in Sri Lanka to which he could return year after year.

The last two examples I know of only from what guides told me, but the selection of guesthouses discussed in the rest of this section were known to me personally, and will serve to illustrate both the ties with the guides and ambiguity over the nature of tourism. The first was run by a semi-retired businessman who occasionally had tourists staying at his house. Between 1979 when his involvement began and 1982, he had had 82 tourists. It was not his habit deliberately to seek out tourists, he claimed, and he certainly would have nothing to do with guides, believing their activities to be a scurrilous way of earning a living. His story was of walking to and from work at lunch time and occasionally seeing tourists who seemed to be lost. In 1979 during the *perahera*, he approached two tourists who appeared not to know where they were going, asked them what they wanted and, on finding out that they were without accommodation, offered them a spare room in his own house. The rent of 100 rupees per day for a double room which he thought of then and still charged in 1982 was simply "a round sum". In fact, for a home with no tourist facilities whatever, 100 rupees in 1979 was exceedingly high. An owner of other properties in Kandy and still a very successful salesman, he explained that the little money he got from tourism helped him and his wife "to get by". Despite the declared casual nature of his involvement in tourism, on first meeting me he had thought of charging 100 rupees for the spare double room, even though I was on my own. He told me that he would have to ask his wife whether she would allow someone in the house for half this amount, so clearly they were not indifferent to financial considerations. On the other hand, when I stayed a number of days, I received free a sumptuous evening meal, specially prepared for me by his daughter, which would easily have cost the equivalent of one day's rent if purchased in a cafe.

A second unlicensed guesthouse was owned by a school teacher. His wife had given up school teaching to look after the children, and doing a little tourism was a way of bringing in some extra money. On a low, government-regulated salary,[3] he spoke enviously and contemptuously of the uneducated cashing in on the opportunities for manual work in the Middle East where fabulous salaries could be earned compared to what was available in Sri Lanka. Tourism, for him, was a vital way of "keeping up with the rising cost of living". Bit by bit, he was building an extension to his home whenever he had money to spare, in order to leave his two children a good home. He had elaborate plans, but was very wary about the future of tourism and therefore had shelved ideas about taking out a bank loan to finance

---

[3] In 1982, a qualified teacher was earning approximately 1,100 rupees per month ($U.S. 55) and an unqualified teacher 800 rupees. By contrast, top hotel managers commanded salaries of 7,000 rupees per month, along with perks. Bank managers would earn approximately 4,500 rupees. Shop assistants earned something in the range 500–800 rupees, security guards 700–900 rupees, tailors 600–800 rupees, and waiters 350 rupees along with meals and accommodation; servants earned 100–250 rupees per month. By the mid-1980s there were about 200,000 Sri Lankans working in the Middle East, some of them earning salaries ten times what they would earn at home (Fyson 1987:58).

the improvements. Given the somewhat hard-to-find location of his home, getting tourists required a great deal of personal effort. It meant that he, a respectable middle-aged teacher, had to walk two kilometres or so to the Kandy railway station to see whether the evening train from Colombo had brought anyone who needed a place to stay for the night. This activity itself meant potentially hostile encounters with the street guides. Both he and his wife were acutely anxious about guides, not wanting them in their home in case they started stealing and expecting to mix with the tourists.

When I myself arrived at their establishment with Ali, the owners told him that they did not want any tourists, and it took some effort by Ali to explain that I was working at the University of Peradeniya and so not a normal tourist. My appearance with a guide certainly had something to do with their initial reluctance. I knew full well that arriving in this way at some establishments would be making difficulties for myself, but it was a way of allowing some of my street corner informants to make a little money as well as affording me the opportunity to observe guesthouse owners and guides interacting. In the case of this particular guesthouse, however, it was my being single that created the real problem. For this respectable, lower middle class family, tourism was slightly risqué; they feared for their reputations and were worried about the attitudes of their neighbours. A single male tourist always posed the potential threat of one day returning with a local prostitute. This had actually happened at this guesthouse some years previously and the owners had had to explain to their guest that they could not countenance local women being seen entering their home with foreigners. They had no objections to tourists sleeping with each other since that was simply a part of the western way of life and nothing to do with them, but involving a local woman was quite a different matter, and they could not tolerate the scandal involved.[4]

This particular home had two rooms for tourists, offered at different prices because of the slightly different facilities in each. Providing even this accommodation put the family out considerably. The wife and two children slept in one room and the husband had taken to sleeping on a bunk in the hallway. The toilet facilities had been westernised so that the family itself now simply used the back garden. The husband made it clear that certain standards had to be maintained because this was a "family home". There could be some negotiation about the price of rooms, but they would not "degrade themselves". If they did not like the look of any tourists on their doorstep they would simply claim to be "full up" and send them away. Tourism had, in fact, back-fired on them several times. Since November 1981, they

---

[4] Sri Lankans are highly conscious about status (*tatvaya*) and Obeyesekere has argued that they are extremely vulnerable to the reaction of others, shaming, ridicule, and so on (1984b:500, 504, 506–7).

had had 90 tourists and had asked six to leave. Some Dutch visitors had made a habit of walking naked about the house in front of them and their children and the tourists had got very angry when they were told to stop doing this. Another group had made a habit of buying food in town, bringing it back and putting it in the fridge and then asking continually for crockery and boiling water instead of eating the meals the guesthouse provided. They had caused a scene when a service charge was added to the bill to cover the extra costs. On another occasion, four tourists wanted to stay in one room, with two of them sleeping on the floor to save money. They made a habit of asking for more food at each meal, but were not prepared to pay any extra. When this group finally left, the school teacher and his wife apparently had a blazing row about why he had brought such types to their house in the first place.

A number of unlicensed guesthouses had a variant on a 'spill over' origin myth. Just outside Kandy, a high ranking family had several homes, three of which catered to tourists of different types. In the early 1970s, tourism was started by one of the home owners and soon there was inadequate accommodation to cope with the ever growing number of inquiries. So the woman's relatives in the adjacent homes got involved, "just to help out" with the excess. A slight distance away, a couple told me that they started simply because a neighbour was sending them tourists when they were full up. This guesthouse, run by the ex-school teacher wife of a local bank manager, was proud of the fact that the majority of her tourists came on the recommendation of previous guests. Neither the husband nor wife made any efforts actively to seek out tourists. But they did have a card which they gave to their guests who could then pass it on to other foreigners. This card was the only one I saw which printed a message to the effect that the holder had been given it by a fellow tourist and that they had not learned about the guesthouse from any guide. It was at this guesthouse, when I arrived accompanied by Felix, that the owner's wife stated: "We do not do tourism on a commercial basis". Felix later commented: "If they do not do it on a commercial basis, why do they not do it for free?" There was a mocking tone in his voice as he posed the question, but he was also angry with the owners because they were not in an easily accessible location and he claimed that the guides had effectively set them up some years earlier by taking them tourists; now, once established, they had turned their backs on the guides.

Since I had arrived with Felix, the owner asked me later that day very pointedly whether I actually had been brought by the guide or whether I knew of the guesthouse already. I replied that I had asked Felix to take me to a guesthouse where I could talk to the proprietors about tourism in Kandy and he had recommended their establishment. I added that since I would be staying some time I felt it would not make a great deal of difference to their finances, but would certainly help Felix, if he received payment for his assistance. The owners made a point of telling me that Felix would receive a commission, but they were still somewhat bemused that I had knowingly brought a guide with me to enable him to earn a little money. They did not mind guides earning money when they did actually provide genuine assistance to a tourist or did give valuable information, they claimed. But they objected to the "parasites" who escorted tourists who already knew where they were going, thus getting an income by doing nothing other than being a general nuisance and intercepting people en route to a particular guesthouse. They also objected to the guides who arrived with tourists and demanded that the proprietors double the prices of their rooms so that they would get a higher commission. Guides setting prices in this way they regarded as quite outrageous. They were also worried that guides, once used to arriving at their home, would start stealing, demanding food, using the telephone, and even interfering with their servants. They were also suspicious about some of their neighbours whom they believed were waylaying their guests, even fraudulently claiming to be them, and so taking them to the wrong address.

The owners of this guesthouse were certainly comfortably off, and being involved in tourism was said by the husband to be "something for the wife to do to keep her busy" after she had left the teaching profession. There was no pressure on guests to eat meals in the guesthouse and tourists were quite free to bring their own food back and put it in the fridge. Local phone calls were free. There was no service charge, but any money a tourist wished to leave would go into bank accounts for the four young servants. There was a very pronounced stress upon it being a family home where standards had to be maintained. Like other guesthouses they had had their share of troubles with foreign guests. Some hippies had blocked the toilets with rotting food. Some Americans had paid considerable rent in advance and then started doing drug deals with local guides. In one incident, a tourist had made sexual overtures to one of their servants, who being a young village girl, was very afraid. Since that time the owner had not allowed any of her servants to go alone into the annexe next to the home where most of the tourists stayed. So conscious was she of her reputation that when neighbours phoned her up to find out how many tourists she had staying there, she would often say there were only two or three even if she was full up, in case rumours spread that her popularity was due to any unseemly activities going on. She told me that Sri Lankans were not envious of the wealth of foreigners, but that they were extremely suspicious of and jealous of each other.

As for the expression "not doing tourism on a commercial basis", she later told me that what she had meant was that bank loans had not been taken out to build large-scale tourist accommodation. What they had done was to modify two rooms in their home and convert a large garage on their property, which had previously housed two lorries, into four rooms with tourist facilities. The owner claimed that the money he could obtain by letting rooms to tourists was far higher than from renting the whole place to local people on a long-term basis. He also remarked that the previous owners of his property must have been very wealthy to own two lorries. He described himself as "comfortable", and tourism was a way of affording "little luxuries". The husband was happy to provide information to tourists and would phone shop keepers in town to tell them that his guests should be treated well, but he claimed that he would accept no commission on sales. He told me that as a bank manager he needed a good reputation and thus could not do "two kinds of business". Felix dismissed this account. The phone calls were bound to lead to commission, in fact were designed for this, he suggested.

The ambiguity over economic and other motivations in the guesthouse was consciously acknowledged by the bank manager when he used the expression "walking a tightrope" to describe his efforts to steer a middle way between hospitality and greed. It was also evident in the way the owner's wife represented the role of her servants. For a small guesthouse, four servants was extremely high. All four — three girls and one boy — were of school age. The owner's wife described them all as from the villages and claimed that she was "always thinking of the poor". Giving guests the choice of leaving something extra for the servants was one way they were made "part of the family". Her servants were paid 200 rupees per month, with all meals provided, and she went out of her way to explain that she had to cook food specially for them since they did not like what was served to tourists. Their wages went into bank accounts to provide for their future needs. She, a low country Sinhalese, claimed that in some guesthouses servants were paid as little as 50 rupees per month, were worked very long hours and were treated "like slaves" by Kandyans. She claimed that, when well treated, servants would stay a long time and that one would send clothes and so on to their families, provide a training in various skills and also contribute substantially towards the costs of marriage. Clearly, in any guesthouse which does not employ more servants as a result of doing tourism, the value to a household of a servant's contribution increases enormously once they become part and parcel of the provision of tourist services. One might also add a comment made by one of my guide informants, that for all the rhetoric about giving these servants a useful training, their employer, an ex-school teacher herself, would have known that they should all still have been at school.

The last guesthouse I discuss here was also a home run by a school teacher, who in January 1980 perceived that tourism was likely to provide a good supplementary income to the 1100 rupees he and the 800 rupees his wife (an unqualified primary school teacher), earned each month. Being a school teacher he had the time, after school each day and during vacations, to catch tourists himself, mainly on the Colombo-Kandy train where he frequently travelled armed with a family photo album and a guest book which showed how many foreigners had already stayed with him. His father-in-law, a public servant, also occasionally helped out by finding guests. The guesthouse was run with one servant,[5] whom the owners would have had in any case, especially after their first child arrived. Of fairly humble origins from the Ratnapura area, the proprietor was proud to have become a teacher and to "own a house in Kandy town". Being recently married, tourism represented a way in which he could pay off his mortgage more quickly or alternatively extend his home. He was fairly sanguine about the future of tourism, thinking that Kandy might have another five or so good years. He intended to make money while tourism was good and to stop when his home was paid off. In the meanwhile, his young children would have the advantage of seeing and hearing Europeans, which he considered important. Stopping when the home loan was paid off was only one of his plans, however. Another was to move into a smaller house and rent the whole of his home to tourists under the control of a housekeeper. It was quite clear that his wife was not impressed by this more grandiose plan, and

---

[5] Despite the prevalence of 'familistic' over economic images, good servants were hard to come by, I was told, in a number of guesthouses. Some stole; some were unreliable; others were lazy. In the normal touristic experience, servants are very much background figures as compared to the proprietors. Language difficulties and shyness have much to do with this. But in most guesthouses, despite being represented as "family affairs", servants are absolutely crucial to the smooth operation of tourism. In one home where I stayed, the provision of services virtually collapsed when it became clear that a servant was so unsatisfactory that she would have to be returned to her home. Other members of the family tried to help out, but the guests were complaining about the quality of the food, and an atmosphere of tension and chaos descended on the guesthouse, relieved only when the servant was escorted back to her village and her money paid to her family. The proprietor was forced to reemploy a much older servant who had left some months earlier amidst suspicions that she had stolen and then subsequently sold some of his mother's jewellery. As for the young servant, he complained that she was not interested in improving herself, learning about housework, cooking or looking after children, and that she was giving up a good opportunity through which she could remain in employment till of marriageable age, at which time she would have accumulated considerable savings, beside the gifts that her employers would contribute to her marriage, and indeed the active role they would play in securing her a good marriage. From the proprietor's perspective, the servant simply did not realise how much good her employers were doing for her. There is another very different form of discourse about servants which is told both by guides and by guesthouse owners about each other. Some servants, I was told on a number of occasions, are dismissed after several years' service without receiving any of their accumulated wages. In one such instance, a theft occurred, and the employer suspected the servant. The employer then told the servant that no action would be taken by the police if she agreed to leave after first signing a declaration that all her back wages had already been paid. To avoid trouble, the servant did so, effectively meaning that she had been working for years for nothing.

indeed did not really like being involved in tourism at all. Living some way out of Kandy in a fairly inaccessible location, for a long time his guesthouse was the only one in the immediate vicinity, and this meant that any foreigners seen travelling along certain paths must be heading for his home. This added considerably to his wife's embarrassment who was conscious of the fact that many of her neighbours looked down on them for being engaged in tourism. This was a household already acutely conscious of status differences given that the husband and wife came from very different backgrounds.

In examining closely the economics of a small unlicensed guesthouse, we need to bear in mind the combined monthly salary of the couple in order to appreciate what a windfall tourism can be. A tourist staying in a top grade hotel in Kandy during 1982 could well spend a school teacher's monthly salary in two days. Alternatively put, a tourist staying for one night in the cheapest room in this guesthouse (approximately 40 rupees) would double the daily income of the owner. On the rare occasions when the guesthouse had its four rooms full (prices ranging from 40–150 rupees), especially if the guests were also staying in for some of their meals, he could easily earn his monthly salary in just a few days. Escorting his guests around town was not a regular part of the guesthouse owner's practice; he was quite happy for the tourists to do whatever they pleased. However, because his home was a long way out of Kandy, he would on occasions escort them to the evening performances of Kandyan dancing to ensure that they found their way back safely after dark. Such an activity earned him commission on the entrance tickets, just as if he had been a street guide. Also, occasionally, he would show tourists some batik shops in Kandy run by his friends, and this too meant further income. These 'guiding' activities were quite casual affairs. He explained to me that while he earned a little money from it, he could also ensure that his guests were not cheated. However, I seriously underestimated the significance of these 'extras' to him. One evening I explained to a group of Danish tourists staying with him how the commission system operated and learned some days later via his wife how put out he had been that I had shared my understanding of how tourism worked with his guests.

As profitable as catching tourists looks, however, when one goes into all the factors which enter into running guest accommodation, a somewhat different picture can emerge. Although no extra servants were engaged in this particular establishment, expensive modifications were needed to the house, in particular toilet and shower facilities the household itself would never use. Other equipment, such as a refrigerator, was required for the storage of cold drinks. Whilst in a successful season some of these items could be paid off in a few months, for the most part they initially required the taking out of bank loans. With a small salary, a bad season with few tourists meant worries, even if only that the debts would take much longer to pay off. The guesthouse owner described himself as a "poor man" for whom the costs incurred in "catching the tourists" in the first place were significant. For instance, a trip to Colombo and back on the train in 1982 amounted to just over 42 rupees, about the same as the husband's daily wage. On top of the train fare, there was the added expense of lunch away from home. On some days, inevitably, this was money simply wasted since he could not always persuade those foreigners he met on the train to stay at his home. When he did catch some, often they were unwilling to walk all the way to his home, so that meant his having to hire a taxi at his own expense. A taxi from Kandy railway station would cost 25 rupees (although to ensure a fast, non-roundabout drive and good service on future occasions, he used to pay 30 rupees). If he had with him only one tourist, given train, meal and taxi costs, a guest would have to stay two days before he would break even, and frequently they did not stay that long.

This particular guesthouse relied far less on guides bringing tourists than was normal in the informal sector. To an extent this was because the home was twenty minutes walk out of town, but also because the working hours of a teacher allowed the owner to do much of the catching himself. But the owner and his wife were also very conscious about upholding standards. This was their family home where his very young children and elderly parents lived and where other relatives and friends were frequent visitors. Because of this, they would not take just anyone in. He preferred to get couples, and always people of a reasonable standard of dress. Even with such precautions, the guesthouse had had a number of bad incidents over the years. One couple had got up very early one morning before anyone else after staying several days and simply left without paying the bill. There had been a few incidents of tourists stealing money from each other. Perhaps the most serious incident was when two Australians involved the tourist police. The couple had paid six months rent in advance and had then been unsuccessful in getting their visas renewed. They then demanded back their rent which the owner had already spent on home improvements. The owner did try to return as much as he could in the way of goods, such as batiks, which the tourists could sell. The tourists were annoyed and complained to the Tourist Police. They also stole from the home some presents which had been left by other guests for the owner's father-in-law.

Another source of upset to the owner was the extreme meanness of some of his tourists. He told me of one incident where four tourists all wanted to share one room with a single bed, with three of them on the floor in order to save rent. On another occasion a couple who had arrived in a taxi promised to stay for several days, so the owner paid the taxi fare. Upon arrival they requested 'half serves' of food at reduced prices because they did not eat much, but then at their evening meal requested more food. They left the next morning, even asking for directions from their host as to how to get to another guesthouse. Whilst in general the owner liked having foreigners at his home, he was deeply offended by this type of behaviour in a way which went beyond the anger caused by the financial losses which it occasioned. He did not mind too greatly when tourists took drinks from the fridge without letting him know; he could not police such matters and so left it to people's conscience. If they stole, their ill deeds would catch up with them later on, he said. Other matters, though, rankled him considerably. On the other hand, good tourists were more than sources of extra income to him. They became his "friends overseas". Several of them had sent gifts and letters and particularly clothes for his children. The gifts he proudly displayed in a glass case in his living room for other tourists to see, telling guests who had sent them, which country they came from and what they were like. Tourists coming back a second time paid a lower rent and were regarded as "friends".

Doing tourism had always been a source of tension between husband and wife. Some of their arguments were over the fact that he spent too much of his time getting tourists and not enough time with his children. In January 1981, he had decided to cut down on the amount of time he spent trying to catch tourists and he asked some guides in Colombo to bring tourists to his place. The guides did bring tourists, but they had also arranged to bring prostitutes for the tourists too. The owner's wife refused to feed the guides when they demanded a meal and her husband made it clear to the tourists that prostitutes could not come to his home. During 1982, he was again thinking of spending more time at home and so needed once again to find another way of getting tourists. As his prior encounters with guides had not worked out, he asked me to choose a local guide for him, one who was reliable and who would understand the sort of tourists he wanted in his home. He knew that as part of my research I spent a great deal of time on street corners with the guides in Kandy so thought that I could make a good selection for him. The very fact that I was asked is itself some indication of the anxious dependence which exists between guesthouse proprietors and the unlicensed guide population.

The two people whom I could contemplate recommending both had serious drawbacks. Felix was friendly and experienced enough, but among other things liked to catch attractive female tourists to sleep with them. Ali had other business interests and so I was not sure that he could spend the time going to Colombo three or four times a week to collect tourists. I approached both of them setting out the conditions of the job, as explained to me by the guesthouse proprietor. The guide would receive a rail pass and a copy of his guest book and would have to travel on the Colombo-Kandy train, picking up tourists either at Colombo station or en route. The guide would get one third of all rent and all commission from shopping. Felix was not in the slightest interested in taking on the job, although 1982 was a very bad year for him when weeks went by without his making any money. He gave me a number of reasons for not wanting the job. Firstly, he was finding guiding too competitive; there were far too many guides around in Kandy, so that catching tourists had become almost impossible. Secondly, some guesthouse owners had given him a difficult time in the past, making him return two or three times before giving him any commission, and so he simply could not tolerate the suggestion that he be in the employ of one. Thirdly, he thought the conditions unrealistic. One simply could not go up to tourists, invite them to a guesthouse and then inform them that drugs and prostitutes were not allowed, he claimed.

Ali, however, who had tried his hand at many fields of employment, volunteered to attempt the job and came to see the guesthouse owner. Ali was not that well experienced in catching tourists since "doing tourism" was only a side line to his pavement hawking activities, but equipped with photos of the family and the guest book, he made a number of trips to Colombo, all of them without success. One day the owner too was at Colombo station and managed to pick up some tourists while Ali was still having no luck. Less than a fortnight later Ali gave up, leaving the owner with a real problem. Given the location of his establishment, it was not possible to opt out of the difficult, demanding side of tourism himself, simply running the place while letting others do the catching. He had no other way of getting tourists to his home than putting in his own time and effort. To make things worse, towards the end of 1982 he started being charged at commercial rates for his electricity and water consumption because the municipality knew that he was using part of his home for tourism. The increase in tariffs was extremely steep and he was very bitter because he knew that others in Kandy doing tourism were paying ordinary domestic rates because they bribed the people who came to read the meters or else had influence over those higher up in the relevant public bodies. This state of affairs rankled him considerably, for during much of 1982 he had no tourists at all and during the peak season far fewer than normally. Consequently, he was, as he put it, "paying commercial rates to do the cooking and wash my children".

Of course, running an unlicensed guesthouse, there was no way that he could advertise in Tourist Board literature. He was also keenly aware of the impending Specified Tourist Services Code and knew that it could mean a fine if caught. He thought the risk worth taking, although he was certainly worried about being found out. He had tried from the beginning in 1980 to be established as a licensed guesthouse because he did not like operating outside the law. Initially, however, his facilities were deemed inadequate and so he went to a great deal of expense to have proper facilities installed. On a second visit from the Tourist Board inspectors he was told that the inaccessibility of the establishment was an impediment and that approval could not be given until a properly sealed road led to his home. He had for years been urging the municipality to seal the road, but had made no progress. He was sure that he could get Tourist Board approval for his home simply by offering the inspectors a large bribe, but he was not prepared to do this.

Doing tourism would therefore have to remain, for him, a time-consuming and somewhat risky business. He would either have to do the catching himself, thus risking encounters with the guides, or else have guides arrive at his house with their own catches: he did not relish either.

THE STREET GUIDES

On any day in Kandy during 1982 one could see numerous unlicensed guides strategically positioned in shop doors, outside cafes, on street corners, near hotels or in alleyways. At the railway station, guides emerged from the train with tourists 'caught' during the journey, steering their charges through the ranks of guides at the station entrance who tried to attract tourists with offers of cheaper accommodation. Those tourists who proceeded alone from the bus or railway station, tired after the three hour journey from Colombo, inevitably ran the gauntlet of several guides. Having rebuffed one, they would move on quickly, only to be approached a few yards further down the street by another. For tourists on their own or in pairs, particularly women, it could be quite intimidating. Many tourists resorted to telling anyone who approached them simply to "fuck off", and the guides often replied in kind. Often, too, when a tourist was 'caught', unsuccessful guides followed, hurling abuse at the successful guide in a combination of Sinhala and English and alleging that he was a "robber". Many of the older generation looking on would denounce such individuals as "young semi-literates out of the drain"; one academic somewhat creatively labelled them the "lumpen bourgeoisie".

The hundred or so guides frequently seen in the streets of Kandy came from diverse ethnic and social backgrounds. The overwhelming majority were young men in their late teens and early twenties, most of whom spoke broken English or, indeed, knew English only via the repetitive encounters with tourists themselves (Cohen and Cooper 1986:543). Many were physically small, appeared very much younger than they were, and some were regarded as physically very attractive. It was suggested to me by a number of informants that there were so many small, youthful guides because tourists felt safer with them than with more robust-looking characters. In addition, I was often told that many Europeans, both men and women, had a strong desire for sex with youngish boys. Despite the preponderance of young men, Kandy's street guide population also included a number of characters who did not fit the above description at all. A few middle-aged or elderly men were guides. One of these even had a municipal guide's licence,[6] but of the dozen or

---

[6] Such a licence required a small annual fee and vetting by the police; it did not involve any rigorous training as with the Tourist Board's training scheme.

so municipally licensed guides in 1982, he was the only one I recognised as actively working the streets. Another middle-aged guide appeared to be constantly drunk, and seemed incapable of knowing what he was doing. He spent most of his time abusing other guides for stealing what he saw as his clients; in seven months I never saw him actually catch a tourist. Some other middle-aged men like Ali took up guiding on the spur of the moment, but were really business men or pavement hawkers.

Some 'occasional' guides were students from the nearby University of Peradeniya, trying to earn a little money. Others were school-aged children, truanting for the day; some had permanently dropped out of school. One young teenage girl supporting her unemployed father had developed a working knowledge of three European languages over the years and combined shopping with tourists with, so other guides told me, occasional sex. Apart from her, most of the other females constantly in the streets were very young children who simply followed tourists, begging for money. One or two guides seemed to be bordering on emotional disturbance. One well educated man in his late twenties, so the story went, had been introduced to drugs by a German woman some years previously. He had taken them thinking they were some kind of confectionery, had become very ill and had then been hospitalised. Since that time he had developed an alcohol addiction and used to hang about in the streets in an extremely dishevelled state, trying to escort tourists to Kandyan dance performances. One or two tourists taken to a show would earn him 20 to 30 rupees (just over $U.S. 1), enough to keep him in alcohol for a day or so.

There seems to be very little 'social structure' to the street guide population in Kandy in the sense of 'structure' used by Whyte for street gangs in his classic study of Cornerville (1955). In Kandy we are not dealing with large gangs with established leaders which routinely perform a number of joint activities. Although some people spent most of their time on the streets, the guide population in the informal sector is not well circumscribed; indeed, for many, guiding is an instantaneous and short-lived role. Furthermore, many services provided by street guides were regularly provided by others in Kandy. Waiters in cafes, for instance, sometimes tried to find accommodation for tourists and taxi drivers also attempted to meet their needs, not only for accommodation but also for drugs and prostitutes. Because of the proximity of the bus and fire stations, off-duty firemen would also convey tourists to accommodation. A security guard at the bus station was often seen picking up foreigners on his way to and from work. My guide friends also told me that even off-duty policemen would try to get into the act. One business man, too, would 'casually' bump into tourists, warn them about the guides and explain that he was simply a businessman. He would then offer to escort them shopping around the town, so that they would not be bothered by anyone else; he mean-

Photo 7   Kandyan dancers.

while, of course, was collecting commissions on purchases just like any other guide. Clearly, given these circumstances, the question of how many guides there were in Kandy — variously estimated by my informants at between 100 and 300 — cannot really be answered. Given the opportunity, on the spur of the moment, almost anyone can become a guide. Not only that, but guides were also mobile. Kandy guides would sometimes get dispirited and try their luck elsewhere, just as others would occasionally turn up from other tourist spots.

Just how large the 'latent' guide population was became very clear to me when talking to Ali by the lake late one night. We saw an elderly American woman get out of a minibus in the dark, weighed down by several suit cases. As I escorted her to a hotel, with Ali going on ahead so that he could make some commission, I told the guides who approached us that the woman was with me, hoping that they would leave us alone. Instead, several were extra persistent. They abused Ali and me, claiming that the woman was their catch, and scuffling broke out among them. When we passed a cigarette boutique where some middle-aged men were quietly enjoying an evening smoke, I thought the situation would be saved. Several came forward to offer their assistance, "just to help". Then they started arguing among themselves about who had offered to help first and began displaying the same sort of behaviour as the youths from whom they were nominally trying to protect us. I later realised what a mistake I had made in claiming that the woman was with me, for instead of making her 'out of bounds', it was interpreted by the guides that I myself was now "doing the tourism" and so was in competition with them. In 1982, in fact, several European tourists had set themselves up as guides in Kandy and were making money from other tourists who felt safer being with someone who spoke their own language fluently than being escorted by a local. On several occasions groups of tourists who had been approached by local guides were whisked away by compatriots, who on delivering them to a guesthouse received the commission themselves.

A second factor to bear in mind when discussing any 'structural' dimension to guiding activities is that whereas in Whyte's 'Cornerville' definite hierarchies were identifiable, street guiding is normally a highly individualistic occupation. It is very much a matter of one against the rest. There were, to be sure, groups of two or three guides who would regularly hang around together in cafes or on specific street corners. Part of this was to do with protection, I suspect, but when it came to business, this was a solitary matter in the overwhelming number of instances. Some guides were always on their own. Others would split from their peers when getting business seemed likely and, on occasions, there was acute rivalry between them. I frequently heard stories about how greedy, stupid, naive or reckless someone was when my informant had just been sitting with and chatting amicably to the person in question. There was, indeed, a quality to life and social relations on the streets very similar to that commonly described for 'ghetto' situations. Myth-making, exaggeration and bravado abound, personal failures are converted into triumph, exaggerated amity is quickly undone by competition over women or by the sheer need to survive (Hannerz 1969:86, 105–7; Liebow 1967:176, 206–7, 213–4, 217) — all told, a collection of individuals permanently fluctuating between "competence and incompetence, success and failure, good and evil" (Hannerz 1969:112).

If there was little 'structural' quality to the activities of the unlicensed guides, there was nonetheless a degree of territoriality (cf. Skar 1985:159). Some guides worked the bus or railway stations, others around the lake, others hung out in specific cafes; some had special relationships with particular guesthouses. For new guides from out of town, a rough welcome was frequent. Felix, normally fairly amiable, could not contain his anger when a Tamil from Jaffna decided to "do some tourism" in Kandy one weekend. The appearance of this well-spoken university graduate trying to make money on his pitch made him explode with rage, roughing up the newcomer somewhat. Felix told him to go back where he came from, that he owned land and had money and should not come to Kandy to deprive poor people of their living. There is also something of a division of labour among the guides, although this should not be over-stated. Most tried to meet the wide range of tourist requirements but there was also some specialisation evident. Some simply accompanied tourists to guesthouses to obtain commission; others avoided that role but tried to escort tourists on shopping expeditions; yet others specialised in taking tourists to the Kandyan dancing performances; and finally, some guides were drug specialists.

Many street guides provided sexual services for some of their 'catches'. Indeed, "sex mad" was how many described tourists, both male and female, of several nationalities. Felix talked about sex being "free" for Europeans, meaning that one could have several partners. Ali spoke of tourists who "acted like dogs … when they have the feeling any bitch will do". Some commented that I would be surprised to learn who those with the largest appetites were. A very experienced hire car driver, who had also acted as a guide on tourist coaches, told me that some of the worst were the quiet middle-aged English women: "they like little boys, and they like darkies like me", he commented. Some individuals on the street corners specialised in homosexual prostitution, and they were fairly reticent about discussing their trade. Not so the others, most of whom would brag about their sexual conquests with European women, although acknowledging that they sometimes had to perform with women they did not want. But 'making it' with a strikingly attractive European was a source of great kudos, acting perhaps, in some cases, as a compensation mechanism whereby those who lack status can utilise the sexual arena to create the experience of personal power (Bowman 1989). Where a tourism industry flourishes in ex-colonial territories, sexual behaviour is bound to be historically over-determined (Karch and Dann 1981:256–8), and people often said of Felix that his sexual behaviour was very much bound up with the "chip on his shoulder" that he had about whites in general, but particularly the British. At the same time, sex for the guides was still also very much of a business tactic. One self-assured guide, who certainly enjoyed his sexual liaisons, told me: "I spend 100 rupees [approximately $U.S. 5] on them and sleep with them and in return I get back 1000 rupees or more".

Having outlined various guiding activities, it should be recognised that when a street guide first strikes up a relationship with a foreigner, he never knows exactly what any tourist is after. A guide may thus spend half a day escorting someone around town, only to find that they spend nothing — thus earning the guide no commission. On the other hand, a conversation may start around buying batiks and then move to drugs. A guide who takes tourists to a guesthouse may end up escorting them around the island for a ten-day trip, being fed and housed by the tourists for the duration. Occasionally, guides obtain business which they know will occur only once in a lifetime. A young man who, for over a decade had special-ised in taking tourists to Kandyan dance performances, approached me one day in a highly excited state. He was hoping to obtain 100,000 rupees ($U.S. 5,000) for arranging the temporary marriage of a Dane to a local prostitute which would ena-ble him to stay permanently in Sri Lanka. This involved making payments to sev-eral officials for the drawing up of a contract which would allow the marriage to be annulled almost as soon as it was confirmed, but without the woman being able to claim any of the man's estate beyond the agreed fee for entering into such a union in the first place.

I do not possess reliable quantitative data on guides' earnings, but their income is certainly very irregular. On some days windfall gains are made, but guides may also go for many weeks without any business at all. Over the longer term, partly because of the tourist lifestyle which they must, to some extent, partic-ipate in, few were secure financially. Theirs was very much an 'easy come, easy go' existence. Certainly, a few guides claimed to be putting aside savings but, for many, the proceeds of a lucrative catch would soon disappear on clothes, beer, cafe food, and so on. A metal craftsman told me how he had once given 600 rupees commis-sion to a guide (a month's salary for some Sri Lankans) who was back only three days later wanting to borrow 10 rupees. Such spending habits meant that some guides not only worked the streets, but also slept on them, especially when times were rough. Some of the younger guides lived at home. Some came from respecta-ble homes where their parents were in work, but others slept on concrete floors or in alleys. Felix, for example, used to sleep at the top of a flight of concrete steps in a building where the night watchman was a friend of his. Sometimes he would be without food for three days.

Along with the unpredictability of income, making a living from the streets also involved difficult relationships with the authorities. Occasionally street guides were arrested and fined under the Vagrancy Ordinance,[7] but some achieved a *modus vivendi* with the police by bribing them. Other guides were occasionally 'roughed up'. There were also instances of extortion, as Ali himself could personally testify to. Ali had also been warned by other guides to keep out of tourism altogether. I myself witnessed only one serious fight, although scuffles were quite frequent, but Felix told me that serious fights were, in fact, a daily occurrence between guides in places that tourists did not know about. Such fights involved the use of broken bottles, knives and, on occasions, serious injury was inflicted. Several years previously, I was told, a guide had been thrown out of a moving train on the outskirts of Kandy. Incidents of this sort are by no means unique to the tourism arena, for we need to bear in mind that violence, corruption and coercion are part of daily experience in many areas of Sri Lankan life. During the 1983 riots, for instance, gangs of thugs operated under the control, and even in the pay of some Members of Parliament, while monks and even police looked on passively (Obeyesekere 1984a:159–60, 163–4; Kapferer 1988:232–3). In the wake of elections, strong-arm tactics are often employed where businessmen use thugs to drive out rivals who supported the losing party. Simply because foreigners are involved there is no reason to jump to the conclusion that the conduct of the guides is a symptom of some disintegrative 'demonstration effect' and so represents a breakdown in Sri Lankan norms. Acquiring benefits by establishing oneself as an intermediary, which is essentially what a guide does between tourists and either shop keepers or guesthouse owners, being given gifts and commissions rather than a specific salary, is common in many areas of political and economic life in Sri Lanka; it certainly is not unique to tourism.

I have emphasised above some of the less savoury aspects of the guiding role in the informal arena. Felix described 'friendship' in tourism as a "tactic", as "business", and no doubt he was right. For him, one could not do tourism in a "fully

---

[7] The Vagrancy Ordinance was, according to the head of the Tourist Police unit in Kandy, the only piece of legislation usable in respect of the guides. First enacted in 1845 and revised on several occasions subsequently it spoke in archaic terms about fining and whipping "idlers" and "rogues" who "persistently and without lawful excuse follow, accost and address by words or signs any person against his will and to his annoyance" (*Legislative Enactments of Ceylon*). Felix had several times been taken to court under this enactment and was extremely bitter about it. Sri Lanka was a "free country", so how could anyone be committing as offence just by speaking to foreigners, he asked me. The police Inspector stated that there needed to be specific legislation drawn up to deal with the guide problem, for he admitted that one could not reasonably apprehend people for speaking to tourists, especially if tourism was said by the authorities to be about people from different cultures meeting each other.

honest" way, for "real friendship required time", and this was precisely what was missing in nearly all relationships between tourists and locals. Nonetheless, it is important to recognise that some guide/tourist relationships do acquire characteristics other than those of straightforward manipulation or exploitation, just as some of what goes on in unlicensed guesthouses cannot be described as solely commercial. Felix himself had a small list of addresses of tourists with whom he had been friendly over the years. He still wrote to some and waited expectantly for letters to arrive from them (cf. Cohen 1986). One day he was very distressed to find that while returning on the train from Nuwara Eliya to Kandy he had lost his wallet which contained the address list. Most of those on it were women with whom he had been on trips around the island. At the start of such trips, he told me, he would state the price of his company, but if he grew to like his companion, he would tell them at the end that they could give him whatever gifts they liked. Of course he would have enjoyed several days travel, good food, good accommodation and more than likely sex as well, but he made a qualitative distinction between such relationships and a simple business arrangement. As has been recognised in other cultures, such relationships that grow up with foreigners can acquire a profound psychological significance, which terms like "tout" or "prostitute" do not adequately convey (Cohen, 1971:228–9 1982a:411–2; 1986; 1993:16). Certain elements of what might be referred to as 'friendship' can grow up, even if both parties do not quite share the same understanding of the term (Wagner 1981:200–1). Gifts given by tourists to Felix and to other street guides in Kandy, for instance, meant a great deal, even when in monetary terms they were comparatively worthless. Umbrellas, cast-off clothes, goods which do not fit into luggage on the flight out — such items often end up with the guides. Despite the hand-to-mouth existence which many guides lead, such gifts were frequently treasured as mementos of relationships, and several guides told me that they would never sell them. There was also great joy when a guide received a letter, clothes, or other presents from foreigners they had met.

Felix had had nearly a decade of guiding experience. His earlier enthusiasm for things foreign had waned appreciably and his view of Europeans had become somewhat jaundiced. Whilst admitting the calculating nature of guide behaviour, he felt that people had too harsh a view of the guides. Of all the street guides in Kandy, he claimed, only six or so would rob a tourist or do them real harm. Tourists wanted to be shown around in a short space of time and the guides could do this and also keep them safe from criminals. He added that if some guides were "rogues", the guesthouses were also out to take the foreigner's money, only they were "robbers in a gentlemanly way"; guesthouse proprietors, in his words, were "rogues behind a curtain". Certainly there was plenty of evidence that some guesthouses were employing the same strategies as the guides whom they condemned. They told their guests how guides would raise prices for them and then escorted their guests on shopping expeditions themselves to make the commission. They complained at how the guides were ruining the reputation of Kandy, while allowing their own servants to be used as prostitutes. In one incident known to me, a woman who ran a guesthouse warned her guests not to meet up with the touts on the way to the Kandy dancing because they would increase the price of the tickets. She gave her guests tickets with her own initials marked clearly on them, and the price they then paid for entry was actually higher than if they had gained admittance accompanied by one of the street guides.

STREET GUIDES, SHOPKEEPERS AND GUESTHOUSE PROPRIETORS: TRANSACTIONS AND CONFLICTS

Having described both the activities of the unlicensed guides of Kandy and the operations of the unlicensed guesthouses, it is time to concentrate on the patterns of relationships between guides, guesthouses and shopkeepers. As reported in Chapter 3, a number of conflicts within the tourism industry, both at a national and a local level, were surfacing during 1982 and leading to dramatic newspaper headlines. Stories about touts "running tourism" in Kandy were among them, but undoubtedly exaggerated the situation. For a start, street guides normally have access only to independent travellers. Those on 'package tours' or in chauffeur-driven hired cars are usually beyond their reach. In addition, major hotels and the more expensive private guesthouses will often have nothing to do with local guides. Nonetheless, concern in Kandy was widespread, for the power of the street guides was very real, particularly in regard to their ability to direct the flow of certain types of tourist towards or away from various shops and guesthouses, and to influence what went on inside such establishments between their proprietors and the foreigners. For instance, at most of the six venues in Kandy where there were regular dance performances, it was physically almost impossible for a tourist to gain entrance without being accompanied by a local guide. Not only did the guides line the routes leading to these locales asking everybody passing them whether they wanted to go to the dancing, they also clustered at the entrance itself. At a standard entrance fee of 35–50 rupees, the 5 or 10 rupees commission to a guide was a sizeable proportion of the organiser's profit.

A guide escorting a tourist into a shop is able to claim a percentage of a priced article or to influence the bargaining process between shopkeeper and tourist. Indeed, a shopkeeper is sometimes forced into two processes of bargaining at once, one (covert) with the guide and one (overt) with the customer. Because the guide has to be paid a commission, tourists will normally pay more than if they had arrived on their own because they can not beat the vendor down as far as they might be able to when there is no commission to calculate. More than that, though, a guide may demand in Sinhala that a shopkeeper substantially raise his prices so that he can receive a large commission. If the shopkeeper refuses, the guide may simply tell the customer to leave because the articles are inferior or because he knows of a better place to buy them. Some shopkeepers resist such pressures. One semi-retired businessman stated that he would not "rob Peter to pay Paul". In other words, he would not allow the guide's demands to lead to the tourist being cheated. The tout who, in his eyes, did virtually nothing to earn his money could have 5% and if he did not accept that he could leave empty handed. However, other shopkeepers felt far less confident about acting in this resolute fashion, fearing the trouble that might arise if they had an argument with one of the guides. For a shop-keeper, having a heated argument in the presence of a customer can be very embarrassing, and he is therefore in a rather weak position. If the price is too high, the tourist may not purchase an item; if the commission level is high, the trader's profit margin is significantly reduced; if the commission is too low the guide may leave in a huff, taking his catch with him and threatening never to bring any more tourists to the shop.

The situation above understates the bravado of some guides in Kandy, for some tried to obtain commission from shopkeepers without having "made a catch" at all. Outside a popular batik shop. there were normally three or four guides leaning against a metal fence. They simply watched tourists going up the steps into the shop, and then followed them in a few seconds later, said something briefly to them while they were inspecting the wares on display, and then told the shop assistant in Sinhala that they had brought the tourist. They then hung around in the shop, leaving with the tourist. Later in the day they would come back to ask the shop assistant for commission on sales. In some instances, guides even watched for tourists emerging from shops with their purchases and then went into the shop, claiming that they had sent in the tourist who had just left. Naturally, most tourists were completely unaware of the significance of being followed into the shop by a guide, or of responding to a few words from such a person, whom they might well take to be a shop employee. For the shop assistant, however, such scenes were fraught with difficulties and some had begun to check with the tourists as to whether the guide had actually escorted them in or not. They were in a weak position, however, for if they annoyed the guides too much, they could simply stand outside a shop and tell tourists not to go in.

If the above scenario looks decidedly one-sided, some guides had a different view of the matter. As Felix explained, if shopkeepers did not want any dealings with guides they had only to put over their doors a 'No guides allowed' notice. But shops did not display such notices, because many were partly reliant upon tourists brought by the guides. Not all shops were centrally located and, with limited time at their disposal, tourists cannot see all available establishments. In these circumstances, directing tourists into one shop rather than another is a significant service. Felix suggested that many shopkeepers complaining about touts in Kandy were really aggrieved because guides did not visit their particular shop rather than because they did.[8]

A similar pattern is evident in the relationship of street guides to unlicensed guesthouse owners. Hotels and registered guesthouses do most of their business with groups on package tours or with tourists in hire cars booked in advance into accommodation in Kandy by travel agents in Colombo. Little of their trade consists of individual tourists searching for accommodation. Some hotels have a standard rate of 10% commission to guides bringing such people, but others give no commission at all to discourage street guides from frequenting their premises. Some of the larger licensed guesthouses adopt the same policy. The story is very different, however, for the guesthouses in the informal sector for they lack the licenses to operate in an open manner. Since they are unlicensed, they cannot advertise in Tourist Board literature and most are so small that they have no links with travel agents. The source of their guests, therefore, is somewhat variable, and, for many, tourists picked up by guides while casually wandering around the streets of Kandy are a significant source of custom. That, however, does little to change the rhetoric of opposed interests between guesthouse proprietors and guides.

At one guesthouse, I received the standard story about guides being "good for nothing". However, staying there on a semi-permanent basis were at least two individuals who were always catching tourists in the streets of Kandy. I later discovered that they were actually employed by the guesthouse, frequently eating and sleeping there and, in fact, possessing rail passes purchased by the owner so that they could go each day on the train to Colombo to bring tourists. When asked about tourism in Kandy, another guesthouse owner told me the guides were dishonest, that she would have nothing to do with them and that I should avoid them, adding that the foreigners staying with her were friends of her son, who lived in England. The claim was curious, given that the tourists staying at her establishment were French or German. On leaving, I had to ask several times for a receipt and when it finally arrived it had the wrong address and a false name as well as the

---

[8] The formal sector is meant to operate according to a completely different set of rules. Guides trained by the Tourist Board are meant to receive lecturing fees and *per diem* allowances and not to be a party to these covert commission deals. However, none of my street guide informants believed that they acted in that way. Indeed, in Kandy lived one trained guide whose accommodation and living expenses were paid for throughout the eight month off season by the owner of a craft and jewellery store in return for his regularly bringing coachloads of tourists during the peak season.

wrong date. My guide also received no commission, the owner claiming that someone else had brought me. Some weeks later this same woman walked past a group
of guides on a street corner, and in my earshot told them to bring her more tourists.

When a street guide takes a tourist to a guesthouse, he is entitled to commission. Whereas a hotel might give a guide 10% for every day that a tourist is in residence, guesthouses often give 25–50% for a one day stay and, if a tourist stays for
three or four days, the entire rent received for the first day. Commission to the
guide does not always mean higher room rates to the tourist. Some guesthouse proprietors have a fairly fixed idea of charges for their rooms, and this is paid by tourists whether they arrive with a guide or unaccompanied. In the former case it is the
guesthouse owner whose profit is reduced as some of the rent is pocketed by the
guide. Where room rates are not written down, however, the arrival of any new
tourist is an opportunity for bargaining and many guesthouse owners raise their
charges to take account of the guide's commission. Indeed, some proprietors allege
that guides have arrived at the front door and demanded in Sinhala that the room
prices be doubled so that they can have a high commission. Not unnaturally, this
might mean that the tourist refuses to stay, but some owners also found it embarrassing because it made them look greedy. It also infuriated them because it seemed
to allow those they regarded as the *hoi poloi* to dictate to them.

Because room rates are normally not fixed, and because the rules concerning
commission are also somewhat loose, there is much room for misunderstanding or
deception between guide and guesthouse proprietor. I heard guides complain that
commission they deserved was refused, with the proprietor either claiming to have
already paid it, or alleging that the guide did not really help the tourist. Sometimes
proprietors force guides to come back several times before they give them any
money. There are also disputes about the percentages agreed upon or even over
how long a tourist stayed in an establishment. Some guesthouse owners are convinced that guides deliberately move tourists on when they would themselves like
to stay longer, because it is in the guide's interest to receive several commissions of
25%, rather than to have a full day's rent, but collectable only at the end of a period
of several days.

It is not only room prices that lead to conflict between guide and guesthouse
owner, for often much more is involved in the relationship of guide and tourist and
tourist and guesthouse proprietor. For instance, Felix once arrived at a guesthouse
with a young woman, only to be refused entry because, according to him, the
owner wanted to have sex with her. The tourist, who had already struck up a good
relationship with Felix, was unwilling to comply and, three days later when she
left, her bill was much greater than she had been led to expect. There was an argument and when Felix arrived he told her a reasonable figure and suggested she pay
that and leave. In a somewhat different context, Ali told me how he had become

friendly with an Italian couple who had come to Sri Lanka to learn about street vending before establishing a business back home. They wanted him to export goods to them in Italy. When he went to the guesthouse where they were staying to work out the details of the business arrangement, the proprietor refused him permission to enter. The tourists explained that their business dealings had nothing to do with the guesthouse owner and a row erupted. The tourists immediately left with Ali, who then arranged alternative accommodation for them.

Another potential source of conflict involves the arrangement of transport for tourists. Siri had delivered a group of tourists to a guesthouse and then, at their request, arranged a trip for them to visit the Veddah (aboriginal) people living in the jungle at Mahiyangana, an appreciable distance outside Kandy. The guesthouse owners tried to dissuade the tourists, saying that it was not safe and that they should go in the guesthouse's own vehicle, a much more expensive mode of travel than the one Siri intended, namely a car driven by a taxi driver friend who would give Siri commission of 1 rupee per mile. Siri protested to the guesthouse owners that whereas they had a right to room rent, anything else the tourists wanted to do was his concern and not theirs. He told me that it was unfair for wealthy guesthouse proprietors to try to deprive him of his livelihood. Siri insisted on taking the tourists, for which he was well qualified, having been on several such trips before and even having a slight knowledge of the Veddah language. The guesthouse owners were incensed and Siri told me that for some weeks after the incident he went in fear of reprisals, giving me graphic accounts of how he had had several "close shaves" as they tried to run him down with their car.

Guesthouse owners sometimes claim that their profits come less from room rents than from the provision of meals. Some, in fact, deliberately offer low room rates to attract tourists, aiming to compensate by providing relatively expensive meals. If a street guide delivers a tourist to an establishment with the intention of meeting the tourist later, to show him/her around the shops, to have a cafe meal, and so on, the guesthouse proprietor clearly risks losing income. More than that, a guesthouse owner may himself wish to escort the tourist around the town, picking up commissions on shopping purchases, thereby depriving the guides of one of their more lucrative sources of income. In such circumstances, the tourist becomes the recipient of conflicting advice, receiving cautionary tales from both parties. A guide will tell the tourist not to eat at the guesthouse because it will be expensive but, as soon as the guide has departed, the guesthouse owner will endeavour to ensure that the tourist spends no more time with the guide by blackening his character. Conceivably, this may on some occasions be a genuine expression of concern for the tourist, but the guesthouse proprietor may simply want to monopolise the tourist's time and expenditure to maximise his income. Street guides, indeed, told me of a new pattern developing during 1982 which particularly irritated them, where owners sent their guests on shopping expeditions escorted by their own teenage daughters. The guides clearly could not do business with a tourist when accompanied by someone from a guesthouse; indeed, in every shop, the daughter would simply tell the shopkeeper to send the commission to the guesthouse. I witnessed one instance where a young woman had to walk briskly through Kandy, followed by a number of guides hurling abuse at her, while she tried to ignore the whole affair so that the tourists would not understand what was going on.

To avoid such confrontations, many guesthouse owners deliberately confined their role to their own premises and took no interest in tourists' other activities. Escorting tourists shopping not only meant that guesthouse owners had to venture into the streets — the territory of the guides — thus risking potential conflicts, but also that they expose themselves to public opinion. Although some of the well-to-do and respectable in Kandyan society were involved in tourism, it was still an activity looked down upon by many. Many people, conscious of their reputations, simply did not want to be seen accompanying tourists in case onlookers made adverse comments about them. On several occasions, an expected leisurely stroll with an informant to discuss some matter about tourism was made difficult by their obvious embarrassment. They were unwilling to be seen with me in case rumours started that they were now "doing the tourism".

Aggrieved street guides and proprietors of unregistered guesthouses have no easy means of satisfactorily resolving their disputes. Both are engaged in activities on which the Tourist Board and municipal authorities frown, so there can be no ready resort to the tourist police or municipal officials. There are some sanctions, of course. Guesthouse owners can simply tell a guide never to bring tourists again, but at the risk of receiving fewer tourists or simply of being more reliant on other guides. Some guides have been so upset by the demeaning treatment sometimes handed out by guesthouse proprietors that they do indeed, for long periods of time, refuse to take tourists to certain establishments. The manager of a well-known arts and crafts establishment told me that he admitted no guides whatever because if he did and subsequently offended any of them, they would combine to boycott his establishment.

Such a fear is exaggerated, just as the proposal that shopkeepers *en bloc* put up notices forbidding street guides to bring tourists is unrealistic. Neither guides nor guesthouse owners act *en bloc*. Certainly, conflicts between proprietors and guides are conflicts between the relatively affluent and the predominantly poor, between the owners of property and those with only their time and labour to sell, but the two categories do not normally act as antagonistic classes. For a start, neither category is closed: anyone can become a guide, and any home owner can try to let rooms to foreigners; giving up guiding and ceasing to be involved in tourism can also occur very quickly. Also, the class basis is the less obvious because particular individuals in each category are interdependent. Vertical linkages are more visible than solidarity (Bromley 1979:113). Moreover, guesthouse owners are fiercely competitive and jealous of one another and among street guides, too, in the last analysis it is everyone for himself. At least once some 22 shopkeepers in Kandy acted as a group when they presented a petition to the police, requesting that the local tout menace be eliminated (*Sun*, 30 June 1982). I doubt that guesthouse owners would take similar joint action, even though conflicts will certainly continue between individual guesthouse owners and individual guides. As indicated in Chapter 4, no committee of guesthouse proprietors was formed after the Town Hall seminar, even though improving the image of Kandy as a tourist destination would clearly have been in their interests.

LIFE IN THE INFORMAL SECTOR: CONCLUDING THOUGHTS

There was considerable pessimism in Kandy during 1982. Many of those who ran unlicensed guesthouses thought that they might have only two more good years before tourism dried up in the town. Many guides, too, felt that tourism had peaked and those with whom I regularly spoke readily conceded that there were then so many at work in Kandy that guiding was becoming impossible. Indeed, the 'catching zone' already extended to Colombo. One or two guides commented that 1982 was the worst year they had experienced, that in previous years tourists had been considerably more generous. They also felt that tourists would increasingly tell them to "get lost" because of the number of cheap travel books which had become available. Nonetheless, many of them were still sustained by one of the 'founding myths' of the guides, that "doing the tourism" was relatively easy, that fortunes could be earned. Some of the first generation of street guides in Kandy were still around. During the early 1970s, a few had received overseas air tickets from tourists and at least one had married a European woman. The continued affluence of another was evident from his style of dress and the motor cycle he used to ride around the streets. No doubt during 1982 some street guides were still being attracted by the 'bright lights' of tourism, but most were involved simply because they were without regular, or indeed, any employment. I do not know how the decline in tourism in the years after 1982 has affected them,[9] or what impact the enactment of the Specified Tourist Services Code in 1984 has had on those operat-

---

[9] The 1993 edition of the popular Lonely Planet guide *Sri Lanka* states that Kandy "used to be" the tout capital and that the touts have been "cleaned out" (Noble *et al.*, 1993:128), but adds that taxi drivers have stepped into the breach in their place.

ing unlicensed guesthouses. One possibility is that since activity in the informal economy is a "survival mechanism" (Henry 1982:460) for many, legislation could not change things in a fundamental way. It is also hard to see how one can prevent unlicensed operators trying their luck in tourism when national leaders are declaring the 'open economy' as an opportunity for everyone to make money.

Many tourists I met in the streets of Kandy during my seven months of research declared that the touts in Sri Lanka were the most annoying they had met anywhere in Asia. Tired of the incessant approaches of these people, they felt themselves to be 'victims' as they walked the streets of Kandy. At this level, any notion that tourism is a force for international peace and understanding (D'Amore and Jafari 1988 eds; de Alwis 1980) is almost laughable. If the depiction of guide as predator and tourist as victim is understandable at the level of interpersonal interaction, at the 'system' level another perspective emerges. Profits from international tourism, as many contributors to the social scientific literature on the industry argue, have a strong tendency to flow to multinational corporations and to political and economic elites in the developing nations. Seen in this light and given the strategies to which the poor in the Third World have to resort to make ends meet, especially given the forces stacked against them, one perhaps needs to look again at the question of who the beneficiaries and victims in international tourism really are. Having suggested this, however, we also need to acknowledge that few in the streets of Kandy said that tourism was a bad thing, whereas wealthier people, including many involved in tourism, would wax lyrical about how foreigners were corrupting the country and destroying their culture. If international tourism in the Third World frequently creates risky and even demeaning roles for many in the informal sector, the fact is also that tourism at least brings some income and opportunity, even if on an irregular basis. For these individuals, as for some Third World countries which have energetically pursued tourism, we must recognise the fact that there may not be an alternative.

CHAPTER SIX

Tourism in Troubled Times:
1982 to the Present[1]

The international tourism industry, according to some tourism scholars, has an inherently cyclical and therefore decidedly unstable character. Consumer tastes shift, or indeed are consciously shifted by the image-makers in the industry, bringing popularity to hitherto unknown regions, while popular resorts fade. Locals, at first enthusiastic, become either indifferent or positively hostile as saturation point is reached or passed. In some cases, areas which have lost popularity find it again, and hence undergo a second cycle of development. On the other hand, some previously popular tourist sites simply decline after their peak and never again find favour with the travelling public.[1] Whereas the growth in tourist arrivals experienced in Sri Lanka between 1966 and 1982 led many confidently to predict that by the end of the 1980s international tourists would exceed 500,000 (P. Seneviratne 1982:97), others, including those on the streets of Kandy, felt that 1982 itself could turn out to be the peak year. Given the European recession, many were gloomy about the future. The record in the years following 1982 was, in fact, one of considerable decline in tourist numbers, not, however, because of the operation of normal cyclical factors which affect the evolution of touristic systems, but because of the outbreak of widespread civil violence.

It is something of a cruel irony that this should have happened in a country which has so stressed the idea that tourism is a force for peace and understanding, a perspective which, over the last few years, has even found some support among academics (D'Amore and Jafari 1988 eds). There are many, of course, who give no credence whatever to the notion that tourism has this ennobling dimension, especially given the gross economic and political inequalities which normally subsist between tourist generating countries and tourist destinations. In a way, however, de Alwis' views have been vindicated by the Sri Lankan experience, if only in a negative guise. International tourism may have a tenuous link to peace and understanding, but tourism and violence are clearly incompatible; in that sense, peace is a

---

[1] Not only do consumer tastes shift, but even issues as technical as changes in currency rates, variations in the price of aviation fuel and airline reroutings, can substantially affect visitor numbers. Many destination countries in the Third World who thus looked to tourism to provide a secure source of foreign exchange for promoting continued economic growth have learned the hard way that there is much in the tourism industry over which they have little or no control.

prerequisite to a healthy tourism industry (van den Berghe 1988:21). International tourism is almost always one of the first casualties of conflict, so the industry really does have an acute interest in fostering peace.[2]

The far more concrete and practical problem which has confronted the industry in Sri Lanka since the 1983 disturbances has been whether the island would ever again be able to attract mass tourists in such numbers to reach or surpass its 1982 record. Richter voted against tourism delivering the goods for Sri Lanka in 1989 (1989:162), and a past Director of Research at the Central Bank of Ceylon had this to say in 1987:

> quite apart from the internal problems in the country which are causing a serious setback to tourism, the over optimistic projections that government has made regarding tourist traffic do not appear to be realistic. It was believed that after 1977 the high growth rates which prevailed in the seventies would continue unabated throughout the eighties. In the last three years, contrary to expectations, there has been a sharp general decline in tourism in South Asia as a whole ... It cannot, then, be fathomed how Sri Lanka can revitalise this sector, even if the ethnic problem is effectively solved (Karunatilake 1987:259).

During the entire 1966–1982 period, only once had there been a substantial fall in the number of overseas visitors — 1971, a year of armed insurrection led by the Janatha Vimukti Peramuna (People's Liberation Front). Tourists and perhaps even more so tour organisers are highly sensitive to civil disturbances and so are often very quick to choose alternative destinations. It does not take much violence to cripple a tourism industry (Richter 1989:65; 1992) and in that sense the industry can take on more the character of a "high stakes crap game than an economic panacea" (Richter 1993:195). The violence of the past ten years in Sri Lanka has certainly devastated some regions of the country and many who were dependent on tourism for employment have lost their jobs. Hotels have been destroyed by bomb damage. Regions of the country have been declared 'out of bounds'. But besides this, the myriad uncertainties have adversely affected the willingness of overseas investors to put capital into a country which has seemed unable to solve its internal

---

[2] The 'negative proof', of course, is also somewhat less than convincing. Throughout much of South East Asia, for instance, the development of modern tourism industries was significantly spurred along by the need for recreational facilities by the American military during the 1950s and 1960s. There is also a further local irony in the case of Sri Lanka. During 1982 the Sri Lankan Air Force was operating 'Helitours', a project whereby the military allowed its aircraft and helicopters to run pleasure trips for tourists around the island (Jones 1982). This was very much a money-making enterprise by the military to acquire the cash to purchase new equipment. It might therefore be that some tourists have directly, albeit unknowingly, contributed to some of the hardware that has since been unleashed on sections of the population.

difficulties (Manor 1984:83). With communal violence just beginning to flare up in 1983, Obeyesekere observed that it was a truly ugly irony that Air Lanka should still be advertising Sri Lanka as "A Taste of Paradise" when the island was going up in flames (1984:153).[3]

It was in July of 1983 that the civil disturbances in Sri Lanka became head-line news around the world. The effect on tourism arrivals was immediate. For the first six months of 1983 (Ceylon Tourist Board 1983a:1) arrivals were up on the 1982 figures, but for the latter half of the year there were catastrophic falls. In August alone the overall drop was 75.4% and only 2000 instead of the normal 30,000 foreigners attended the Kandy *perahera* that year (Economist Intelligence Unit 1983:13). In addition to the effects of the communal violence, during 1983 India revised its tax concession regulations regarding 'duty free' goods, with the result that the very high number of Indians utilising the Duty Free Shopping Com-plex in Colombo also fell off dramatically (C.T.B. 1983a:9). This was a serious blow, for in 1983 (C.T.B.1984e:1) Indians had actually outnumbered German visi-tors, becoming, for the first time, the major source country for visitors to Sri Lanka. The total number of tourists visiting Sri Lanka in 1983 was 337,342, a fall of 17.2% on 1982. At the end of 1984 Sri Lanka recorded a further fall to 317,734 (C.T.B. 1984b:2), in part caused by the 52.6% drop in visitors from India. Given drops in two consecutive years from the 1982 peak of 407,000 arrivals, Sri Lanka's international tourists fell below the 321,000 reached in 1980, although it must be stressed that had it not been for the declining numbers from India, Sri Lanka would actually have avoided an overall decline (C.T.B. 1984e:Annex iii). Despite such trends, many held out the hope that the 'good times' would soon return after 'tem-porary disturbances'. Planning approval for hotels in Colombo and elsewhere still went ahead (International Travel Review 1983:5), and the Ceylon Tourist Board was spending considerable amounts of foreign exchange on publicity campaigns abroad to restore Sri Lanka's image; in 1985, for instance, it spent 36 million rupees (E.I.U. 1985b:17). Meanwhile, the Central Bank was stating that with such a decline as had already taken place, the industry was so clearly over-capitalised that many recent approvals should, in fact, have been withheld (1983:192).

The disturbances, however, did not turn out to be 'temporary' and in 1984 tourism fell to being the seventh earner of foreign exchange for Sri Lanka (C.T.B.1985a:1–2), bringing in only 5.8% of the total compared with the 10.5% of 1982. In mid 1985 (C.T.B.1985b:1), Business Turnover Tax was reduced from 5% to 1% as relief for the ailing industry. At the end of 1985, however, tourist arrivals,

---

[3] Others, of course, might regard international tourism in the Third World as an ugly irony at all times since it hides the insecurity and poverty of the lives of the masses in those countries underneath glossy images which portray where tourists go to as 'par-adises on earth' (Richter 1992:75).

given the escalating communal violence, fell even further to 257,456, a figure only slightly above that recorded for 1974, and only half of the 506,000 arrivals predicted in the *Annual Statistical Report* for 1981 (Table 24; C.T.B.1985c:1). The downturn was even worse for the optimists working in the industry. The Director-General of the Ceylon Tourist Board, for instance, had expressed the hope in 1981 that the industry would reach 500,000 during 1984, to coincide with Sri Lanka hosting the Pacific Area Travel Association conference (*South Asia Travel Review*, December 1981:8,12). Apart from overall numbers, occupancy rates also reveal the catastrophic dimensions of the problem. Throughout 1982–4 the building of new rooms in graded establishments continued, increasing from 7,539 rooms in 1982 to 9,627 in 1984, but occupancy rates fell from 47.8% to 35.6%, the lowest occupancy rate since 1972 (C.T.B.1984:6,44).

A 1984 newspaper article by a Reuters correspondent entitled "Riots hit tourist boom" (*Geelong Advertiser* 23 August 1984) tells how the clash between the army and Tamil insurgents had "badly damaged Sri Lanka's image of an island favourable both to sunbathers and shareholders". It quoted the Sri Lankan Minister of Finance, speaking about the need for political stability in order to bring back tourists and foreign investments. Many hotels in Colombo were being left uncompleted. Many debts incurred could not be repaid, and massive refinancing and rescheduling schemes had to be put into operation (Monetary Board 1990:96). $U.S.1 million had been spent on overseas publicity campaigns to restore Sri Lanka's image abroad, but to no avail. In addition to the continued closure of the Talaimannar Ferry from south India (the entry point to Sri Lanka for many budget tourists), foreign airlines started to delete Colombo as a landing point. In 1986 it was also widely reported that some countries were thinking of discontinuing foreign aid to the island (approximately 60% of Sri Lanka's national budget consists of such aid), given Sri Lanka's inability to solve its ethnic violence (*Weekend Australian* 18 June 1986). Tamils outside Sri Lanka, it was also claimed, were actively campaigning for aid to be stopped and were also trying to persuade travel agents to stop sending tourists to Sri Lanka.

In May 1986 an Air Lanka plane was destroyed by a bomb blast at Katunayake Airport (E.I.U. 1986b:11), and a few tourists were added to the list of the dead in the island. 12 of 13 hotels had already closed down in the northern and eastern regions (Central Bank 1986:200). According to Ratnatunga: "tourism in Sri Lanka is fading into history ... nine years after a free market economy flourished to give this island nation a new quality of life, Sri Lanka is on the road to economic disaster" (*Weekend Australian* 18 June 1986). Indeed, in 1986 the Ceylon Tourist Board not only downgraded its advertising overseas, it even closed some overseas offices (Central Bank 1986:196). During 1987, too, after years of rumours about the running of Air Lanka, the entire board was sacked after a commission of inquiry found incompetence and corruption on such a scale that it was believed that criminal charges would follow (E.I.U. 1987a:13; 1987b:10–11; 1987c:14). Permission for new hotel construction also came to an end. In 1987 arrivals fell to 187,620, a decline of 55% on the 1982 figures, and income had declined by a comparable 51% (Central Bank 1987:196). Tourism-related employment in 1982 standing at 64,262 had fallen to 48,811 and room occupation rates in the hill areas fell to 24.9%; in the northern and eastern regions occupation rates were so low they were not even recorded (Central Bank 1987:194, 197). To the extent that the armed conflict was consistently reported as distinctly regional (Garcia 1988:101), tourism continued in quite a healthy state in some localities in the island. But in 1988, jut when many expected an upswing to commence (E.I.U. 1989:15–16), the J.V.P. led a second uprising in the south and southwest of the island — both prime beach resort locations. This uprising had little to do with the Sinhalese-Tamil struggle and further crippled the industry. Tourist arrivals fell further to 184,732 and in 1989 the Ceylon Tourist Board actually started sending tourists home, rather than have them caught up in the conflagration (E.I.U. 1989:15–16).

In 1993, ten years after the commencement of the most recent chapter of domestic conflict, reports of widespread killing are still almost a daily occurrence in the international press with precious little evidence of any satisfactory solution on the horizon. But one cannot, for all that, say that the international tourist industry is finished for good in Sri Lanka. Other destinations which have fallen out of favour have regained popularity and Sri Lanka herself in both 1990 and 1991 saw substantial increases in arrivals. 317,703 was the figure reached in 1991, with the Ceylon Tourist Board confidently expecting over 400,000 in 1992 (Ahamath 1992). Some international press agencies were already speaking of a return to "normal times" (A.F.P. 1990). New master plans were being developed and new resorts were being built (E.I.U. 1991:18–19). On the other hand, many hotels were still greatly in debt and the government itself started to sell its stake in a number of hotels to overseas interests. The casino in Colombo which had promised to draw in significant numbers of wealthy tourists from Asian countries such as Taiwan, Singapore and Hong Kong was also shut down, with much publicity about massive criminal racketeering as well as staunch opposition from the Buddhist establishment (E.I.U. 1991:18–19; 1992:15). There is thus some reason to believe that ideas about "normal times" may be premature. Full recovery will surely require a widely perceived effective and long term solution to internal discord so that a Ceylon Tourist Board brochure like "Sri Lanka. A Welcome Change" achieves some semblance of credibility with the tour promoters and with the average holiday-maker.

That brochure, in circulation during 1982, contained the following statement: "Sri Lanka is a happy island ... a land of smiling people ... you will find that the people are always friendly and outgoing ... Over the centuries [different groups] have learned to respect their cultural differences ... In a world in which peace and leisure is becoming more sought after and ever harder to find, Sri Lanka remains a true paradise on earth". Such messages are the very stuff of tourism image-making the world over, of course, and Sri Lanka has merely trod the same sort of route as most tourist destinations in emphasising friendly people, attractive scenery, wonderful beaches, cultural interest, and all the rest. Touristic representations invariably fall short of an accurate portrayal of the social reality of a destination country, but they need to be minimally believable in order to be effective marketing tools. In the case of Sri Lanka, given the communal bloodbath of the past decade, the image is simply unsustainable, even if it is true that a great many tourists know little about the country before they go and little more when they leave (Garcia 1988:93, 98). With no political or military solution in sight, at any time there can be an escalation in violence which could totally undermine any tendency for tourist numbers to pick up. In that sense, "normal times" are still perhaps a long way off. On the other hand, the latest evidence suggests that within Sri Lanka the government and tourism authorities have entered a confident and fully expansionary mode again (Fierz 1993:35). UN development funds are being utilised in significant new tourism planning, many hotels are being renovated and several new developments have already commenced. There are expectations of a trebling of hotel rooms in the next three years and the Minister of Tourism is expecting one million tourists by 1996, more than double the number achieved in the previous peak year of 1982 (Fierz 1993:35). Only time will tell, of course, whether these goals are attained and whether they are then sustainable in the longer term.

Chapter 3 made it clear that the tourism industry in Sri Lanka faced a number of difficult policy decisions in 1982. Disagreements were evident then as to whether the thrust for the future should be in increased numbers of tourists or rather in a restriction of numbers but a maximising of daily expenditure from each. A major unsolved problem involved the tensions between the formal and the informal spheres. Entrepreneurs were complaining that the authorities had started to tax the industry too heavily and were thus "killing the goose that laid the golden egg". Rapidly increasing prices were, it was said, beginning to decrease the attractiveness of Sri Lanka as compared to some other very similar destination countries. Many also were the voices beginning to draw attention to the high moral price being paid for tourism development by reason of the cultural pollution believed to follow in its wake. Some have viewed the downturn of the last decade resulting from the violence as something of a "blessing in disguise"[4] (Sri Lanka Profiles 1987a:4) given

---

[4] Some niche marketers have certainly seen advantages for themselves. Inter Cultural Travel Education Services, for instance, advertised for 'alternative tourists' in 1991 to "visit us before the 'tourists' return" (Sri Lanka Profiles 1987b:2).

such an array of problems in the tourism industry, in that it might provide sufficient breathing space for a solution to be found for some of these dilemmas.

In 1989 a new ministerial portfolio was created for tourism and in 1991 the
Ceylon Tourist Board itself acquired a new chairman, either of which developments could have sparked fresh developments (Seneviratne and Peiris 1991:47). But
it is evident that in 1993 many of the problems apparent in 1982 are still there and
many of the discordant voices are still clearly audible. Some of the voices, indeed,
are very much more organised today, and some of the problems would seem to
have got worse despite the decrease in number of arrivals. If international press
coverage is anything to go by, for instance, the reputation of Sri Lanka as a "haven
for perverts" (Wimaladasa 1992b:16) has actually strengthened. Sri Lanka is widely
recognised as second only to Thailand in respect of sex tourism, and some allege
that the island is now also sitting on an "AIDS volcano" (Wimaladasa 1992b:16).
O'Grady ranks Sri Lanka along with Taiwan, Thailand and the Philippines as destinations for paedophile tourists (1992:134) and it is even possible that given the way
in which the violence tended to divert other tourists elsewhere, that very downturn
may have led to the percentage of paedophile tourists going to the island greatly
increasing over the past decade (O'Grady 1992:92; Seneviratne and Pieris 1991:49).

Richter once argued (1982:108) that tourism development was normally a
relatively easy policy option for governments since, the industry being new, there
were no entrenched, antagonistic interest groups to cause obstruction. This can no
longer be said of Sri Lanka where, in addition to the increasingly critical comments
of a range of voices at home there is the loud denunciation of international groups
such as the Ecumenical Coalition on Third World Tourism. Two recent events
clearly reveal the mounting volume of voices hostile to tourism to the point where
groups otherwise quite separate find common ground in concern about the industry (Wimaladasa 1992a).

Iranawila, a small fishing village on the west coast of Sri Lanka north of
Negombo was chosen to be the site of a new luxury hotel and a 'Voice of America'
relay station (Firth 1993). The developments between them would require the evic-
tion of approximately four hundred local families, some of whom, of course, might
receive temporary employment in constructing the very facilities which displaced
them. Apart from the appropriation of land for the benefit of foreigners so reminiscent of colonial times, there were also concerns that in this fishing locality the
moral degeneration which would follow from the onslaught of wealthy tourists
would be unacceptable. Local leaders, NGOs, human rights workers, Christian
and Buddhist clergy all lent their weight to opposing the development and were
finally successful in having the facilities moved elsewhere as the government, early
in 1991, was forced to withdraw planning approval, largely as a result of the strenuous opposition from the Catholic Church (Fierz 1993:36). In the second case, that

of Kandalama, to date the government and tourism developers have stood firm (Firth 1993; Commission for Justice and Peace 1992; Pravada 1992:1). Near Dambulla, sixty kilometres from Kandy, there were plans to build a 'Four star' hotel in the catchment area of the Kandalama tank, the reservoir which provided water vital to the agriculture of a number of villages. Fears were that the water supply would be both polluted and interrupted, with the villages thus dying whilst tourists luxuriated in the hotel swimming pool nearby.

Elaborate irrigation systems have long been a feature of agriculture in Sri Lanka, and tanks, along with rice and Buddhism are three of the most emotive symbols in the island. The Dambulla local council (*Pradeshiya Sabhawa*) ordered that building be stopped, but the instruction was ignored. An environmental impact assessment was also ignored. The Minister of Tourism was approached but he too refused to halt the development. Then the opposition S.L.F.P. made Kandalama an issue with which to attack the U.N.P. government, thus bringing tourism into the arena of national political dispute, something that had not occurred a decade earlier, although local interests groups were somewhat wary of such a development. The issue was very much seen as the exposure of village folk in the Kandyan heartland to the moral evils of multinational capitalism and the ruination of rural people at the hands of metropolitan developers. No local benefits were expected, for as had happened elsewhere, the objectors claimed, the tourism industry would

Photo 8   Rangiri Temple, Dambulla.

not stimulate local agriculture and ordinary village folk would not be those who would find employment in the tourism industry. Many local interests groups came together in this protest — Christians, Buddhists and Muslims — with tourism thus cementing ties between groups normally quite separate, as had occurred at Iranaw- ila. But the developers and authorities could not easily be diverted this time. Indeed, local village leaders were threatened that they would be 'disappeared' if they continued to protest, a local Buddhist monastery was set alight and gunmen intimidated the local *moulavi* who had signed the protest petition. The protest, however, continued to gather strength and on July 12 1992 at Dambulla 50,000 people of all religious denominations took part in *satyagraha* — mass, non-violent civil protest.

It is some indication of the extent to which tourism is now a source of dis- cord in Sri Lanka that in an island which reached political independence after four hundred years of colonial rule without the mass civil disobedience campaigns that had marked the struggle of her large neighbour India, that she should now, forty years after independence, be witnessing such protests because of tourist develop- ments which are deaf to the voices of so many. As a report by the Commission for Justice and Peace put it: "Will the fifty thousand voices ... be drowned by a few more powerful voices, conveniently overlooking and ignoring the cry of these ... villagers just to satisfy the selfish wants of the affluent ... will a government that has survived thousands of violent deaths be prepared to listen to the voice of its peaceful people?" (1992:3). Clearly, if tourism is a force for peace and understand- ing, many thousands of Sri Lankans still remain to be convinced.

Bibliography

Abu-Lughod, L.
1991   Writing against culture. In R. Fox (ed.), *Recapturing anthropology. Working in the present*. School of American Research Press, Santa Fe, 137–62.

Adler, J.
1989   Origins of sightseeing. *Annals of Tourism Research* **16**: 7–29.

A. F. P.
1990   Sri Lanka's tourism industry back to normal? *Contours* **4**(6): 21.

Ahamath, A.
1992   Paradise regained for Sri Lanka's tourism. *Jakarta*, 13 October.

Ahmed, S. A.
1984   Perceptions of tourism in Sri Lanka. *Vidyodaya* **12**: 280–92.
1985   Tourism in Sri Lanka. In H. V. Kirpalani (ed.), *International marketing*. Random House, New York, 634–45.
1987   Perceptions of socio-economic and cultural impact of tourism in Sri Lanka — a research study. *Marga Quarterly Journal* **8**(4): 34–63.
1989   Psychological profiles of Sri Lankans versus tourists. *Annals of Tourism Research* **16**: 345–59.

Aluwihare, Sir R.
1964   *The Kandy Perahera*. M. D. Gunasena and Co. Ltd, Colombo.

Amunugama, S.
1979   Ideology and class interest in one of Piyadasa Sirisena's novels: the new image of the 'Sinhala-Buddhist' nationalist. In M. Roberts (ed.), *Collective identities, nationalisms and protest in modern Sri Lanka*. Marga Institute, Colombo, 314–36.

Appadurai, A.
1991   Global ethnoscapes. Notes and queries for a transnational anthropology. In R. Fox (ed.), *Recapturing anthropology. Working in the present*. School of American Research Press, Santa Fe, 191–210.

Ariyaratne, A. T.
1970   Promotion of tourism in the context of rural communities in Ceylon. In Association for the Promotion of Tourism in Ceylon 1970, *Proceedings of seminar on tourism for local bodies*, held on 20 September, 1970, Ceylon Chamber of Commerce, Colombo, 49–54.

Association for the Promotion of Tourism in Ceylon
1969   *Proceedings of seminar on tourism*, held on 27 June 1969, Hotel Taprobane, Colombo.

203

1970   *Proceedings of seminar on tourism for local bodies*, held on 20 September, 1970, Ceylon Chamber of Commerce, Colombo.

Attanayake, A., Samaranayake, H. M. S. and Ratnapala, N.
1983   Sri Lanka. In E. A. Pye and T. Lin (eds), *Tourism in Asia. The economic impact.* Singapore University Press, Singapore, 241–351.

Balakrishnan, N.
1979   A review of the economy. In T. Fernando and R. N. Kearney (eds), *Modern Sri Lanka. A society in transition.* Maxwell School of Citizenship and Public Affairs, Syracuse University, New York, 101–130.

Berindranath, D.
1980.   Who benefits from tourists? *Democratic World* 18 May: 5–6.

Bochner, S.
1981   The social psychology of cultural mediation. In S. Bochner (ed.), *The mediating person. Bridges between cultures.* Schenkman Publishing Co., Cambridge, Mass., 6–36.
1981 (ed.) *The mediating person. Bridges between cultures.* Schenkman Publishing Co., Cambridge, Mass.
1982 (ed.) *Cultures in contact.* Pergamon Press, Oxford.

Boissevain, J.
1977   Tourism and development in Malta. *Development and Change* 8: 523–8.

Boissevain, J. and Inglott, P. S.
1979   Tourism in Malta. In E. de Kadt (ed.), *Tourism. Passport to development? Perspectives on the social and cultural effects of tourism in developing countries.* Oxford University Press, New York, 265–84.

Bouhdiba, A.
1981   Mass tourism and cultural traditions. *People's Bank Economic Review*, Colombo, August, 27–9.

Bowman, G.
1989   Fucking tourists. Sexual relations and tourism in Jerusalem's Old City. *Critique of Anthropology* 9(2): 77–93.

Brewer, J. D.
1978   Tourism, business and ethnic categories in a Mexican town. In V. Smith (ed.), *Hosts and guests. The anthropology of tourism.* Blackwell, Oxford, 83–100.

Britton, R. A.
1978   International tourism and indigenous development objectives: a study with special reference to the West Indies. PhD thesis, University of Minnesota.
1979   The image of the Third World in tourism marketing. *Annals of Tourism Research* 6: 318-28.

Britton, S. G.
1982   The political economy of tourism in the Third World. *Annals of Tourism Research* 9: 331-58.

Bromley, R.
1979   Who are the casual poor? In R. Bromley and C. Gerry (eds), *Casual work and poverty in third world cities*. J. Wiley and Sons, Chichester, 3–23.

Bromley, R. and Gerry, C. (eds)
1979   *Casual work and poverty in third world cities*. J. Wiley and Sons, Chichester.

Bruner, E.
1989a   Tourism, creativity and authenticity. *Studies in Symbolic Interaction* 10: 109–14.
1989b   Of cannibals, tourists and ethnographers. *Cultural Anthropology* 4: 438–45.

Burrows, S. M.
1899   *The visitor's guide to Kandy and Nuwara Eliya*. Fifth edition. A. M. and J. Ferguson, Colombo.

Carrithers, M.
1983   *The forest monks of Sri Lanka. An anthropological and historical study*. Oxford University Press, Delhi.

Casson, L.
1979   *Travels in the ancient world*. Allen and Unwin Ltd, London.

Cater, E.
1987   Tourism in the least developed countries. *Annals of Tourism Research* 14: 201–26.

Central Bank
1979   *Review of the Economy.* Central Bank, Colombo.
1980   *Review of the Economy.* Central Bank, Colombo.
1981   *Review of the Economy.* Central Bank, Colombo.
1982   *Review of the Economy.* Central Bank, Colombo
1983   *Review of the Economy.* Central Bank, Colombo.
1984   *Review of the Economy.* Central Bank, Colombo.
1985   *Review of the Economy.* Central Bank, Colombo.
1986   *Review of the Economy.* Central Bank, Colombo.
1987   *Review of the Economy.* Central Bank, Colombo.

Ceylon Tourist Board
1966   Report for the period 1/5/66-30/9/66. Government Printer, Colombo.
1968   Review of activities 1967-8. CTB, Colombo.
1975   Tourism in 1970. A survey of performance. CTB, Colombo.
1980a   Guide lecturers training programme.
1980b   Annual statistical report. CTB, Colombo.
1981a   Annual statistical report. CTB, Colombo.
1981b   December Monthly Bulletin on Tourism. CTB, Colombo.
1981c   Report on the performance of the tourism industry. Colombo
1981d   List of guide lecturers. Colombo.
1982a   Monthly bulletin on tourism (March). CTB, Colombo.
1982b   Monthly bulletin on tourism (August). CTB, Colombo.
1982c   Annual statistical report. CTB, Colombo.
1982d   A guide to investors in hotel projects. CTB, Colombo.
1982e   Tourism on Track. CTB, Colombo.
1982f   Conditions of employment of guide lecturers. CTB, Colombo.

1982g   Performance report for 1/1/82-30/9/82. CTB, Colombo.
1983a   Monthly bulletin on the performance of the tourism sector (November). CTB, Colombo.
1983b   Market intelligence news release (May). CTB, Colombo.
1983c   Annual statistical report. CTB, Colombo.
1984a   Specified Tourist Services Code.
1984b   Annual statistical report.. CTB, Colombo.
1984c   Market intelligence news release (February). CTB, Colombo.
1984d   Market intelligence news release (June). CTB, Colombo.
1984e   Market intelligence news release (December). CTB, Colombo.
1985a   Market intelligence news release (April). CTB, Colombo.
1985b   Market intelligence news release (July/August). CTB, Colombo.
1985c   Market intelligence news release (December). CTB, Colombo.
n. d.   Sri Lanka. official tourist handbook. Colombo.

Chesney-Lind, M. and Lind, I. Y.
1986   Visitors as victims: crimes against tourists in Hawaii. *Annals of Tourism Research* **13**: 167–91.

Chib, S. N.
1967   Tourism in Ceylon. MS.
1980a   Tourism in the Third World. *Third World Quarterly* **11**: 283–94.
1980b   Tourism policy — a political gimmick. *Eastern Economist*, September 5, 584–6.

Cleverdon, R.
1979   *The economic and social impact of tourism in developing countries.* The Economist Intelligence Unit Ltd, London.

Cohen, E.
1971   Arab boys and tourist girls in a mixed Jewish-Arab community. *International Journal of Comparative Sociology* **12**: 212–33.
1972   Towards a sociology of international tourism. *Social Research* **39**: 164–82.
1973   Nomads from affluence. Notes on the phenomenon of drifter tourism. *International Journal of Comparative Sociology* **14**: 89–103.
1979   Rethinking the sociology of tourism. *Annals of Tourism Research* **6**: 18–35.
1982a   Thai girls and farang men. The edge of ambiguity. *Annals of Tourism Research* **9**: 403-28.
1982b   Jungle guides in northern Thailand — the dynamics of a marginal occupational role. *The Sociological Review* **30**: 234–66.
1985   The tourist guide. The origins, structure and dynamics of a role. *Annals of Tourism Research* **12**: 5–29.
1986   Lovelorn farangs: the correspondence between foreign men and Thai girls. *Anthropological Quarterly* **59**: 115–27.
1993   Open-ended prostitution as a skillful game of luck. In M. Hitchcock *et al.* (eds), *Tourism in South-East Asia*. Routledge, London, 155–78.

Cohen, E. and Cooper, R. L.
1986   Language and tourism. *Annals of Tourism Research* **13**: 533–63.

Collignon, R.
1984   La lutte des pouvoirs publics contre les 'encombrements humains' à Dakar. *Canadian Journal of African Studies* **18**: 573–82.

Commission for Justice and Peace
1992   *Kandalama*. National Christian Council, Colombo

Committee for Rational Development
1984   *Sri Lanka. The ethnic conflict. Myths, realities and perspectives*. Navrang, New Delhi.

Cook, T. and Sons
1912   *Information for travellers landing at Colombo*. Cook and Sons, Colombo.

Cooper, J.
1990   Unspoilt, friendly: the real Sri Lanka. *The Weekend Australian Review*, 8–9 December: 13.

Crick, M. R.
1985   'Tracing' the anthropological self: quizzical reflections on fieldwork, tourism, and the ludic. *Social Analysis* **17**: 71–92.
1989a   Representations of international tourism in the social sciences: sun, sex, sights, savings, and servility. *Annual Review of Anthropology* **18**: 307–44.
1989b   Shifting identities in the research process: an essay in personal anthropology. In J. Perry (ed.), *Doing fieldwork. Eight personal accounts of social research*. Deakin University Press, Geelong, 24–40.
1989c   The hippy in Sri Lanka: a symbolic analysis of the imagery of school children in Kandy. *Criticism Heresy and Interpretation* **3**: 37–54.
1991   Tourists, locals and anthropologists: Quizzical reflections on 'otherness' in touristic encounters and in tourism research. *Australian Cultural History* **10**: 6–18.
1992   Ali and me: an essay in street corner anthropology. In J. Okely and H. Callaway (eds), *Anthropology and autobiography*. Routledge, London, 175–92.
1993   Obtaining information from a school-age sub-population in Sri Lanka. In M. Crick and B. Geddes (eds), *Research methods in the field: ten anthropological accounts*. Deakin University Press, Geelong, 162–85.

Crystal, E.
1978   Tourism in Toraja (Sulawesi, Indonesia). In V. Smith (ed.), *Hosts and guests. The anthropology of tourism*. Blackwell, Oxford, 109–25.

D'Amore, L. and Jafari, J. (eds)
1998   *Tourism — a vital force for peace*. First Global Conference, Montreal.

Daniel, E. V.
1990   Afterword: sacred places, violent spaces. In J. Spencer (ed.), *Sri Lanka. History and the roots of conflict*. Routledge, London, 227–46.

Dann, G., Nash, D. and Pearce, P.
1988   Methodology in tourism research. *Annals of Tourism Research* **15**: 1–28.

Davies, R.
1979   Informal sector or subordinate mode of production? A model. In R. Bromley
            and C. Gerry (eds), *Casual work and poverty in third world cities*. J. Wiley and
            Sons, Chichester, 87–104.

Davis, D. E.
1978   Development and the tourism industry in third world countries. *Society and
            Leisure* 1: 301–22.

Davy, J.
1821   *An account of the interior of Ceylon and of its inhabitants*. Longman, Hurst,
            Rees, Orme and Browne, London.

de Alwis, A.
1970   Star sapphire. In *Star sapphire and other stories*. Dinna Dina Press, Colombo, 9–
            45.
1978   A decade of tourism in Sri Lanka. In Department of Information 1978, *Tourism
            in Sri Lanka. The first decade*. Colombo, 35–8.
1980   Tourism the greatest movement for world peace and understanding. Ceylon
            Tourist Board, Colombo.
1981   The "them" and "us" in tourism. Department of Tourism, Colombo.
1982a   A world-wide exercise of human understanding. In Department of Information
            1982, *Sri Lanka Today* (October). Colombo.
1982b   Address to CTB Tourism Marketing Conference, 15 June, Colombo.
n.d.   *Collected speeches of Dr Anandatissa de Alwis*. Department of Information,
            Colombo.

de Beer, P.
1980   Les nouveaux conquistadores. Sri Lanka: la culture dans les griffes de
            l'exoticisme. *Le Monde*, March 1: 27–8.

de Kadt, E.
1979   The issues addressed. In E. de Kadt (ed.), *Tourism. Passport to development?
            Perspectives on the social and cultural effects of tourism in developing countries*.
            Oxford University Press, New York, 3–76.
1979 (ed.) *Tourism. Passport to development? Perspectives on the social and cultural effects
            of tourism in developing countries*. Oxford University Press, New York.

de Mel, V. E. H.
1969   Welcome address. In Association for the Promotion of Tourism in Ceylon 1969,
            Proceedings of seminar on tourism, held on 27 June 1969, Hotel Taprobane,
            Colombo.
1970   Preface. In Association for the Promotion of Tourism in Ceylon 1970,
            Proceedings of Seminar on Tourism for Local Bodies, held on 20 September, 1970,
            Ceylon Chamber of Commerce, Colombo, 1–2.

Department of Information
1978   *Tourism in Sri Lanka. The first decade*. Colombo.
1982   *Sri Lanka Today* (October). Colombo.

de Silva, C. R.

1978   Discussion. In National Science Council, *The role of tourism in social and economic development of Sri Lanka*. Social Science Research Centre, Colombo, 57.

de Silva, K. M.

1979   Resistance movements in nineteenth century Sri Lanka. In M. Roberts 1979 (ed.), *Collective identities, nationalisms and protest in modern Sri Lanka*. Marga Institute, Colombo, 129–52.

de Zoysa, C. N.

1978   Development of tourism in Sri Lanka. In Department of Information 1978, *Tourism in Sri Lanka. The first decade*. Colombo.

Dharmadasa, K. N. O.

1979   The Sinhala-Buddhist identity and the Nayakkar dynasty in the politics of the Kandyan kingdom, 1734–1815. In M. Roberts (ed.), *Collective identities, nationalisms and protest in modern Sri Lanka*. Marga Institute, Colombo, 99–128.

Dogan, H. Z.

1989   Forms of adjustment. Sociocultural impacts of tourism. *Annals of Tourism Research* **6**: 216–36.

Doxey, G. V.

1976   A causation theory of visitor-resident irritants: methodology and research inferences. Proceedings of the Travel Association, Sixth Annual Conference **6**: 195–8.

Due, E.

1980   Tourism and development. Examining the case of Sri Lanka. Unpublished M.A. thesis, McMaster University.

Dumont, J.-P.

1977   Review of MacCannell 1976. *Annals of Tourism Research* **4**: 223–5.
1978   *The headman and I. Ambiguity and ambivalence in the field experience*. University of Texas Press, Austin.

Duncan, J.

1990   *The city as text: the politics of landscape interpretation in the Kandyan kingdom*. Cambridge University Press, Cambridge.

Economist Intelligence Unit Ltd

1972   Quarterly Economic Review of Sri Lanka (Ceylon), No. 2.
1974   Tourism in Sri Lanka. Image Motivation Study. United Nations, New York.
1979   Quarterly Economic Review of Sri Lanka (Ceylon), No. 2.
1981   Quarterly Economic Review of Sri Lanka (Ceylon), No. 4.
1983   Quarterly Economic Review of Sri Lanka (Ceylon), No. 4.
1985a   Quarterly Economic Review of Sri Lanka (Ceylon), No. 2.
1985b   Quarterly Economic Review of Sri Lanka (Ceylon), Annual Supplement.
1986a   Quarterly Economic Review of Sri Lanka (Ceylon), No. 3.
1986b   Quarterly Economic Review of Sri Lanka (Ceylon), No. 4.

1987a   Quarterly Economic Review of Sri Lanka (Ceylon), No. 1.
1987b   Quarterly Economic Review of Sri Lanka (Ceylon), No. 3.
1987c   Quarterly Economic Review of Sri Lanka (Ceylon), No. 4.
1989   Quarterly Economic Review of Sri Lanka (Ceylon), No. 1.
1991   Quarterly Economic Review of Sri Lanka (Ceylon), No. 4.
1992   Quarterly Economic Review of Sri Lanka (Ceylon), No. 2.
1992–3.   Sri Lanka. Country Profile. Annual Survey of Political and Economic
            Background.

Ecumenical Coalition on Third World Tourism
1983   *Tourism Prostitution Development.* ECTWT, Bangkok.

Ediriweera, P. A.
1969   Changing patterns in tourism. In Association for the Promotion of Tourism in
            Ceylon 1969, Proceedings of seminar on tourism, held on 27 June 1969, Hotel
            Taprobane, Colombo.

Endagama, P.
1978   Discussion. In National Science Council, *The role of tourism in social and
            economic development of Sri Lanka.* Social Science Research Centre, Colombo,
            61.

Errington, F. and Gewertz, D.
1989   Tourism and anthropology in a post-modern world. *Oceania* 60: 37–54.

Evans-Pritchard, D.
1989   How "they" see "us". Native American images of tourists. *Annals of Tourism
            Research* 16: 89–105.

Fabian, J.
1983   *Time and the other. How anthropology makes its object.* Cornell University
            Press, New York.

Farrell, B. N.
1979   Tourism's human conflicts. Cases from the Pacific. *Annals of Tourism Research* 6:
            122–36.

Farver, J. A.
1984   Tourism and employment in The Gambia. *Annals of Tourism Research* 11: 249–
            65.

Fernando, P. C. S.
1982   Tourism in turbulent times. In Department of Information 1982, *Sri Lanka
            Today* (October). Colombo.

Fernando, T. and Kearney, R. N. (eds)
1979   *Modern Sri Lanka. A society in transition.* Maxwell School of Citizenship and
            Public Affairs, Syracuse University, New York.

Fierz, G.
1993   Sri Lanka protests over tourism. *Contours* 6(3/4): 34–7.

Finney, B. R. and Watson-Gegeo, K. A.
1979   A new kind of sugar. Tourism in the Pacific. *Annals of Tourism Research* **6**: 469–71.

Firth, Rev. F. O.
1993   A people's march: from Iranawila to Kandalama. *Contours* **6**(1): 17–21.

Fox, R. G. (ed.)
1991   *Recapturing anthropology. Working in the present.* School of American Research Press, Santa Fe.

Fussell, P.
1980   *Abroad. British literary travelling between the wars.* Oxford University Press, New York.

Fyson, N. L.
1987   *People at work in Sri Lanka.* B. T. Batsford Ltd, London.

Gamage, M. A.
1978   Tourism in the economy of Sri Lanka. M.Sc. thesis, University of Strathclyde.
1981   *Commercial profitability of tourism.* CTB, Colombo.

Garcia, A.
1988   And why don't you go to the Seychelles? In P. Rossel (ed.), *Tourism. Manufacturing the exotic*, International Working Group for Indigenous Affairs, Copenhagen, 93–115.

Gibson, T.
1982   Sri Lanka: economic growth and equity. *Contemporary Southeast Asia* **4**(4): 174–83.

Gooneratne, L. V.
1970   Tourism and local bodies. In Association for the Promotion of Tourism in Ceylon 1970, *Proceedings of seminar on tourism for local bodies*, held on 20 September, 1970, Ceylon Chamber of Commerce, Colombo.

Goonatilake, S.
1975   Development thinking as cultural neo-colonialism — the case of Sri Lanka. Institute of Development Studies Bulletin, University of Sussex.
1978   Tourism in Sri Lanka: the mapping of international inequalities and their internal structural effects. Centre for Developing Area Studies, Working Paper No. **19**, McGill University.

Goonetileke, H. A. I. (ed.)
1976   *Images of Sri Lanka through American eyes. Travellers in Ceylon in the nineteenth and twentieth centuries.* International Communication Agency, U.S. Embassy, Colombo.
1984   *Lanka, their Lanka. Cameos of Ceylon through other eyes.* Navrang, New Delhi.

Graburn, N. H.
1978   Tourism: the sacred journey. In V. Smith (ed.), *Hosts and guests. The anthropology of tourism.* Blackwell, Oxford, 17–31.
1983a   Editor's page. *Annals of Tourism Research* **10**: 1–3.

1983b   The anthropology of tourism. *Annals of Tourism Research* **10**: 9–34.
1983 (ed.) The Anthropology of Tourism. *Annals of Tourism Research* **10** (1).

Greenwood, D.
1978   Culture by the pound. An anthropological perspective on tourism as cultural commoditisation. In V. Smith (ed.), *Hosts and guests. The anthropology of tourism*. Blackwell, Oxford, 129–38.

Gunasinghe, N.
1984   The open economy and its impact on ethnic relations in Sri Lanka. In Committee for Rational Development, *Sri Lanka. The ethnic conflict. Myths, realities and perspectives*. Navrang, New Delhi, 192–214.
1990   *Changing socio-economic relations in the Kandyan countryside*. Social Scientists' Association, Colombo.

Gunatilleke, G.
1978   Participatory development and dependence — the case of Sri Lanka. *Marga Quarterly Journal* **5**(3): 38–93.
1981   Tourist development in Sri Lanka. Options and alternatives. Marga Institute, Colombo.

Haas, H.
1984   A decade of alternative tourism in Sri Lanka. In P. Holden (ed.), *Alternative tourism with a focus on Asia*. Ecumenical Coalition on Third World Tourism, Bangkok, 1/1–1/7.

Haekel, E.
1975   A visit to Ceylon. (Originally published 1882). *The Ceylon Historical Journal* **23**: 1–229.

Hannerz, U.
1969   *Soulside. Inquiries into ghetto culture and community*. Columbia University Press, New York.
1985   The informal sector. Some remarks. In H. O. Skar (ed.), *Anthropological contributions to planned change and development*. Acta Universitatis Gothenburgensis, Gothenburg, 143-53.

Harris, Kerr, Forster and Co.
1967   *Ceylon tourism plan*, Hawaii.

Harrison, D.
1992a   International tourism and the less developed countries: the background. In D. Harrison (ed.), *Tourism and the less developed countries*. Belhaven Press, London, 1–18.
1992b   Tourism to less developed countries: the social consequences. In D. Harrison (ed.), *Tourism and the less developed countries*. Belhaven Press, London, 19–34.
1992c   Tradition, modernity and tourism in Swaziland. In D. Harrison (ed.), *Tourism and the less developed countries*. Belhaven Press, London, 148–62.
1992 (ed.) *Tourism and the less developed countries*. Belhaven Press, London.

Hastrup, K.

1993   The native voice — and the anthropological vision. *Social Anthropology* 1: 173–86.

Hawkins, D. E. (ed.)

1982   *Social and economic impact of tourism on Asian Pacific Region.* Asian Productivity Organisation, Tokyo.

Hawkins, D. E., Shafer, E. L. and Rowelstad, J. M. (eds)

1980   *Tourism planning and development issues.* George Washington University, Washington, D.C.

Henry, S.

1982   The working unemployed: perspectives on the informal economy and unemployment. *Sociological Review* 30: 460–77.

Hettiarachchi, W.

1974   Net foreign exchange earnings for tourism with special reference to Sri Lanka. *Staff Studies, Central Bank of Ceylon* 4: 165–84.

Higgins, B.

1982   Why poor people stay poor in Sri Lanka. *Asian Studies Association of Australia Review* 5(3): 15–19.

Hills, T. L. and Lundgren, T.

1977   The impact of tourism in the Caribbean. *Annals of Tourism Research* 4: 248–57.

Hitchcock, M., King, V. T. and Parnwell, M. J. G.

1993   Tourism in South-east Asia: introduction. In M. Hitchcock *et al.* (eds), *Tourism in South-East Asia*, 1–31.

1993 (eds) *Tourism in South-East Asia.* Routledge, London.

Hocart, A. M.

1931   The Temple of the Tooth in Kandy. Memoirs of the Archaeological Survey of Ceylon, Vol. 4. Luzac and Co., London.

Holden, P. (ed.)

1984   *Alternative tourism with a focus on Asia.* Ecumenical Coalition on Third World Tourism, Bangkok.

Husbands, W.

1989   Social status and perceptions of tourism in Zambia. *Annals of Tourism Research* 16: 237–55.

Ilangakoon, B.

1978   The seminar in retrospect: a Marga viewpoint. *Marga Quarterly Journal* 5(3): 30–7.

International Bank for Reconstruction and Development

1968   Report of the prospects for tourism development in Ceylon. Ministry of Planning and Economic Affairs, Colombo.

International Tourism Quarterly

1983   Sri Lanka starts road to recovery. 12(4): 14–15.

Isenman, P.
1980   Basic needs: the case of Sri Lanka. *World Development* **8**: 237–58.

Ivan, V.
1989   *Sri Lanka in crisis. Road to conflict.* Sarvodaya Book Publishing Services, Ratmalana.

Jayewardene, J. R.
1982   Tourism — passport to peace. In Department of Tourism 1982, *Sri Lanka Today* (October). Colombo.

Jennings, W. I.
1958   The opening of the Kandy road. *Ceylon Journal of Historical and Social Studies* **1**(1): 97–104.

Jones, C.
1982   'Moonlighting' air force builds Sri Lanka's tourism. *The Christian Science Monitor* **74**(43):2.

Jules-Rosette, B.
1984   *The messages of tourist art. An African semiotic system in comparative perspective.* Plenum Press, New York.

Kalugalle, P. B. G.
1970   Comment. In Association for the Promotion of Tourism in Ceylon 1970, *Proceedings of seminar on tourism for local bodies*, held on 20 September, 1970, Ceylon Chamber of Commerce, Colombo, 33–5.

Kapferer, B.
1988   *Legends of people. Myths of state. Violence, intolerance and political culture in Sri Lanka and Australia.* Smithsonian Institution Press, Washington.

Karasek, H.
1980   School-pen, rupies, bonbons. *Der Spiegel* **34**(17): 236–40.

Karch, C. A. and Dann, G.
1981   Close encounters of the Third World. *Human Relations* **34**: 249–69.

Karunaratna, N.
1984   *From governor's pavilion to president's palace.* Department of National Archives, Colombo.

Karunatilake, H. N. S.
1978   Foreign exchange earnings from tourism. In National Science Council, *The role of tourism in social and economic development of Sri Lanka.* Social Science Research Centre, Colombo, 25–30.
1987   *The economy of Sri Lanka.* Centre for Demographic and Socio-Economic Studies, Colombo.

Kemper, S.
1991   *The presence of the past. Chronicles, politics and culture in Sinhala life.* Cornell University Press, Ithaca.

Knox, R.
1911   *An historical relation of Ceylon.* (Originally published 1681). James Maclehose and Sons, Glasgow.

Kovach, G. S.
1965   *Report on tourism in Ceylon.* Government Press, Colombo.

Krippendorf, J.
1987   *The holiday makers. Understanding the impact of leisure and travel.* Heinemann, London.

Lanfant, M.-F.
1980   Tourism in the process of internationalisation. *International Social Science Journal* **32**: 14–43.

Legislative Enactments of Ceylon
1958   Volume 2. Government Printer, Colombo.

Lett, J.
1983   Ludic and liminoid aspects of yacht tourism. *Annals of Tourism Research* **10**: 35–56.
1989   Epilogue. In V. Smith 1989 (ed.), *Hosts and guests. The anthropology of tourism.* Second edition. University of Pennsylvania Press, Philadelphia, 275–9.

Lévi-Strauss, C.
1984   *Tristes tropiques.* Atheneum, New York.

Liebow, E.
1967   *Tally's corner. A study of negro streetcorner men.* Little, Brown and Co., Boston.

Ling, T.
1980   Buddhist values and development problems: a case study of Sri Lanka. *World Development* **8**: 577–86.

Liyanage, D. A.
1965   Promotion of tourism and wild life. Colombo.

MacCannell, D.
1973   Staged authenticity: arrangements of social space in tourist settings. *American Journal of Sociology* **79**: 589–603.
1976   *The tourist. A new theory of the leisure class.* Schocken Books, New York.

McGee, T. G.
1979   The poverty syndrome: making out in the Southeast Asian city. In R. Bromley and C. Gerry (eds), *Casual work and poverty in third world cities.* J. Wiley and Sons, Chichester, 45–68.

McKean, P. F.
1976   An anthropological analysis of the culture-brokers of Bali: guides, tourists and Balinese. UNESCO/IBRD, Paris.

McLeod, B.
1981   The mediating personality and cultural identity. In S. Bochner 1981 (ed.), *The mediating person. Bridges between cultures.* Schenkman Publishing Co., Cambridge, Mass., 37–52.

Mabbett, H.
1983   Sri Lanka's naked truth. *The Age*, 14 February.

Manning, F.
1982   The Caribbean experience. *Cultural Survival Quarterly* **6**(3): 13–14.

Manor, J.
1984   Introduction. In J. Manor (ed.), *Sri Lanka. In change and crisis.* Croom Helm, London, 1–31.
1984 (ed.) *Sri Lanka. In change and crisis.* Croom Helm, London.

Marcus, G. E.
1980   The ethnographic subject as ethnographer: a neglected dimension of anthropological research. *Rice University Studies* **66**: 55–68.

Mathieson, A. and Wall, G.
1982   *Tourism. Economic, physical and social impacts.* Longmans, London.

Mattis, A. R.
1978   An experience in need-oriented development. *Marga Quarterly Journal* **5**(3): 1–29.

Mendis, E. D. L.
1981   *The economic, social and cultural impact of tourism on Sri Lanka.* Christian Workers Fellowship, Colombo.

Ministry of Cultural Affairs
1980   UNESCO-Sri Lanka Project of the Cultural Triangle. Colombo.

Ministry of Plan Implementation
1982   *A statistical pocket book of the Democratic Socialist Republic of Sri Lanka.* Colombo.

Mitchell, L. S.
1979   The geography of tourism. An introduction. *Annals of Tourism Research* **6**: 235–44.

Monetary Board
1989   Annual report to the Hon. Minister of Finance and Planning. Central Bank, Colombo.
1990   Annual report to the Hon. Minister of Finance and Planning. Central Bank, Colombo.

Moore, M.
1985   *The state and peasant politics in Sri Lanka.* Cambridge University Press, London.

Moon, O.
1989   *From paddy field to ski slope: the revitalisation of tradition in Japanese village life.* Manchester University Press, Manchester

Morrison, B. M.
1979   Meegama. Seeking livelihood in a Kandyan village. In Morrison *et al.* (eds), 71–113.

Morrison, B. M., Moore, M. P. and Ishak Lebbe, M. U.
1979   Introduction. In Morrison *et al.* (eds), *The disintegrating village. Social change in rural Sri Lanka.* Lake House Investments Ltd, Colombo, 3-41.
1979 (eds) *The disintegrating village. Social change in rural Sri Lanka.* Lake House Investments Ltd, Colombo.

Nanayakkara, V. N. D.
1971   Some aspects of tourism in Ceylon 1968–69. *Staff Studies, Central Bank of Ceylon* 1: 52–66.

Nanayakkara, V.
1977   *A return to Kandy. Over Balana and beyond.* Revised edition. Arasan Printers, Colombo.

Nash, D.
1978   Tourism as a form of imperialism. In V. Smith (ed.), *Hosts and guests. The anthropology of tourism.* Blackwell, Oxford, 33–47.
1981   Tourism as an anthropological subject. *Current Anthropology* 22: 461–81.
1984   The ritualisation of tourism. *Annals of Tourism Research* 11: 505–7.

Nash, D. and Smith, V.
1991   Anthropology and tourism. *Annals of Tourism Research* 18(1): 12–25.

National Science Council of Sri Lanka
1978   *The role of tourism in social and economic development of Sri Lanka.* Social Science Research Centre, Colombo.

Nissan, E.
1987   The work of Sri Lankan anthropologists: a bibliographical survey. *Contributions to Indian Sociology* 21(1): 1–25.
1988   Polity and pilgrimage centres in Sri Lanka. *Man* 23: 253–74.
1989   History in the making. Anuradhapura and the Sinhalese Buddhist nation. In H. L. Seneviratne (ed.), Identity, consciousness and the past. The South Asian scene. *Social Analysis* (Special Issue) No. 25: 64–77.

Noble, J., Forsyth, S. and Wheeler, T.
1993   *Sri Lanka. A travel survival kit.* Fifth edition. Lonely Planet Publications, Melbourne.

Nolan, S. D. and Nolan, M. L.
1978   Variations in travel behavior and the cultural impact of tourism. In M. Zamora *et al.* (eds), *Tourism and behaviour.* (Studies in Third World Societies No. 5). Department of Anthropology, College of William and Mary, Virginia, 1–17.

Nuñez, T.
1963   Tourism, tradition and acculturation. *Weekendismo* in a Mexican village. *Southwestern Journal of Anthropology* 34: 328–36.
1978   Touristic studies in anthropological perspective. In V. Smith (ed.), *Hosts and guests. The anthropology of tourism.* Blackwell, Oxford, 207–16.

Obeyesekere, G.
1967   *Land tenure in village Ceylon. A sociological and historical study.* Cambridge
           University Press, Cambridge.
1976   Personal identity and cultural crisis. The case of Anagarika Dharmapala. In F. D.
           Reynolds and D. Capps (eds), *The biographical process. Studies in the history and
           psychology of religion.* Mouton, The Hague, 221–52.
1979   The vicissitudes of the Sinhala-Buddhist identity through time and change. In M.
           Roberts (ed.), *Collective identities, nationalisms and protest in modern Sri Lanka.*
           Marga Institute, Colombo, 279–313.
1984a   The origins and institutionalization of political violence. In J. Manor (ed.) *Sri
           Lanka. In change and crisis.* Croom Helm, London, 153–74.
1984b   *The cult of the goddess Pattini.* University of Chicago Press, Chicago.

Okely, J. and Callaway, H. (eds)
1992   *Anthropology and autobiography.* Routledge, London.

O'Grady, R.
1992   *The child and the tourist. The story behind the escalation of child prostitution in
           Asia.* ECPAT, Bangkok/Pace Publications, Auckland.

Palmer, A. and Palmer, V.
1976   *Quotations in history.* Harvester Press, Sussex.

Panditharatne, B. L.
1978   Opening address. In National Science Council of Sri Lanka, *The role of tourism
           in social and economic development of Sri Lanka.* Social Science Research Centre,
           Colombo, 9.

Pearce, P.
1988   *The Ulysses factor. Evaluating visitors in tourist settings.* Springer-Verlag Inc.,
           New York.

Peebles, P.
1982   *Sri Lanka. A handbook of historical statistics.* G. K. Hall and Co., Boston.

People's Bank
1982a   The need for monitoring trends in tourism. *People's Bank Economic Review*
           7(11): 21–2.
1982b   The case for high cost, low density tourism. *People's Bank Economic Review*
           8(2): 14–15.

Percival, Capt. R.
1975   An account of the island of Ceylon. (Originally published 1803). *The Ceylon
           Historical Journal* 22: 122–80.

Perera, L.
1978   Case study: Hikkaduwa. In National Science Council of Sri Lanka, *The role of
           tourism in social and economic development of Sri Lanka.* Social Science Research
           Centre, Colombo, 47–56.

Perera, R.
1985   Tourism: from commodity to human relations. *Sri Lanka Profiles* 2(1): 3–4.

Pfaffenberger, B.
1983   Serious pilgrims and frivolous tourists: the chimera of tourism in the pilgrimages
            of Sri Lanka. *Annals of Tourism Research* **10**(1): 57–74.

Picard, M.
1993   'Cultural tourism' in Bali. National integration and cultural differentiation. In M.
            Hitchcock *et al.* (eds), *Tourism in South-East Asia*. Routledge, London, 71–98.

Pieris, G.
1971   Kalapura: the colony of craftsmen in Patha-Dumbara. *Modern Ceylon Studies* **2**:
            88–122.
1982   Basic needs and the provision of government services in Sri Lanka. A case study
            of Kandy District. Working paper no. 35. World Employment Programme
            Research, International Labour Office, Geneva.

Pi-Sunyer, O.
1978   Through native eyes. Tourists and tourism in a Catalan maritime community. In
            V. Smith (ed.), *Hosts and guests. The anthropology of tourism*. Blackwell, Oxford,
            149–55.
1981   Tourism and anthropology. *Annals of Tourism Research* **8**: 271–84.

Ponnambalam, S.
1981   *Dependent capitalism in crisis. The Sri Lankan economy, 1948–80.* Zed Press,
            London.

Pravada
1992   Kandalama, capital and environment. *Pravada* **1**(7): 1–2.

Pye, E. A. and Lin, T. (eds)
1983   *Tourism in Asia. The economic impact.* Singapore University Press, Singapore.

Radke, D. *et al.*
1975   Contribution of the international tourism to the economic and social
            development of Sri Lanka. Occasional Paper No. 26, German Development
            Institute, Berlin.

Research Surveys of Great Britain Ltd
n.d.   Tourism in Sri Lanka. Image motivation study. Book 2 Data Presentation.
            London.

Richter, L. K.
1982   *Land reform and tourism development. Policy-making in the Philippines.*
            Schenkman Publications Co. Ltd, Cambridge, Mass.
1989   *The politics of tourism in Asia.* University of Hawaii Press, Honolulu.
1992   Political instability and tourism in the Third World. In D. Harrison (ed.),
            Tourism and the less developed countries. Belhaven Press, London, 35-46.
1993   Tourism policy-making in South-east Asia. In M. Hitchcock *et al.* (eds), *Tourism
            in South-East Asia.* Routledge, London, 179–99.

Richter, L. K. and Richter, W. L.
1985   Policy choices in South Asian tourism development. *Annals of Tourism Research*
            12: 210–17.

Riley, P.

1988   Road culture of international long-term budget travellers. *Annals of Tourism Research* **15**: 313–28.

Roberts, M.

1979   Meanderings in the pathways of collective identity and nationalism. In M. Roberts (ed.), *Collective identities, nationalisms and protest in modern Sri Lanka*. Marga Institute, Colombo, 1–96.

1989   Apocalypse or accommodation? Two contrasting views of Sinhala–Tamil relations in Sri Lanka. *South Asia* **12**(1): 67–83.

1979 (ed.) *Collective identities, nationalisms and protest in modern Sri Lanka*. Marga Institute, Colombo.

Roberts, M., Raheem, I. and Colin-Thomé, P.

1989   *People inbetween. The Burghers and the middle class in the transformations within Sri Lanka 1790s–1960s.* Sarvodaya Book Publishing Services, Ratmalana.

Rojek, C.

1985   *Capitalism and leisure theory.* Tavistock Publications, London.

Rossel, P. (ed.)

1988   *Tourism. Manufacturing the exotic.* International Working Group for Indigenous Affairs, Copenhagen.

Rupasinghe, K.

1978   Discussion. In National Science Council, *The role of tourism in social and economic development of Sri Lanka*. Social Science Research Centre, Colombo, 58–9.

Rupesinghe, W.

1983   Whither tourism? *Travel Horizons Asia* **1**: 42–3.

Ryan, B.

1953   *Caste in modern Ceylon. The Sinhalese system in transition.* Rutgers University Press, New Brunswick.

Samaranayake, H. M. S.

1970   Charter tourist survey, January–April. CTB, Colombo.

1978   Economic effects of tourism. In Department of Information 1978, *Tourism in Sri Lanka. The first decade.* Colombo, 4–7.

n.d.   Employment generation in the tourist industry.

Samarasuriya, S.

1982   *Who needs tourism? Employment for women in the holiday-industry of Sudugama, Sri Lanka.* Research Project: Women and Development, Colombo/ Leiden.

Samaraweera, V.

1981   Land, labour, capital and sectional interests in the national policies of Sri Lanka. *Modern Asian Studies* **15**(1): 127–62.

Sarachandra, E. R.
1965   Traditional values and the modernization of a Buddhist society: the case of Ceylon. In Bellah (ed.), *Religion and Progress in Modern Asia*. Free Press, New York, 109–23.

Sathiendrakumar, R. and Tisdell, C.
1989   Tourism and the economic development of the Maldives. *Annals of Tourism Research* **16**: 254–69.

Schwimmer, E.
1979   Feasting and tourism: a comparison. In I. Portis-Winner and J. Umiker-Sebeok (eds), *Semiotics of culture*. Mouton, The Hague, 221–35.

Selwyn, T.
1993   Peter Pan in South-East Asia. Views from the brochures. In M. Hitchcock *et al.* (eds), *Tourism in South-East Asia*. Routledge, London, 117–37.

Seneviratna, A.
1983   Kandy. An illustrative survey of ancient monuments with the historical, archaeological and literary descriptions including maps of the city and its suburbs. Central Cultural Fund, Ministry of Cultural Affairs, Colombo.

Seneviratne, H. L.
1963   The Äsala perahära in Kandy. *Ceylon Journal of Historical and Social Studies* **6**: 169–80.
1977   Politics and pageantry: universalization of ritual in Sri Lanka. *Man* **12**: 65–75.
1978   *Rituals of the Kandyan state*. Cambridge University Press, Cambridge.
1989 (ed.) Identity, consciousness and the past. The South Asian scene. *Social Analysis* (Special Issue) No. **25**.

Seneviratne, M.
1984   Tourism patterns in Sri Lanka and its potential for alternative tourism. In P. Holden (ed.), *Alternative tourism with a focus on Asia*. Ecumenical Coalition on Third World Tourism, Bangkok, 16/1–16/6.

Seneviratne, M. and Peiris, S.
1991   Tourism and child prostitution in Sri Lanka. In K. Srisang (ed.), *Caught in modern slavery. Tourism and child prostitution in Asia*. Ecumenical Coalition on Third World Tourism, Bangkok, 47–52.

Seneviratne, P.
1982   Sri Lanka. In D. E. Hawkins (ed.), *Social and economic impact of tourism on Asian Pacific Region*. Asian Productivity Organisation, Tokyo, 96–104.

Sievers, A.
1983   *Der Tourismus in Sri Lanka (Ceylon). Ein social geographischer beitrag zum tourismus phänomen in tropischen entwicklungsländern ins besondere in Südasien*. F. Steiner Verlag, Wiesbaden.

Silva, K. T.
1979   Welivita: the demise of Kandyan feudalism. In B. M. Morrison *et al.* (eds), *The disintegrating village. Social change in rural Sri Lanka*. Lake House Investments Ltd, Colombo, 47–70.

Silva, N.
1970   The government's plan for the development of domestic tourism in Ceylon. In Association for the Promotion of Tourism in Ceylon 1970, *Proceedings of seminar on tourism for local bodies,* held on 20 September 1970, Ceylon Chamber of Commerce, Colombo, 41–8.
1978   Policies and programmes for tourism. In National Science Council, *The role of tourism in social and economic development of Sri Lanka.* Social Science Research Centre, Colombo, 10–16.
1982   Regional cooperation in tourism. The role of Sri Lanka. In Department of Information 1982, *Sri Lanka Today* (October). Colombo.

Simmel, G.
1980   The stranger. In D. Levine (ed.), *On individualism and social forms.* Chicago University Press, Chicago, 143–9.

Simpson, B.
1993   Tourism and tradition. From healing to heritage. *Annals of Tourism Research* **20**(1): 164–81.

Sinclair, M. T., Alizadeh, P. and Onunga, E. A. A.
1992   The structure of international tourism and tourism development in Kenya. In D. Harrison (ed.), *Tourism and the less developed countries.* Belhaven Press, London, 47–63.

Siriwardhana, H. P.
1982   Tourism development in Sri Lanka. In Department of Information 1982, *Sri Lanka Today* (October). Colombo.

Skar, H. O.
1985   Questioning three assumptions about the informal urban sector. In H. O. Skar (ed.), *Anthropological contributions to planned change and development.* Acta Universitatis Gothenburgensis, Gothenburg, 154–75.
1985 (ed.) *Anthropological contributions to planned change and development.* Acta Universitatis Gothenburgensis, Gothenburg

Smith, V.
1977   Recent research on tourism and culture change: 1976 Symposium. *Annals of Tourism Research* **4**: 129–34.
1978a   Hosts and guests. *Annals of Tourism Research* **5**: 274–7.
1978b   Introduction. In V. Smith (ed.), *Hosts and guests. The anthropology of tourism.* Blackwell, Oxford, 1–14.
1978 (ed.) *Hosts and guests. The anthropology of tourism.* Blackwell, Oxford.
1980   Anthropology and tourism. A science-industry evaluation. *Annals of Tourism Research* **7**: 13–33.
1989   Preface. In Smith (ed.), *Hosts and guests. The anthropology of tourism.* Second edition. University of Pennsylvania Press, Philadelphia, ix–xi.
1989 (ed.) *Hosts and guests. The anthropology of tourism.* Second edition. University of Pennsylvania Press, Philadelphia.
1992 (ed.) Pilgrimage and tourism. The quest in guest. *Annals of Tourism Research* (Special Issue) **19**(1).

Spencer, J.
1990   *A Sinhala village in a time of trouble. Politics and change in rural Sri Lanka.*
            Oxford University Press, Delhi.
1990 (ed.) *Sri Lanka. History and the roots of conflict.* Routledge, London.

Sri Lanka Profiles
1987a   Turning tide in tourism? *Sri Lanka Profiles* (Special Issue) **3**: 4–6.
1987b   Visit us before the 'tourists' return. *Sri Lanka Profiles* (Special Issue) Preview
            1988:2.

Srisang, K. (ed.)
1991   *Caught in modern slavery. Tourism and child prostitution in Asia.* Ecumenical
            Coalition on Third World Tourism, Bangkok.

Stringer, P. F.
1981   Hosts and guests. The bed and breakfast phenomenon. *Annals of Tourism
            Research* **8**: 357–76.

Swearer, D. K.
1982   The Kataragama and Kandy Äsala perahäras: juxtaposing religious elements in
            Sri Lanka. In G. R. Welbon and G. E. Yokum (eds), *Religious festivals in South
            India and Sri Lanka.* Manohar, New Delhi, 295–311.

Sweet, J. D.
1985   *Dances of the Tewa Pueblo Indians. Expressions of new life.* School of American
            Research Press, Santa Fe.
1989   Burlesquing 'the other' in pueblo performance. *Annals of Tourism Research* **16**:
            62–75.

Taft, R.
1981   The role and personality of the mediator. In S. Bochner 1981 (ed.), *The mediating
            person. Bridges between cultures.* Schenkman Publishing Co., Cambridge, Mass.,
            53–88.

Tambiah, S. J.
1985   An anthropologist's creed. In *Culture thought and social action. An
            anthroplogical perspective.* Harvard University Press, Cambridge, Mass., 339–58.

Tennekoon, N. S.
1988   Rituals of development: the accelerated Mahaväli development program of Sri
            Lanka. *American Ethnologist* **15**: 294–310.

Tennent, Sir J. E.
1859   *Ceylon. An account of the Island.* Volume 2. Longman, Green and Roberts,
            London.

Tokman, V. E.
1978   An exploration into the nature of informal–formal sector relationships. *World
            Development* **6**(9/10): 1065–75.

Truong, T.-D.
1990   *Sex, money and morality: prostitution and tourism in Southeast Asia.* Zed Books
            Ltd, London.

Turner, L. and Ash, J.
1975   *The golden hordes. International tourism and the pleasure periphery.* Constable, London.

van den Abbeele, G.
1980   Sightseers: the tourist as theorist. *Diacritics* 10: 3–14.

van den Berghe, P.
1980   Tourism as ethnic relations: a case study of Cuzco, Peru. *Ethnic and Racial Studies* 3: 375–92.
1988   Tourism and peace. Some critical reflections. In L. D'Amore and J. Jafari (eds), *Tourism — a vital force for peace.* First Global Conference, Montreal, 20–4.

van den Berghe, P. and Keyes, C.
1984   Tourism and re-created ethnicity. *Annals of Tourism Research* 11: 343–52.

Vijayavardhana, D. C.
1953   *The revolt in the temple. Composed to commemorate 2500 years of the land, the race and the faith.* Sinha Publications, Colombo.

Wagner, U.
1977   Out of time and place — mass tourism and charter trips. *Ethnos* 42: 38–52.
1981   Tourism in The Gambia. *Ethnos* 46: 190–206.
1982   *Catching the tourist. Women handicraft traders in The Gambia.* Department of Social Anthropology, University of Stockholm.

Wahnschaft, R.
1982   Formal and informal tourism sectors. A case study in Pattaya, Thailand. *Annals of Tourism Research* 9: 429–51.

Warrell, L.
1983   The Kandy asala perahara. An analysis of the relationship between religion and power in Sri Lanka as expressed in ritual. BA Hons thesis, Anthropology Department, University of Adelaide.
1990a   Historicising the cosmogony: naming the Asala perahara in Buddhist Sri Lanka. *The Australian Journal of Anthropology* 1(1): 3–17.
1990b   Cosmic horizons and social voices. PhD thesis, Department of Anthroplogy, University of Adelaide.
1990c   Conflict in hierarchy: jealousy among the sinhalese Buddhists. *South Asia* 13(1): 19–41.

Wheeler, T.
1980   *Sri Lanka: a travel survival kit.* Lonely Planet Publications, Melbourne.
1987   *Sri Lanka: a travel survival kit with Maldives supplement.* Fourth edition. Lonely Planet Publications, Melbourne.

Whyte, W. F.
1955   *Street corner society. The social structure of an Italian slum.* University of Chicago Press, Chicago.

Wijeratne, R.
1982   Tourism: a challenge for the private sector. In Department of Information 1982, *Sri Lanka Today* (October). Colombo.

Wilson, D.

1993   Time and tides in the anthropology of tourism. In M. Hitchcock *et al.* (eds),
            Tourism in South-East Asia. Routledge, London, 32–47.

Wimaladasa, V.

1992a   Sex tour fears halt Sri Lankan resort. *The Weekend Australian,* March 11–12: 11.
1992b   Perverts discover paradise in Sri Lanka. *The Weekend Australian,* March 7–8: 16.

Wood, R. E.

1984   Ethnic tourism, the State and culture change in Asia. *Annals of Tourism Research*
            11: 353–74.
1993   Tourism, culture and the sociology of development. In M. Hitchcock *et al.* (eds),
            Tourism in South-East Asia. Routledge, London, 48–70.

Wriggins, W. H.

1960   *Ceylon: dilemmas of a new nation.* Princeton University Press, Princeton N.J.

Yacoumis, J.

1980   Tackling seasonality. The case of Sri Lanka. *International Journal of Tourism
            Management* **1**(2): 84–98.

Index

Printed in the United Kingdom by
Lightning Source UK Ltd., Milton Keynes
138689UK00009BA/1/A

9 783718 655649